I0891359

COASTAL SCENES IN WATERCOLOUR

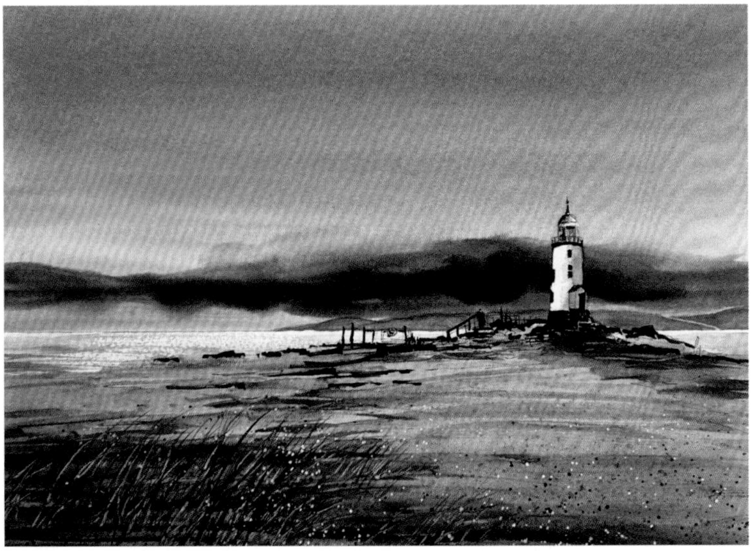

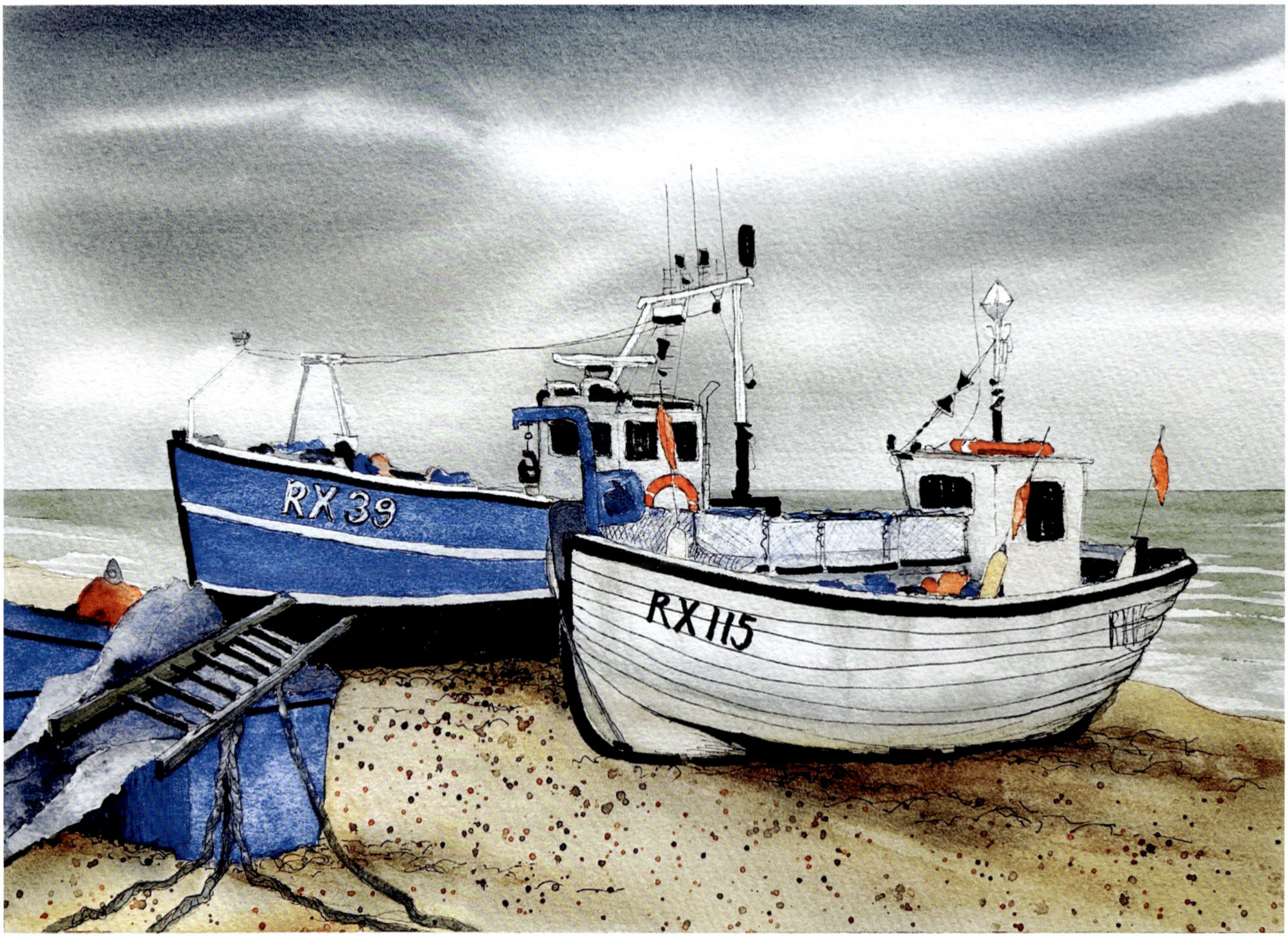
RX 39
RX 115

COASTAL SCENES IN WATERCOLOUR

TECHNIQUES AND TUTORIALS FOR THE COMPLETE BEGINNER

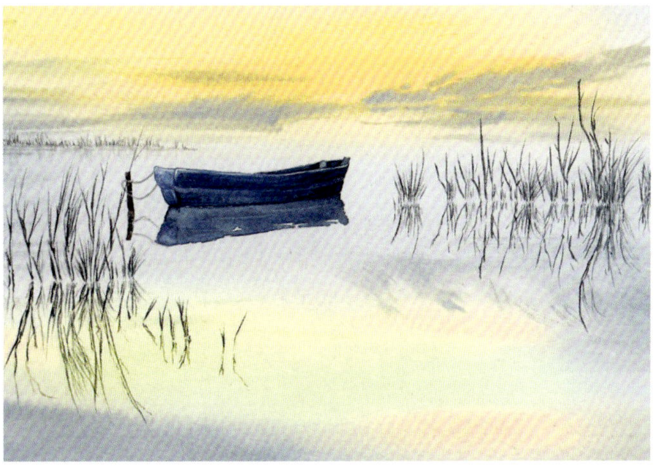

LOIS DAVIDSON AND MORGAINE DAVIDSON

THE GUILD OF MASTER CRAFTSMAN PUBLICATIONS

First published 2026 by
Guild of Master Craftsman Publications Ltd
Castle Place, 166 High Street, Lewes,
East Sussex, BN7 1XU, UK
www.gmcbooks.com

ISBN 978 1 78494 726 2

The EEA authorised representative is Authorised Rep Compliance Ltd., Ground Floor, 71 Baggot Street Lower, Dublin, DO2 P593, Ireland, www.arccompliance.com

A catalogue record for this book is available from the British Library.

PUBLISHER **Jonathan Bailey**
PRODUCTION MANAGER **Jim Bulley**
MANAGING ART EDITOR **Robin Shields**
SENIOR PROJECT EDITOR **Tom Kitch**
DESIGNER **Ellie Smith**
EDITOR **Theresa Bebbington**
PHOTOGRAPHY **Morgaine Davidson and Lois Davidson**

The publisher would like to thank Gahbane/Shutterstock (page 32, top right), kirill_makarov/Shutterstock (page 32, bottom left), Yari Ghidone/Shutterstock (page 32, bottom right), Pop95/Shutterstock (page 55, bottom), WhyNotChannel/Shutterstock (page 67, bottom), Chris Klonowski/Shutterstock (page 75, bottom) and Ronald Rozema/Shutterstock (page 87, bottom) for permission to reproduce copyright material.

Colour origination by GMC Reprographics
Printed and bound in China

Dedicated to the wild and beautiful coastline we call home.

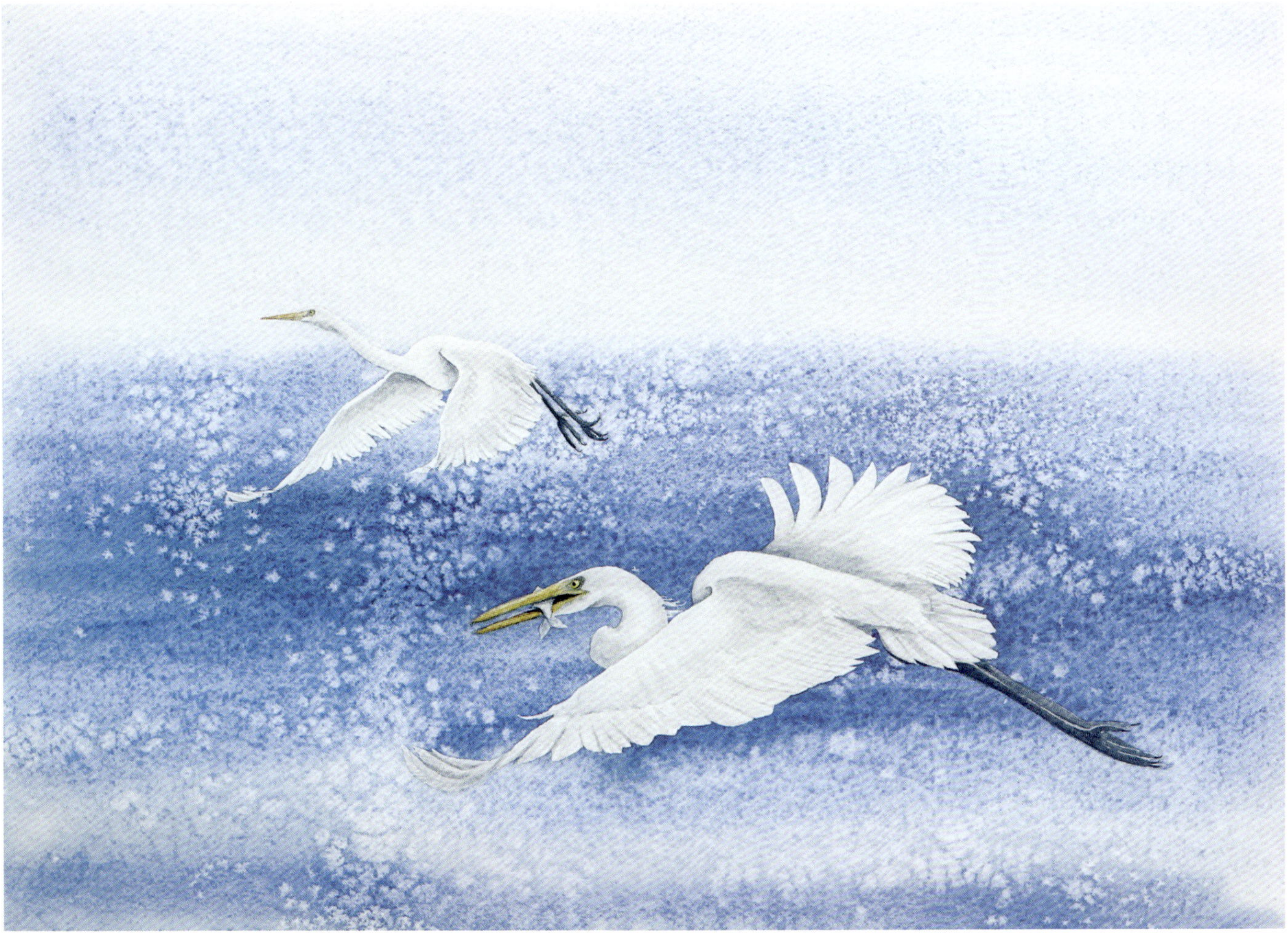

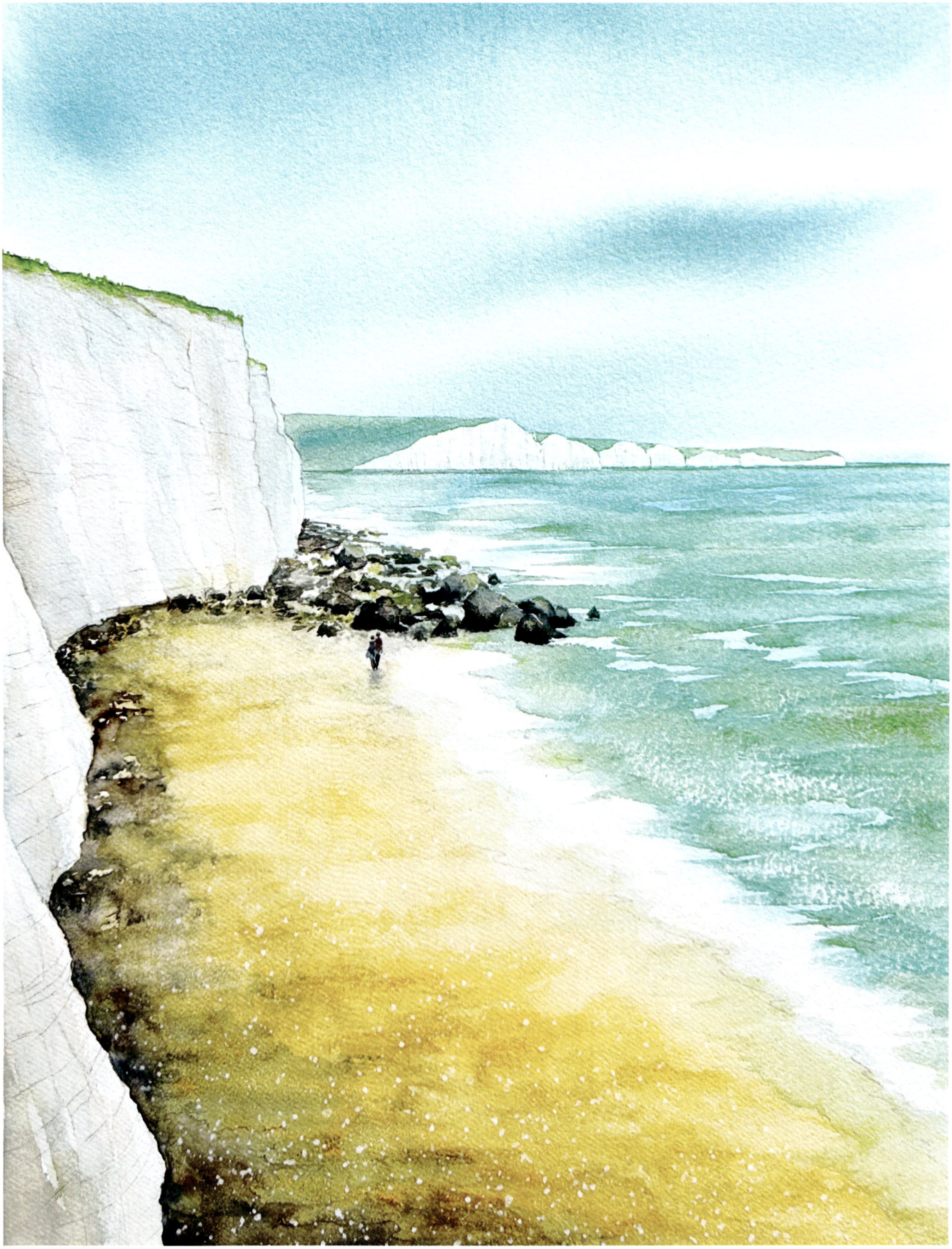

Contents

Introduction

The sea is a source of endless inspiration. What other aspect of our landscape changes so quickly, constantly and dramatically? Our oceans are constantly in flux: tides rise and fall with the pull of the moon; sunlight casts a kaleidoscope of colours across the waters day by day; waves roll in and out, soft and calm one minute, then whipped into a fury by an oncoming storm the next. Capturing such moments in paint and paper can seem like an endless task – but, fortunately, it can also be an extremely enjoyable one.

Learning to paint coastal scenes in watercolour has proved to be an incredibly rewarding experience for both of us, and we hope it will prove the same for everybody who picks up this book. Inside, you will find details on how to paint a variety of different coastal subjects, from stormy skies to quiet sunsets. There are also helpful sections on tools, paper, paints and the various different pieces of equipment that will prove useful on your watercolour journey, as well as notes on stepping outdoors and painting beside the sea – one of the loveliest of pastimes.

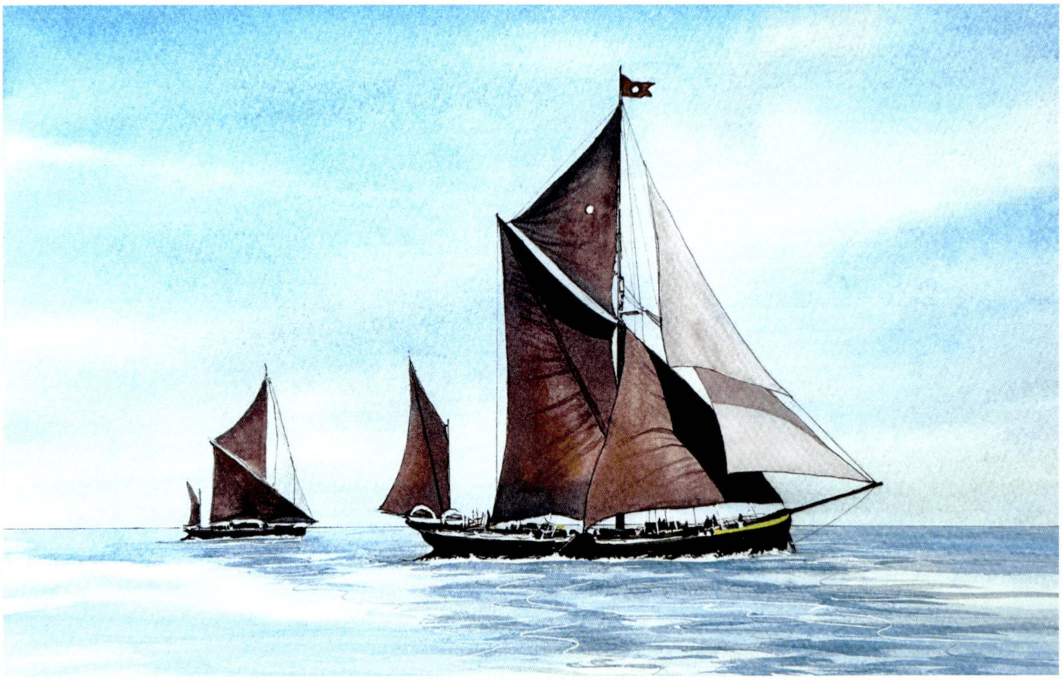

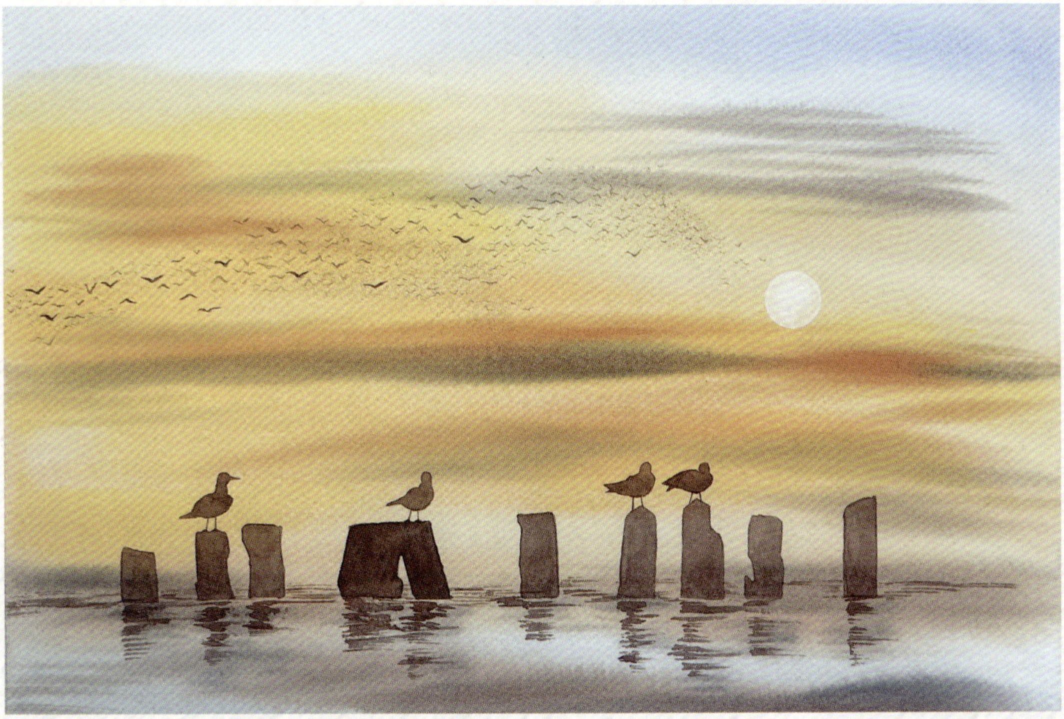

Each project inside this book has been carefully broken down into four step-by-step stages to help inspire a fledgling painter to create their own versions of a variety of scenes. Our goal is to turn what can be a slightly intimidating, and certainly complex, subject matter into something manageable and practicable. We hope you will enjoy working on these projects just as much as we have enjoyed creating them.

Equipment and Materials

Watercolour painting is a technique that is easy to learn, but it can be difficult to master. The first step in this journey is familiarizing yourself with the essential tools of the trade, and understanding the way watercolour paints work as a medium.

Watercolour Paints

As a transparent medium, there are lots of opportunities when applying watercolour paints for layering and blending beautiful glazes and rich hues. However, this also means that mistakes, when made, are harder to erase! Understanding the basics about your paints, tools and other equipment will give you the best possible foundation for beginning your watercolour painting journey.

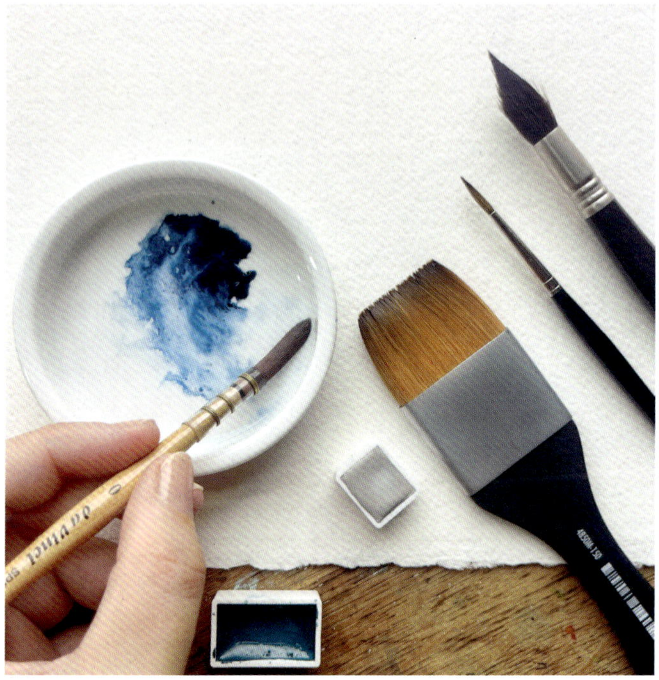

PAN PAINTS VERSUS TUBE PAINTS

The most practical form of watercolour paints is available in pans: these are hard little cubes or discs of solid colour that must be 'activated' with clean water before using. Pan paints are wonderful for *plein-air* work, where portability is key; and they also last a long time, provided they receive the proper care. They usually come in basic colour sets containing primaries, secondaries, lights and darks – and some brands offer limited-edition sets with specialist colours. Pans and half-pans can also be purchased individually: you can slot these into metal watercolour tins to create a custom palette of your own preferred hues.

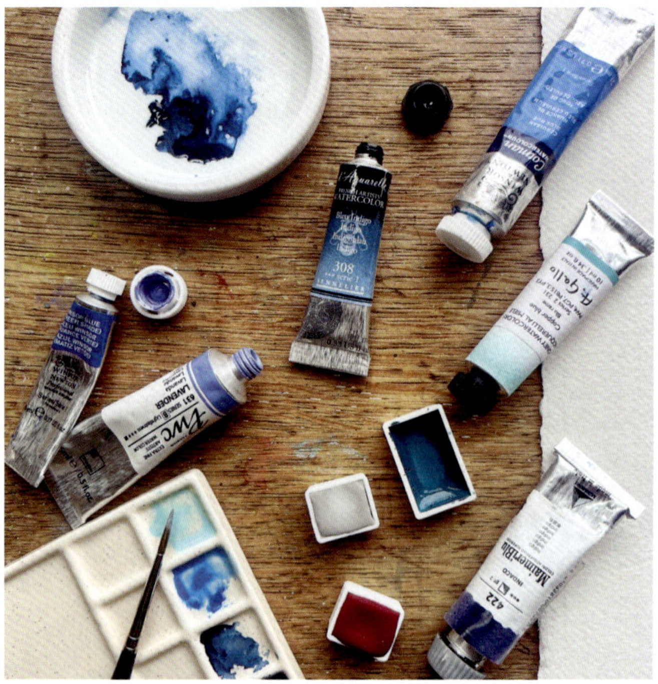

Watercolour paints come in tube form, too. They have a thick, creamy consistency, and must be mixed with a little water on a palette before use. The more water you mix in will determine the intensity of a paint's hue: more water will result in light-value colour, and less will give intense, dark-value shades. Again, these can be bought as sets or individually.

Both pan and tube paints have their plus points. For smaller areas of detailed colour, pans are a great option, as there is generally less wastage; the pans can be individually activated, used, then left to dry. For larger areas of rich colour, such as big seas and open skies, tube paints are a simple way to achieve intensely saturated washes.

Both types of paint are suitable to use when working through the projects in this book; you shouldn't feel like you need to necessarily stick to using either pans or tubes! Try experimenting with both and see which suits you best.

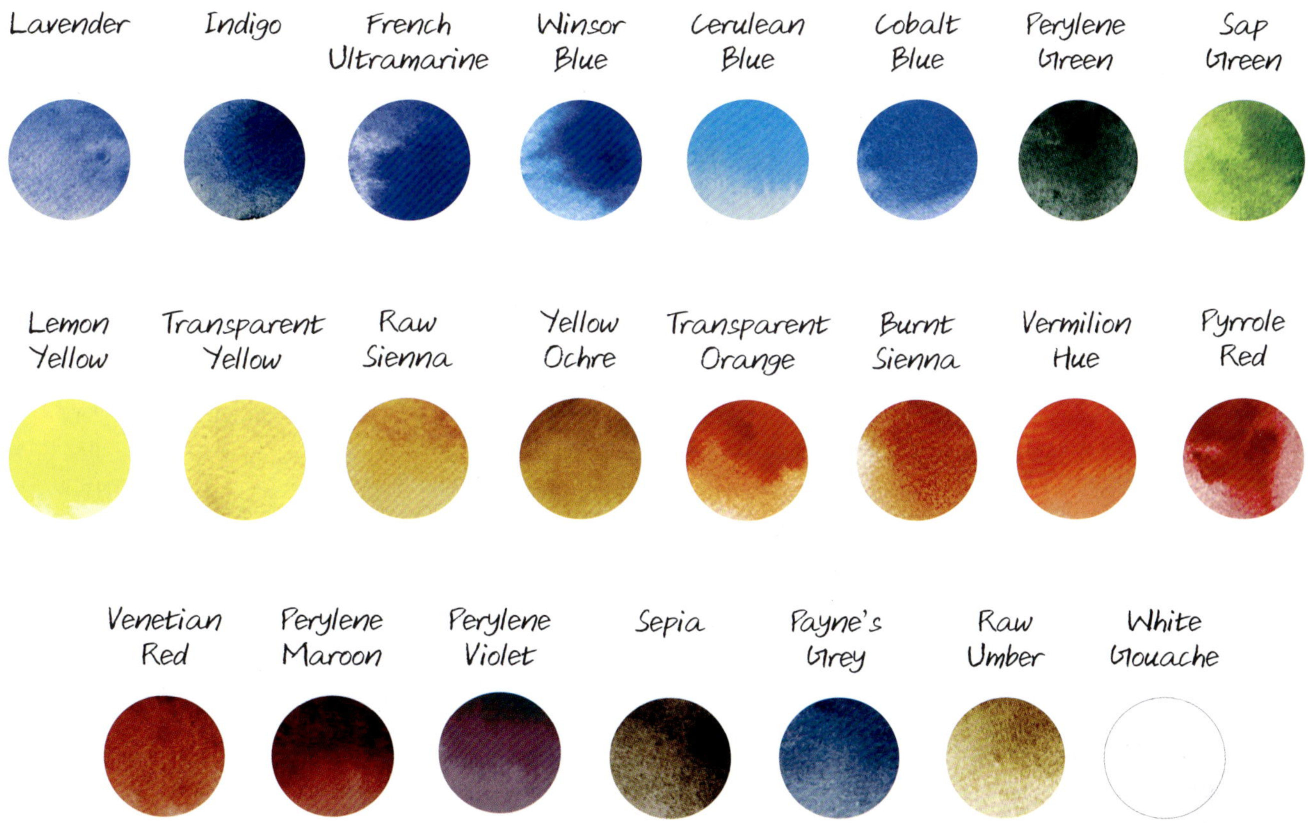

Helpful Hints

After painting with pan paints, especially those in a tin, leave them to fully dry out before closing the lid and putting them away. This will help preserve the colours and prevent them from becoming mouldy, which can occasionally happen if paints are put away damp.

You should always test your colours on a piece of scrap paper before adding them to your painting! It can sometimes be difficult to gauge the intensity of a colour mix when it's sitting on a non-absorbent palette surface. By swiping a little colour onto some spare paper, you will gain a clear view of how light or dark the paint will appear in your finished work. Remember, too, that watercolour paint will usually dry to be roughly 30 per cent paler than it appears when wet; so, don't be afraid of those lovely rich colour mixes!

After purchasing a new set of colours, a great way to start using them is by swatching them out in a sketchbook. This is a doubly helpful exercise: it will allow you to familiarize yourself with the strength and tone of the individual colours, and it will help you to build up your own personal reference library of beautiful hues. You may naturally be drawn more to certain hues above others; for this reason, specially curated paint sets can be worthwhile investments.

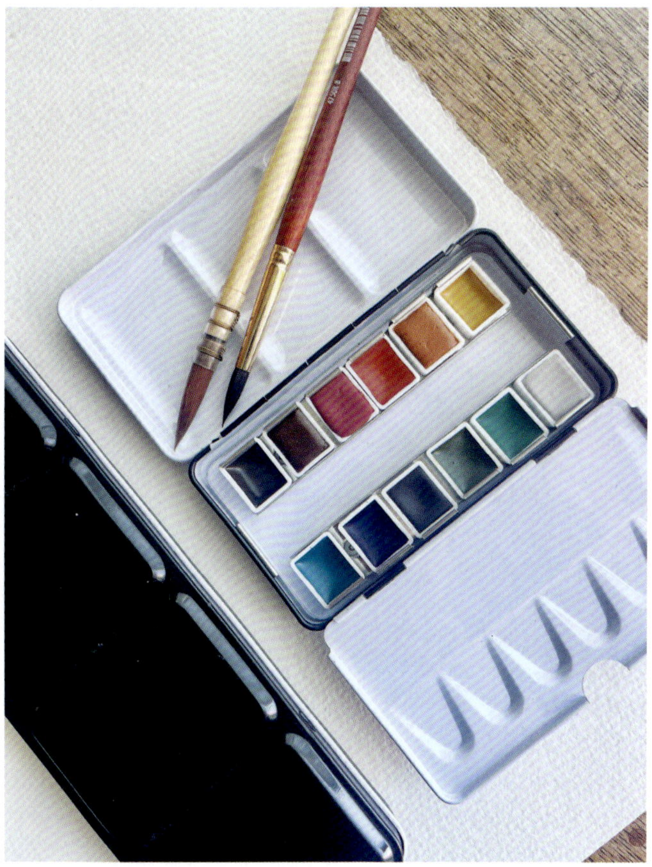

Watercolour Paper

Paper size, weight, texture and format is usually a very personal choice. However, the many different types of watercolour paper that are available to purchase can make such choices bewildering to begin with; especially as the weight and texture of your paper will directly affect the way the paint will react when applied. Different shades of toned paper are also available (see page 53); however, you will only need regular white watercolour paper for the projects in this book.

TEXTURE

Watercolour papers come in three basic textures: hot press, which has a smooth, satin-like finish; cold press (sometimes called NOT), which has some grain/texture; and rough, which is very highly textured. Each type of paper has its own merit, and it's worth experimenting with these different textures to discover what works best for you. Many art suppliers will offer paper sample packs, and these can be a handy and cost-efficient way of trying out a variety of different brands and finishes.

WEIGHT

Paper weight is important to note as it affects the quantity of paint and water the paper can handle. Lower weight, e.g. 90lb (180gsm), is considered thinner, so it will buckle quickly under heavy application of water. For landscape paintings, we recommend a minimum of 140lb (300gsm) weight paper, as this is able to support dramatic washes of colour; and while it will buckle a little if not pre-stretched (see below), it will usually flatten down nicely as it dries.

STRETCHING THE PAPER

Stretching is a technique used to pre-flatten lighter weight papers, to prevent them from buckling and becoming warped when water is added. Usually, this involves thoroughly wetting the paper all over on both sides to allow the water to soak all the way through; then laying it flat on a board and taping the sides down firmly with brown gummed tape that is water-activated (masking tape will peel away). As the paper dries, it will be held in place by the tape, allowing the fibres to relax and 'stretch'. Once fully dry, the paper is ready to be used.

Comparing various paper brands and surfaces can help make it clear just how much variety is out there. Certain painting techniques can be made simpler through choosing the right paper; for example, dry-brush technique (see page 38) is much easier to do on rough/cold press paper that has texture than on hot press paper with a smooth texture.

Paintbrushes

For the ten projects in this book, we've curated a small set of paintbrushes that have a broad range of use and are suitable for creating a variety of beautiful marks and painterly effects. These can be either synthetic fibre or natural hair brushes, according to your personal preference; these days, high-quality synthetic alternatives to natural hair or bristle brushes are readily available to purchase from most art suppliers.

The paintbrushes you will need for the projects are:

1 1½in (38mm) mottler brush
2 ¾in (20mm) flat brush
3 Size 20 mop brush
4 Size 10 mop brush
5 Size 2 quill brush
6 Size 3 round brush
7 Size 0 round brush
8 Small sword liner brush
9 Size 2 fan brush

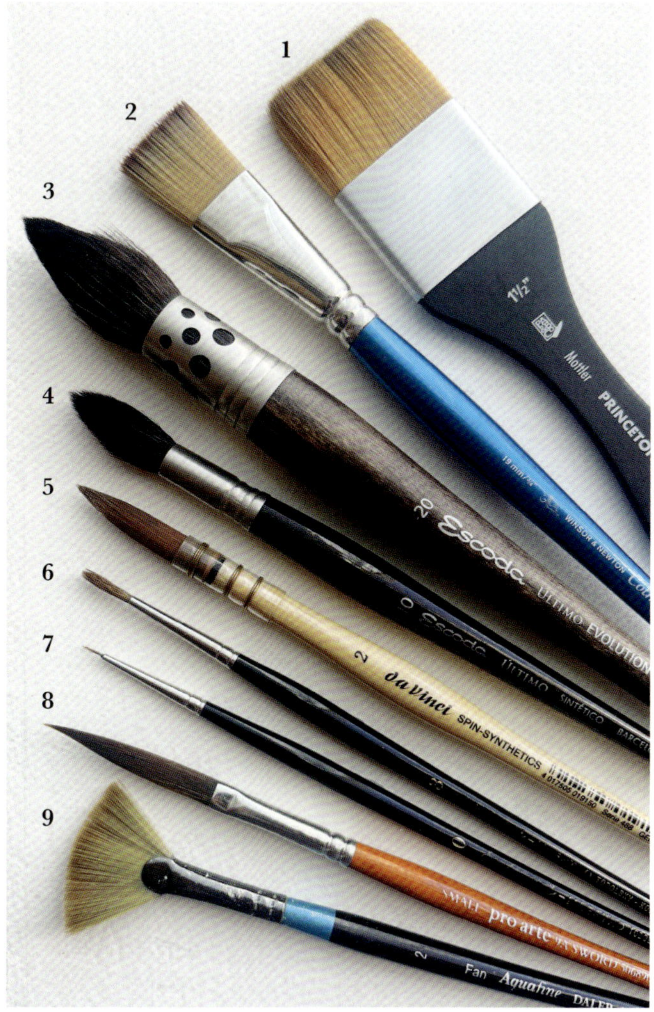

1½IN (38MM) MOTTLER BRUSH

This is a fantastic all-round flat brush. It will help you create beautiful vistas and washes of colour, as it holds a large amount of paint and water that can be applied in broad, sweeping motions to create dramatic seas and skies. Its crisp, flat edge means that the tip and corners can also be used to create flat lines and geometrical shapes.

¾IN (20MM) FLAT BRUSH

The thin profile of this more diminutive flat brush is ideal for painting smaller elements that would be difficult with the mottler. It works well to create simple lines and hard edges, as well as for sweeping colour over smaller areas.

SIZES 10 AND 20 MOP BRUSHES

These are soft round brushes that can hold a large amount of paint and water. Their shape makes them ideal for covering areas of colour quickly while avoiding the broad, straight-edged lines that a flat brush can sometimes create. They also taper to a fine point, which means they can be used for creating smaller marks, making them extremely versatile.

SIZE 2 QUILL BRUSH

This is a mid-sized round brush that has a lovely fine tip, making it ideal for filling complex areas of colour. Unlike the mop brushes, the hairs on this quill are flexible and springy, offering a different style of mark making.

SIZE 3 ROUND BRUSH

This is a real workhorse brush for filling in those smaller details. It can get into the intricate spaces of a painting, yet it's not so small that it constantly needs refilling with colour.

SIZE 0 ROUND BRUSH

Here is a fine round brush that is perfect for details and those small, fiddly areas that require a delicate touch. It is ideal for adding finishing touches to paintings such as highlights.

SMALL SWORD LINER BRUSH

The long, slender hairs on this shapely brush hold a large amount of paint and water, making it ideal for painting long, unbroken thin lines, as well as sweeping curved shapes.

SIZE 2 FAN BRUSH

A versatile brush, it has wide-splayed, fan-like bristles. It can be used to make a variety of marks, including fine lines and spatter detail.

Other Equipment

PALETTES

Sets of pan watercolours will often come with a small, built-in palette. However, it can be very helpful to have a larger, separate palette on hand, too. Having a variety of mixing wells is useful for scenes that require several colours to be applied quickly, one after the other. Palettes come in many shapes and sizes, usually made from plastic, ceramic or metal. You can also use plates or saucers as paint palettes – just ensure you wash them thoroughly after use!

MASKING FLUID

This fluid is handy for preserving areas of white paper. To apply the mask, we recommend a small paintbrush with a good point, but use an old one as the fluid can damage the hairs of the brush if allowed to dry out. Be sure to first prep your brush with a little soap; this will protect the hairs and allow the masking fluid to be thoroughly washed away, which you should do immediately after use. You can purchase a specialist brush soap from an art shop, but ordinary hand soap works, too. Specialist masking fluid 'pens' are also available in most art shops; these can be useful for very fine, detailed work.

Once the painting is dry, you can easily remove the mask (see Basic Watercolour Techniques, page 24). For larger areas, we recommend an adhesive eraser pick-up to remove the mask cleanly without damaging the paper.

Tip

Some cheaper papers will tear on removing the mask, so do test your paper first to ensure it is suitable to use with masking fluid.

MASKING TAPE

Used to tape down sheets of watercolour paper firmly to a board, masking tape will prevent them from moving around or heavily buckling while you work. As a low-tack tape, it can be easily removed at the end of the project to reveal the finished painting.

SPONGE/KITCHEN PAPER

When working with a water-based medium, it's important to have something absorbent on hand – both for mopping up spills and to aid with water control. Dabbing your brush on clean kitchen paper is a great way to remove excess water that could potentially flood your painting and cause unwanted blooms or marks.

SANDPAPER

This abrasive is handy for adding texture or highlights once the paint is bone dry. Add these effects in last, as over-use can damage the paper surface. It is best used on textured paper, such as cold press or rough. It could also be used on hot press, but the textural effect would be less pronounced.

PALETTE KNIFE

More often used for oils and acrylics, a palette knife can also be used for watercolour: use it either as an alternative brush to add bold, distinctive marks, or to scrape into wet paint to add variety and texture.

SPRAY BOTTLE

Keeping a small spray bottle of water on hand is useful for a variety of reasons. A quick, careful mist can prevent your painting from drying out too fast, especially if you're working in a hot or arid environment. It can also be useful for activating watercolour paint pans, as well as to create soft, diffused effects when sprayed directly onto your work.

FINE-LINER PENS

These are vital for line and wash paintings, such as in 'Red Sails' (see page 40). They come in a variety of thicknesses and colours, but the projects in this book will only use black in sizes 0.1mm, 0.3mm and brush nib. Ensure you use pens with waterproof ink; otherwise, the outlines will be destroyed as soon as you start adding colour.

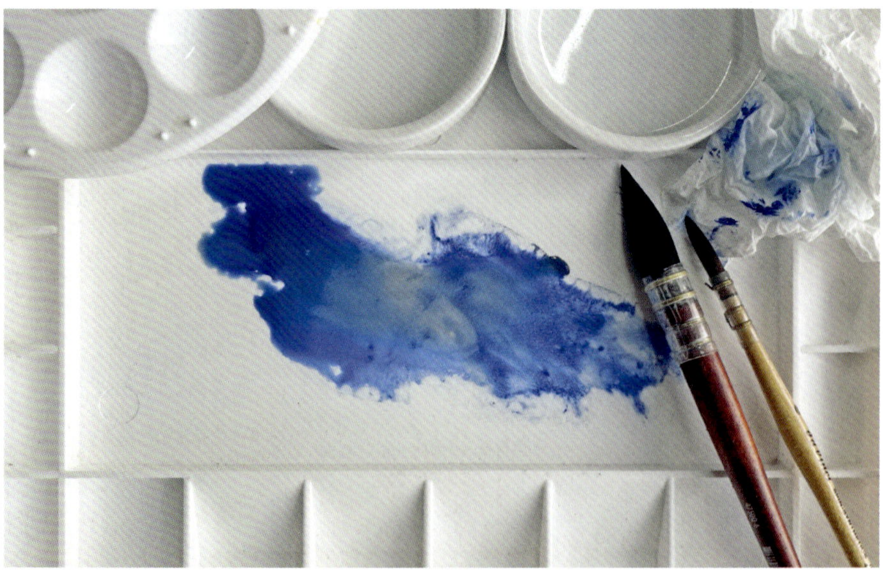

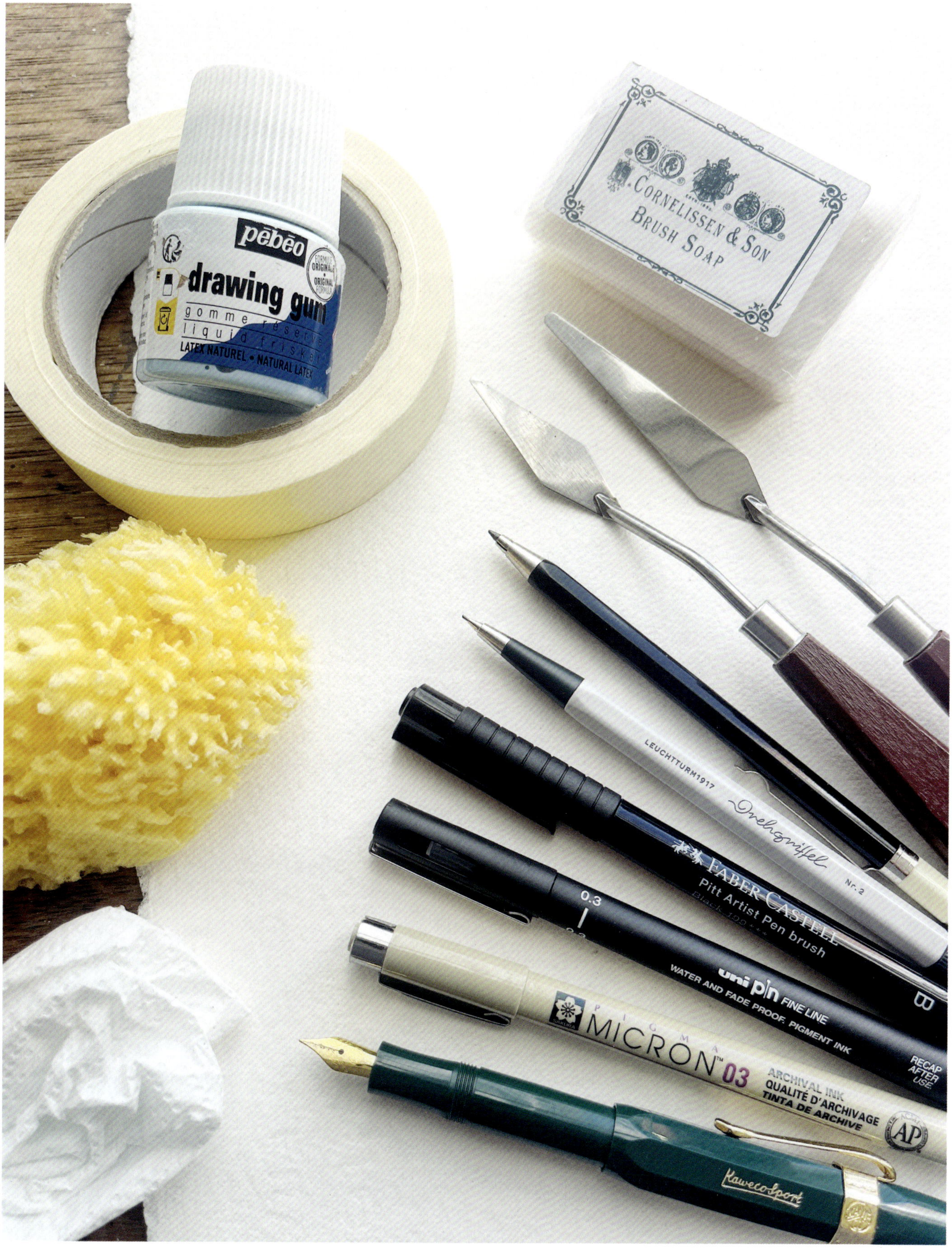
pébéo
drawing gum
gomme réserve
liquid frisket
LATEX NATUREL • NATURAL LATEX
CORNELISSEN & SON
BRUSH SOAP
LEUCHTTURM1917
Drehgriffel
Nr. 2
FABER-CASTELL
Pitt Artist Pen brush
0.3
uni pin FINE LINE
WATER AND FADE PROOF, PIGMENT INK
RECAP AFTER USE
PIGMA
MICRON 03
ARCHIVAL INK
QUALITÉ D'ARCHIVAGE
TINTA DE ARCHIVE
Kaweco Sport

Applying Colour

Colour is one of the key elements that acts as a way to create meaning in art. It enables a painter to convey a sense of place, focus and emotion that communicates without the need for using words. Because of this, understanding the how, why and when of applying colour is an important stage of familiarizing yourself with the overall process of watercolour painting.

The 'How' of Colour

When it comes to applying colour, the 'how' can be best approached in two different ways. The first of these is to familiarize yourself with the technical side by practising the various different brush techniques and methods for applying colour, which are covered in 'Basic Watercolour Techniques' (see pages 22–25). The second way is to take a look at what we actually mean when we use the word 'colour'.

When selecting colours for a project, there are three main elements to consider: hue, value and saturation. Hue is what we mean when we speak of colours in general; it refers to the actual colour itself. For example, Cerulean Blue and Ultramarine Blue are both blue hues. The value refers to how light or dark a colour appears, and in watercolour painting this is usually determined by how much water is used to dilute a paint solution. The saturation refers to the colour's intensity. There are ways to both brighten and lower (desaturate) your colours; mixing a little of the main colour's complementary colour (see below) will temper its brightness. For example, to desaturate a livid green, try mixing in a little red to tone down its brightness and give it an earthier hue.

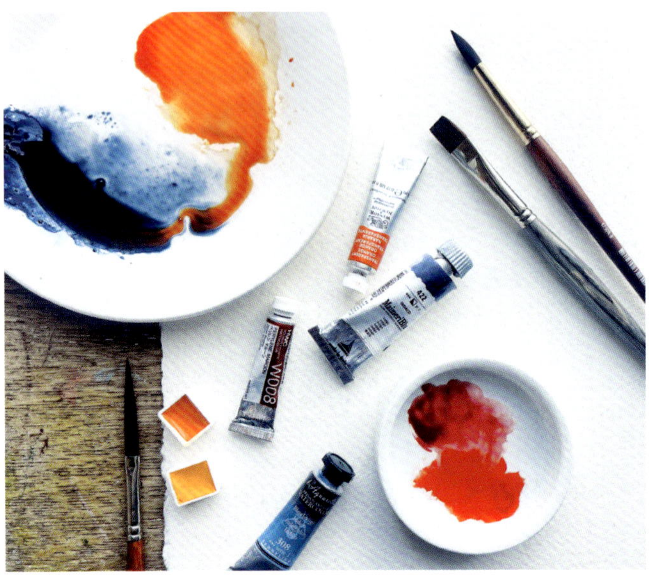

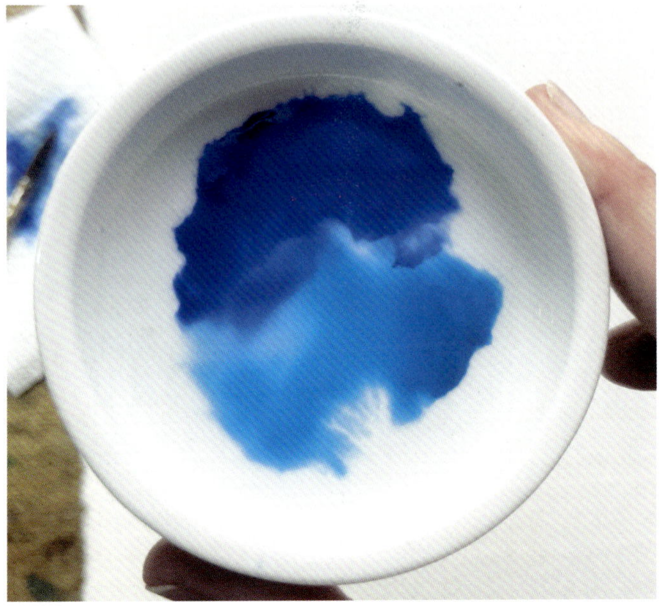

There is a difference in hue between Ultramarine Blue (top) and Cerulean Blue (bottom). Both are intense and lovely shades of blue, and they work well alongside one another when painting seas and skies.

The 'Why' of Colour

Why use one colour over another? Why use Cerulean Blue if one prefers Cobalt Blue? All painters have their personal preferences, and this so often dictates the overall palettes of their paintings. We have provided a selection of recommended colours that are used over the course of the ten projects in this book, which will allow you to follow along and complete each demonstration. However, always remember that it is perfectly acceptable to use substitute colours for any reason – even if the reason is simply because you prefer them!

Tip

Spend a little time colour mixing and swatching in your sketchbook. You may be amazed at the many variations that different combinations can produce!

Colour Theory Basics

Having said that, there are some colour theory basics that should always be kept in mind when setting up your palette. The three primary colours are always going to be useful, in one way or another: these are red, yellow and blue. From these hues, we may mix a variety of secondary colours: red and yellow mix to make orange, red and blue will combine to create violet, and yellow with blue will create green.

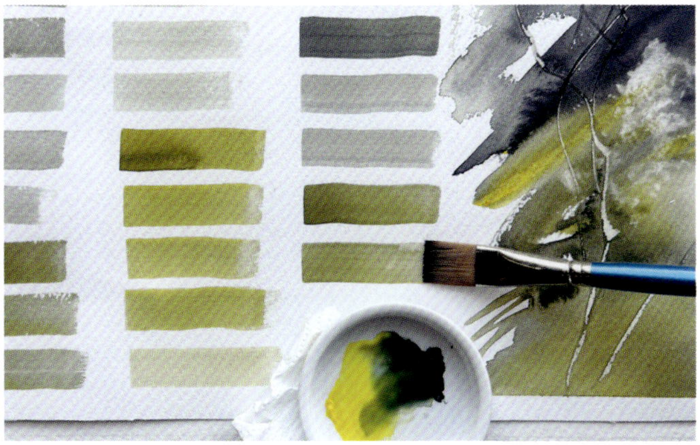

These secondary colours are also known as complementary colours: each primary has a corresponding secondary, or complementary, colour, which is mixed from the other two primaries. For example, the complement of blue is orange, mixed from yellow and red. Using complementary colours side-by-side in your paintings provides contrast, and can be a useful visual cue to indicate points of interest. For example, a scattering of crimson flowers against a wash of green grass is a great way to draw a viewer's eye to that area of the composition.

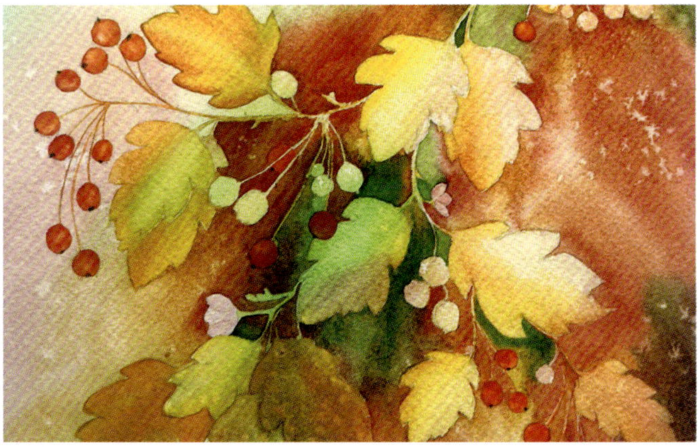

The use of the complementary pairing of red and green in various hues turns this simple tangle of hawthorn leaves and berries into a more interesting composition.

The 'When' of Colour

Knowing when to choose a warm colour over a cool one is something best learned through doing. There are no hard rules here; however, when painting a landscape scene, it can be handy to remember that warm colours tend to stand out and come forward, while cool colours recede. For this reason, warm tones are ideal to use for painting foregrounds and points of interest, while cool tones are perfect for panoramic vistas that include features, such as distant forests or cliffs, that need to fade into the distance.

WARM VERSUS COOL

Traditionally, green, blue and purple are classed as cool colours, while yellow, red and orange are classed as warm. However, there is some variation within these colours – for example, there are cool reds and warm reds, and the key to determining which is which lies in how well they react with other tones. Cool reds will lean towards the blue end of the spectrum and tend to create the prettiest violet hues; while warm reds will lean more heavily towards the yellow side of the spectrum and will mix well with other warm colours. For example, Cadmium Scarlet is a warm red, as it inclines towards orange and mixes beautifully with yellows and pinks; while Alizarin Crimson is a cool red that mixes wonderfully with other cool colours, such as purples and blues.

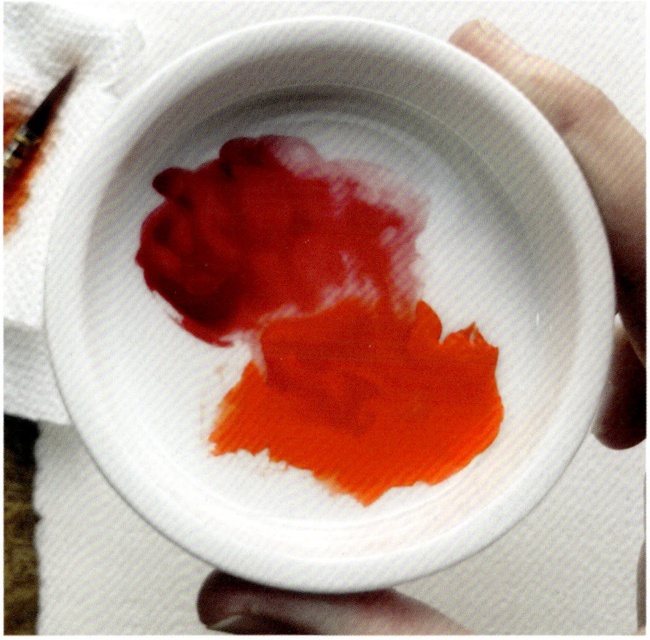

When placed side by side, the difference between these cool (Alizarin Crimson at top) and warm (Cadmium Scarlet at bottom) reds becomes readily apparent.

Design, Depth and Distance

When planning your paintings, it's worth bearing in mind that you are trying to create an artistic interpretation – not an exact copy of a reference. Following a few simple guidelines will help you to create well-crafted designs with depth and distance.

Design

Taking a little time to plan out your painting can create a more successful and engaging outcome. There are many ways of doing this, but it can be helpful to start to think about composition in terms of a few simple shapes that can act as a guide when positioning other elements in your painting. This ensures that everything works together as a whole, and viewers will be effectively guided to your points of interest.

V AND Z COMPOSITIONS

A sideways V composition creates a dynamic yet simple design that will help to guide a viewer's eye around the painting.

Z- (or S-) shaped designs work in a similar way to the sideways V, but you can add as many 'bends' to the compositional pathway as you need if you wish to create a little more complexity.

CROSS AND L COMPOSITIONS

Cross and L shapes work well where a strong horizontal element crosses or meets a strong vertical one, such as the horizon line and a tree. These compositional pathways and nodes are the perfect position to place points of interest, where they will draw the eye towards what we want the viewer to notice in our paintings.

THE RULE OF THIRDS

Using this simple principle can also help you to create a pleasing design. Imagine your paper as a grid of nine equal sections. Any of the points where the grid lines intersect are considered to be good places to position points of interest, because the eye is drawn to elements that are slightly off-centre. This effect can be enhanced if you add more detail and contrast to these elements.

Tip

Do remember that when it comes to design, you can take a flexible approach as you grow in confidence, and be prepared to break the rules sometimes; after all, they are simply guidelines to get you started.

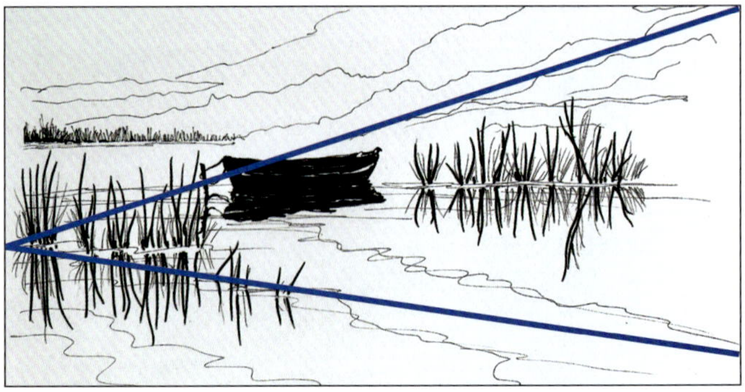

The subtle upward tilt of the horizontal elements add to the dynamic effects in this classic V-shaped composition.

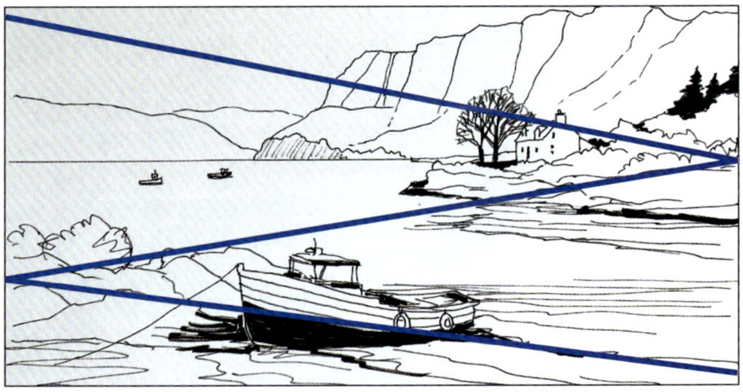

Using a Z-shaped design can add clarity when you wish to include a number of different design elements.

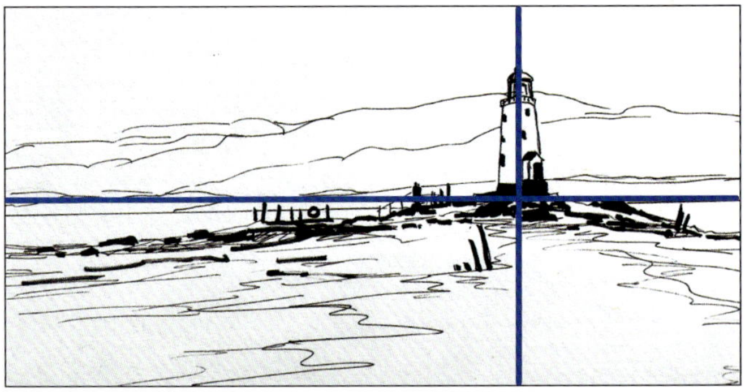

Here, the strong horizontal contrast provided by the sea, land and low cloud creates a pleasing cross-shaped design when combined with the vertical 'pull' of the lighthouse.

Depth and Distance

As you learn to paint coastal scenes in watercolour, it will help to follow a few basic principles when creating your painting. They will enable you to simplify what you see, thereby helping you to represent the depth and distance of a three-dimensional world on a two-dimensional surface (your watercolour paper).

To create a convincing illusion of depth and distance in your paintings you will need to use these three principles: linear perspective, aerial perspective and foreshortening. A basic understanding of simple linear perspective and foreshortening will enable you to draft your design accurately at the sketching stage, while the principle of aerial perspective, applied during the painting process, can help to create a convincing sense of depth and distance in your work.

LINEAR PERSPECTIVE

Elements will recede in size as they get closer to a vanishing point on the horizon. You can create linear guidelines to follow in order to position receding elements on the picture plane, so that they reduce in size the closer they get to the vanishing point. Place a vanishing point on the horizon line, and then imagine converging lines radiating out from this point (or converging at the point). This will keep things in proportion and create a sense of depth and distance.

Sketch these lines lightly in pencil on watercolour paper first. Once you are happy with the position of all your elements and the scale of your drawing, simply erase the converging lines and you will be ready to paint.

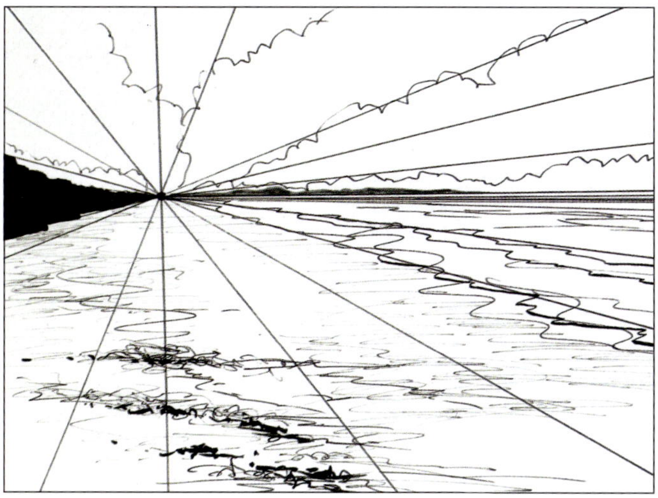

The lines of perspective 'converge' at the vanishing point on the horizon line. Don't forget to pay attention to perspective in the sky as the type of clouds you wish to paint may need it.

AERIAL PERSPECTIVE

You can create the effects of aerial or atmospheric perspective by using subtle tonal and colour-temperature changes as you paint these distant elements. By using paler, cooler colours for distant areas, and warmer colours and stronger contrasts in middle and foreground elements, things will appear to recede into the distance. (See 'Applying Colour', pages 16–17.)

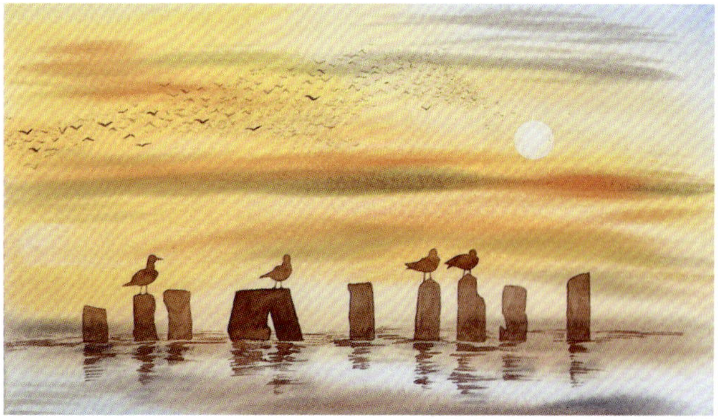

The flock of birds is suggested by loose marks that become smaller, paler and less distinct, creating the impression of the flock disappearing into the distance.

FORESHORTENING

If you want to show an element in your painting at an angle – let's use a boat as an example – its overall shape will look very different to the typical view seen from the side or front. The illustration below demonstrates this. Through careful observation and lots of practice in your sketchbook, you should get used to rendering objects at different angles, paying close attention to the shapes that can be seen at particular angles.

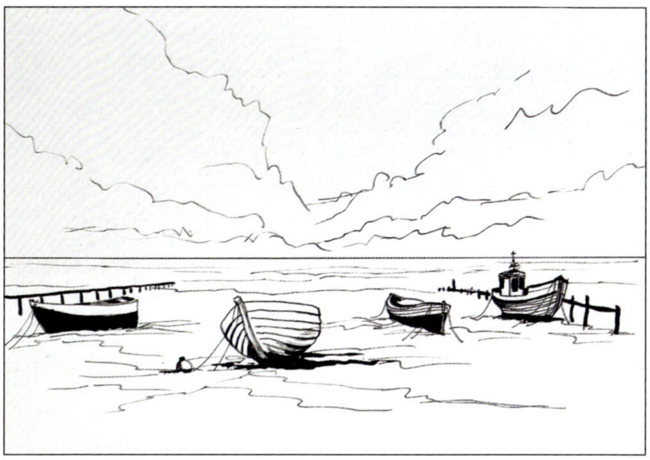

The different shapes of the boats depend on whether they are viewed front-on or angled to the left or right.

Sketching and Drawing

Much like learning to play an instrument or learning a new language, sketching and drawing are skills that anyone can learn. With regular practice, you can develop the fundamental skills that will help you to form a firm foundation for painting coastal scenes.

Sketching is a great way to practise and improve your drawing and painting skills, to try out ideas for future paintings, and to develop your observational skills. You don't have to worry about creating masterpieces in a sketchbook; it is simply a place to play around with ideas, test compositions and build the skills you need for painting coastal scenes in watercolour.

You can sketch outdoors with very few specialist art supplies, or if you prefer to work at home, take lots of photos of your favourite places, and then use them to try out ideas and plan future paintings back home in your studio space.

Safety First

If you plan to go sketching on beaches at low tide, ensure you are fully informed about tide times and any safety information you need for that location. In this way you shouldn't be caught out when the tide comes in, which can be very quick!

Drawing Outlines for the Projects

The projects in this book are set up in two ways: the pure watercolour paintings start by lightly sketching the outline with an HB pencil; the ink and watercolour projects require drawing over the pencil sketch with waterproof black fine-liner pens to create inked line work. You then erase any pencil marks, and tape the paper to a painting board, ready to begin.

If you prefer, you can practise sketching the outline in your sketchbook first, then when you are happy with it, use tracing paper to transfer the sketch onto watercolour paper.

Sketching at Home

If you sketch and draw at home, you will have access to all your regular art supplies. However, it can be handy to have a dedicated sketchbook or two just for sketching and drawing: somewhere to experiment, play with ideas and test out designs for paintings.

Sketching Outdoors

I love to sketch outdoors, *en plein air*. When I'm out and about, I always try to travel light. You don't need expensive equipment and materials, just a pencil and a small sketchbook, and maybe a set of portable travel paints and a water brush, so you can quickly capture the essence of anything that catches your eye: the gentle curve of a distant headland, a fishing boat dragged up on the shingle, or dappled sunlight sparkling on a river as it flows out to the sea.

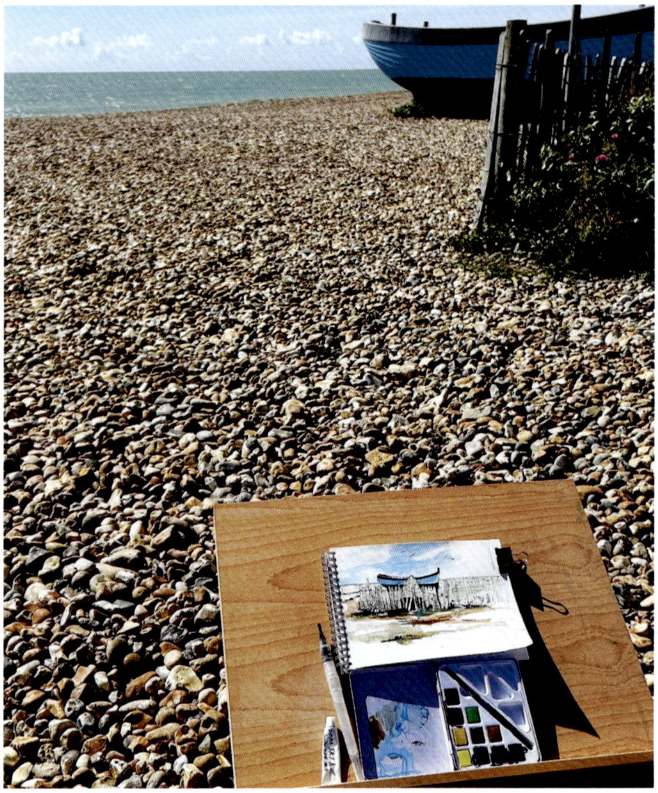

Nothing beats going for a long coastal walk, armed with a small bag of sketching supplies and a flask of coffee. There's always something new to see and sketch.

Outdoor Sketching Supplies

Portability is key when sketching outdoors, which means small sketchbooks are ideal. I prefer those with mixed media paper so I can sketch in watercolour as well as pencil and other dry mediums. A sketchbook with a stiff cover will suffice, but if space allows, a small table easel or drawing board can be a useful addition to your kit.

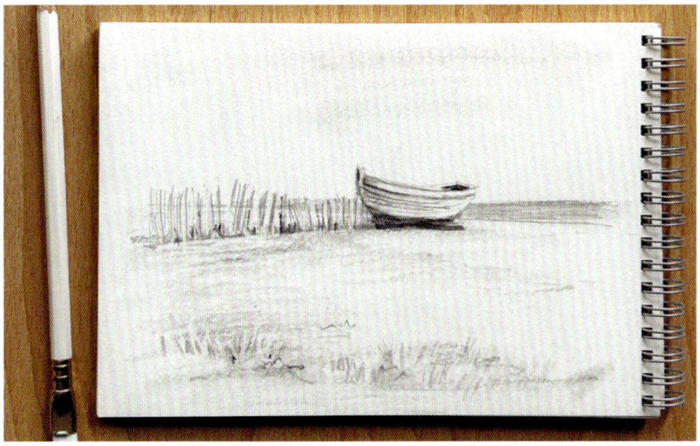

My small sketchbook is ring-bound and opens flat, so it is really easy to whip out and start sketching when I spot something interesting! A pencil with an eraser on the end is very handy.

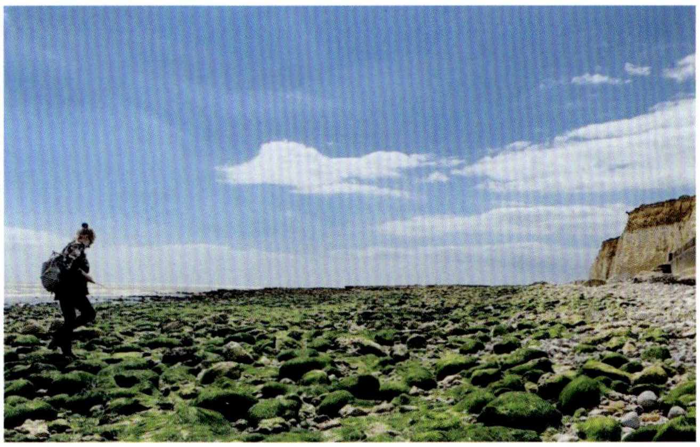

A backpack makes light work of carrying all your supplies while you search for suitable locations to draw or paint.

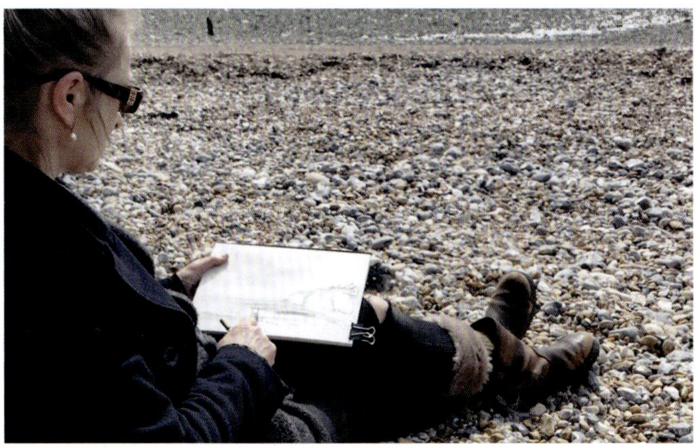

Try to find a sheltered spot for sketching. Bulldog clips can be useful to keep your sketchbook pages from flapping about in the winds that are common on the coast.

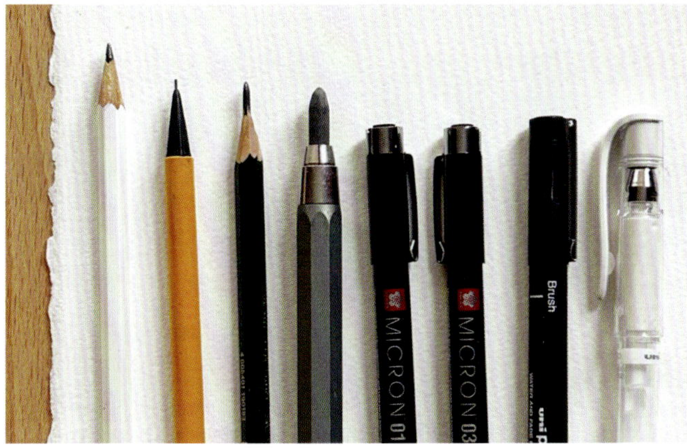

Here are my favourite pencils and pens for sketching: 2B wood case pencil, HB mechanical pencil, HB wood case pencil, clutch pencil with large lead, black 0.1mm, 0.3mm and brush-nib fine-liner pens, and white gel pen.

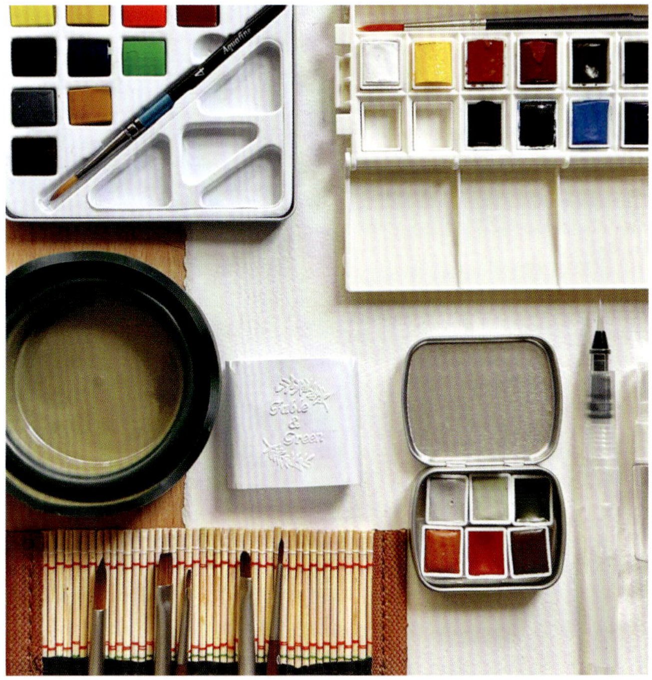

Small paint sets are perfect to take with you for sketching, or you can choose a few of your favourite pan colours and keep them in a small tin. Brush rolls are very handy for keeping pencils, pens, paintbrushes, etc. together and easily accessible. Water brushes do away with the need to carry heavy bottles of water around. If you prefer to use traditional brushes and water, you can purchase collapsible water pots that are light and durable, and travel paintbrushes that are either shorter than studio brushes, or that come in small protective cases where the handle and heads can be put together on location.

Basic Watercolour Techniques

Watercolour painting has a reputation for being quite a challenging medium, and it can be, but if you practise the basic techniques outlined in this section, and familiarize yourself with them before tackling the projects, you will begin to develop the necessary skills, and above all, the confidence to learn to work with watercolour's unique characteristics.

A good place to start is with the big brush techniques: how to create the large, softly diffused wet-in-wet washes that will help you to establish the background, as well as the overall atmosphere of your painting.

Next come the smaller brush techniques: the crisper, hard-edged wet-on-dry brushstrokes and marks that will build up value, texture and detail.

Lastly, we share some of our favourite techniques, such as glazing, lifting paint, preserving the white paper and salt effects. These can add a little extra magic to your work.

Wet-in-wet Technique

This technique can be defined as painting onto a wet surface so the marks soften and diffuse on the page. All the projects start with a wet-in-wet wash: wetting the paper with clean water first, then using a large brush to create a 'wash' of colour – a thin layer of graduated, variegated or flat paint.

GRADUATED WASH

In a graduated wash, the colour is graded from dark to light, or from light to dark. Wet the paper with clean water, then starting at the top, apply the paint with a large wash brush, working down the page and adding a little more water to the paint to lighten it – or a little more pigment to darken it.

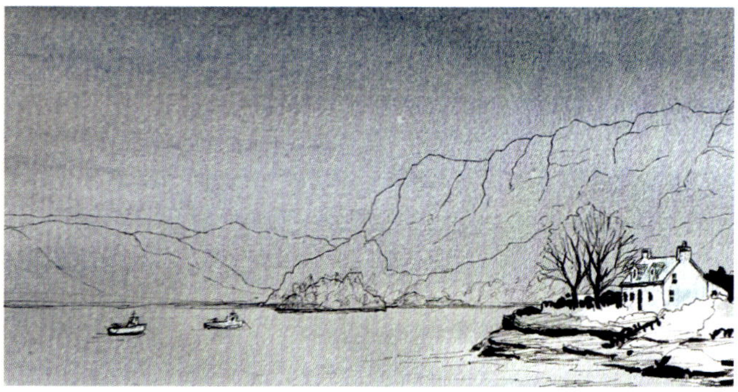

This wash is graduated from dark to light, which creates the atmosphere of the painting right from the start.

VARIEGATED WASH

A variegated wash is painted in the same way, but with more than one colour – a great way to add sunset effects and clouds.

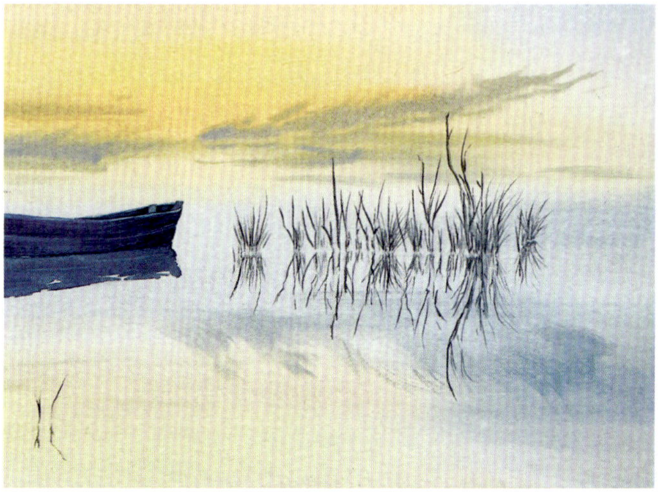

In a variegated wash, the colours blend on the paper, creating a variety of subtle hues.

FLAT WASH

We don't often use flat washes as we generally prefer a little variation in tone and colour, but a flat wash consists of an even wash of one colour, maintaining the same hue and value across the whole wash.

ALLA PRIMA

Painting *alla prima* is an exciting technique where the whole painting is completed wet-in-wet in one sitting, without leaving things to dry between stages. Sea Fret (see pages 80–85) uses this technique for most of the painting, working swiftly from one stage to the next, only pausing to wait for the painting to dry before adding the gulls and finishing touches at the end. This painting approach is best planned and prepared for, as it can be quite a full-on process. Pre-mix all the colours you need, and assemble all your brushes and tools beforehand.

WATER MISTING SPRAY

Wet-in-wet washes can be encouraged to flow by using a water misting spray. It can help to seamlessly blend between colours, and can remove all signs of brushstrokes. Tipping and tilting the board will help the paint to flow where you want it to go.

Dry Brush Technique

Mix a creamier paint using a little less water than you would for a more fluid wash. Load the brush, then dab on kitchen paper to absorb excess moisture. Hold the brush at a shallow angle to the paper as you make the brushstroke, and with practice, the paint will transfer to the raised texture, leaving the dimples of the paper unpainted. It can be painted onto dry paper, or a wash that has been allowed to dry to produce a sparkling effect.

Wet-on-dry Technique

This technique involves painting onto dry paper or a dried wash to create hard-edged brushwork and crisper detail.

FLICKED AND CALLIGRAPHIC BRUSHSTROKES

With a little practice, you can use the long-haired liner brushes, such as the sword liner, to create a wide range of loose brushstrokes. Using a flicking motion of the wrist, the brush is perfect for creating birds in flight, reeds and grasses.

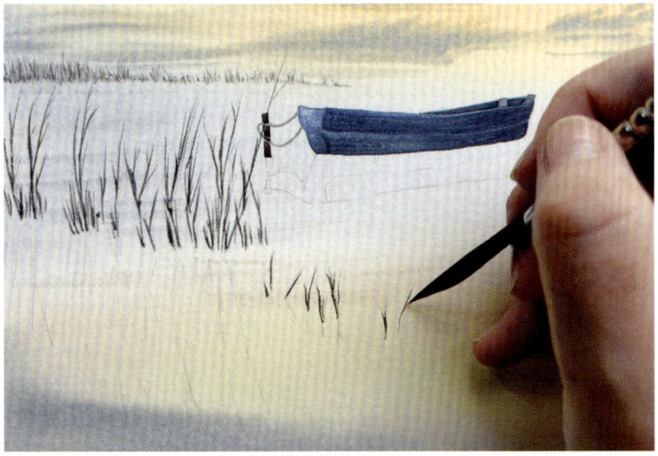

By using the fine tip of the sword liner brush and a flicking motion, you can create really delicate brushstrokes.

Inspired by the art of calligraphy, loose patterns and textures can be painted by 'dancing' the tip of the brush across the paper, filling the area with fresh, spontaneous calligraphic marks that work especially well for foliage; or in the case of the flat brush, using fluid, side-to-side motions with the tip can create lively and effective reflections or ripples. Practise these brushstrokes in your sketchbook to familiarize yourself with the techniques.

SPATTER PATTERNING

We love to use the fan brush to create spatter patterns – its fan-shaped bristles deliver an interesting, random pattern of spots. Load the brush with inky consistency paint, and then tap it with a finger or against another brush handle.

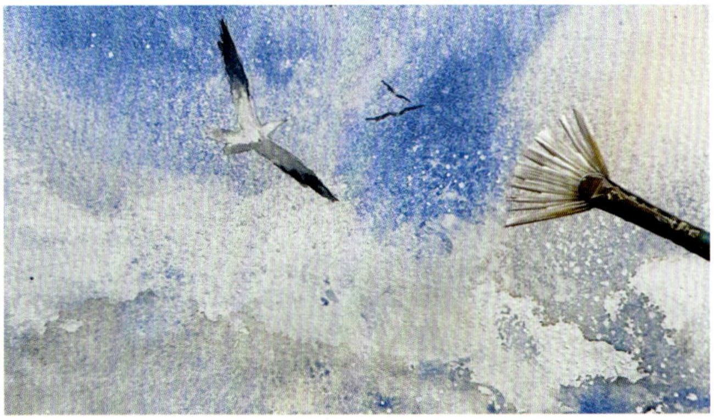

Tap the brush handle or ferrule sharply with your finger to release a random spread of spatter droplets.

MIXED COLOUR BRUSHSTROKES

This involves dipping your brush into more than one colour at the same time to create a mixed colour brushstroke. The effects here can be quite random, but unique. Experiment in your sketchbook with this technique, either wet-in-wet, or wet-on-dry, to discover the wonderful effects you can create!

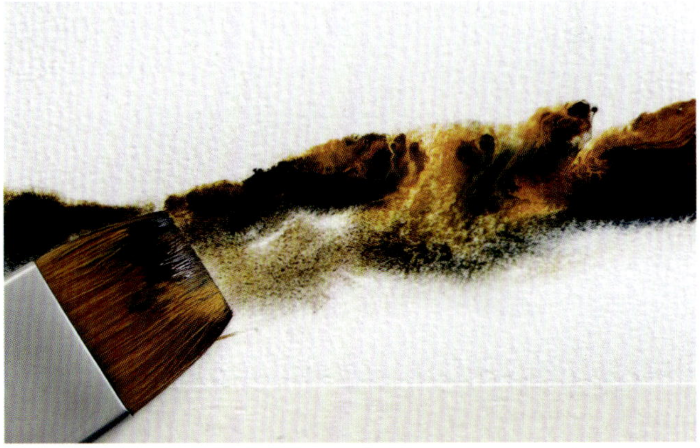

These beautiful effects were created by loading the brush with a dark value Indigo, Sepia, Burnt Sienna and Raw Umber, and then painting onto damp paper so that the colours blend together and diffuse.

Miscellaneous Techniques

This list of techniques is not exhaustive, but the information should give you an idea of some of the creative possibilities you can bring to life in your work.

PRESERVING THE WHITE PAPER

Unpainted white paper is highly prized in watercolour painting, as it provides the lightest value and, therefore, the greatest contrast. The white of the paper can be preserved as you paint, or you can add white highlights afterwards.

NEGATIVE PAINTING OR MASKING FLUID

You can preserve the white on the paper by carefully painting around the area you wish to keep white – in other words, painting the negative space around the white area. Or you can protect the area you wish to stay white with masking fluid (see Equipment and Materials, page 14). After applying this fluid to the paper with an old pointed small paintbrush, allow it to dry before painting with any subsequent washes. Once the painting is bone dry, you can remove the mask. For small areas, gently rub it away with a clean fingertip; you can use an adhesive eraser to remove the mask from larger areas.

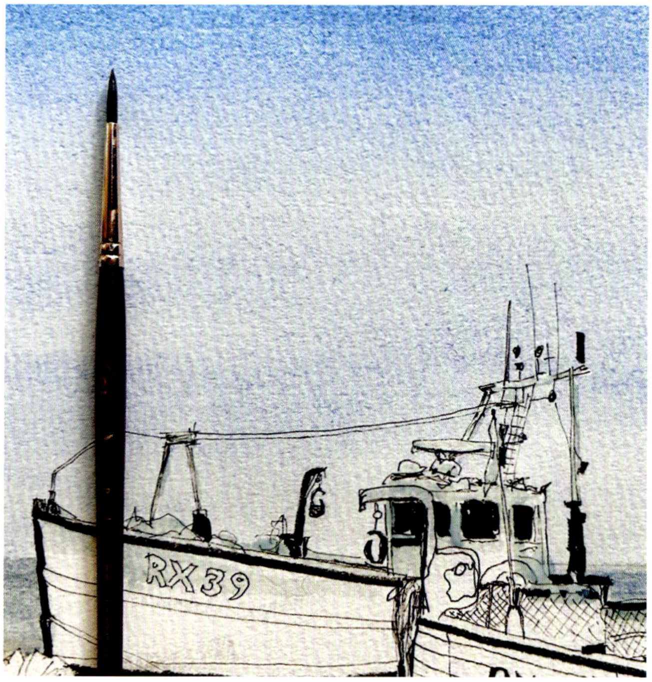

Apply a thin layer of masking fluid only to the areas you wish to keep white. Take care not to allow the dried masking fluid to 'sit' on the paper surface for too long, or you may find that it is difficult to remove or will otherwise damage the soft surface of your watercolour paper.

WHITE GOUACHE AND INK

Sometimes it is more suitable to add highlights on top of painted areas, so using opaque media, such as white ink or white gouache, can create effective white highlights.

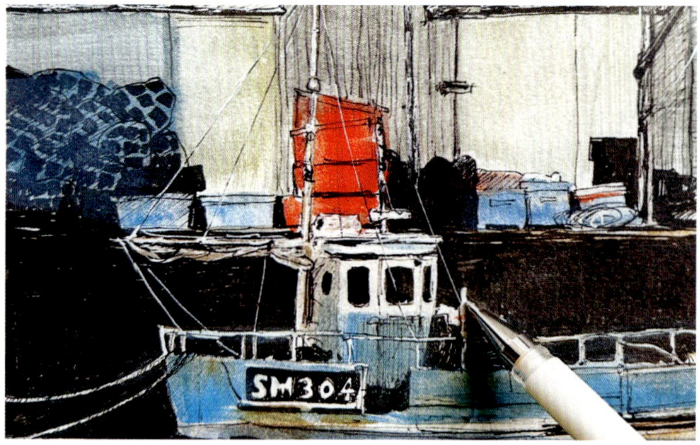

White highlights work especially well when added to a dark background.

LIFTING PAINT

You can lift wet paint with a damp paintbrush or kitchen paper – and you can also lift dry paint. Re-wet an area of paint by carefully brushing it with a little water. Leave it for a few seconds, then gently dab with kitchen paper to remove the paint. Repeat until the paint has been lifted.

LIFTING OUT A MOON OR SUN SHAPE

This is a fun trick to create a perfectly round shape: Take a small coin, and a piece of kitchen paper. Wrap the coin in the kitchen paper, and press lightly into a wet wash to lift out a perfect circle!

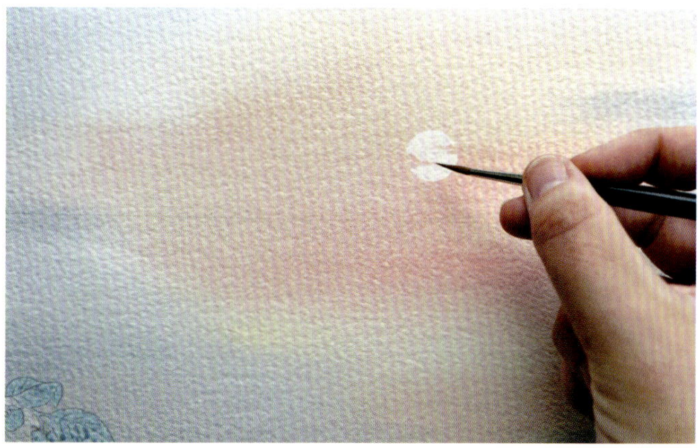

Paint a little of the sky colour over the lifted moon to suggest delicate clouds drifting in front of it.

GLAZING

As watercolour is a transparent medium, you can 'glaze' over areas of your painting with thin washes, so that the colour beneath shows through. This can be a very useful way to adjust the colour temperature of the painting; for example, a warm yellow glaze will add a sunlit look to foreground grass, whereas a glaze of grey or pale blue over the same area will cool it a little so it appears to be in shadow.

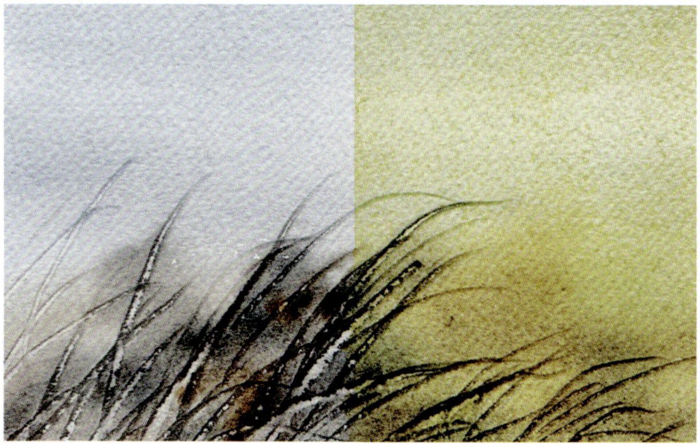

Glazing Transparent Yellow over this grey marsh scene creates an interesting and atmospheric effect.

SALT EFFECTS

A little ordinary table salt sprinkled into a damp wash can create beautiful textural effects. The salt grains repel the watery paint, leaving a tiny flower or fern-like 'bloom'. It won't work if the wash is too wet or too dry, so practise on the back of an old painting first to see how factors like the wetness of the paper, as well as the warmth and humidity in your painting space, affect the way the salt behaves.

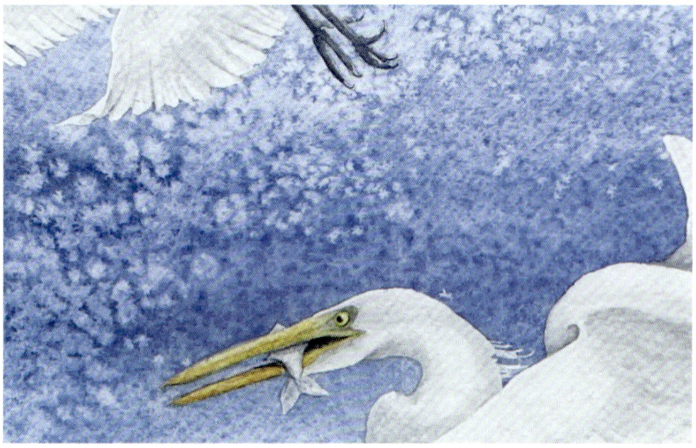

A small amount of salt grains sprinkled into the damp wash can produce very pretty textural effects.

SGRAFFITO AND SANDING

You can reveal the white paper by scratching into the surface of a bone-dry painting with a craft knife, or lightly sand the painted surface to create effects similar to painting with a dry brush (see page 38). Don't try this on a damp painting as the paper will tear! Do bear in mind that these effects damage the paper and are permanent, so they should be used sparingly, and when you are sure the painting is finished.

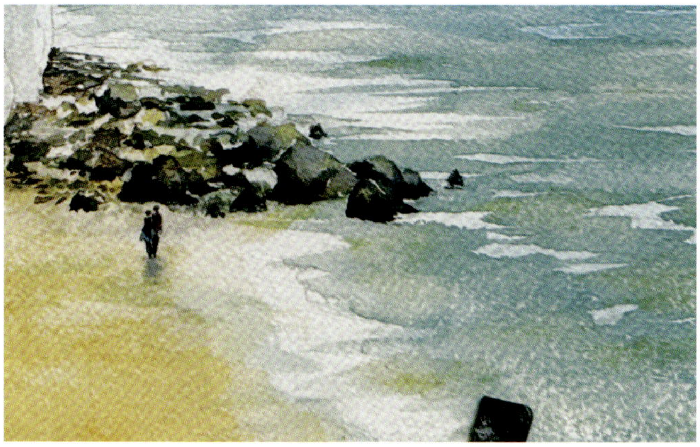

A little light sanding in the shallows has revealed subtle sea-foam highlights, giving an effect similar to dry brush.

MARKS WITH A PALETTE KNIFE OR OTHER TOOLS

The pointed tip of a palette knife can be used to scrape through damp paint to reveal the paper or paint below. This is useful for creating rock and strata textures, or tree branches and grasses. This versatile tool, or other alternative tools, can also be used in place of a brush to apply paint to the paper, either when wet or dry for interesting effects (see Focus On: Creating Atmospheric Scenes, page 53).

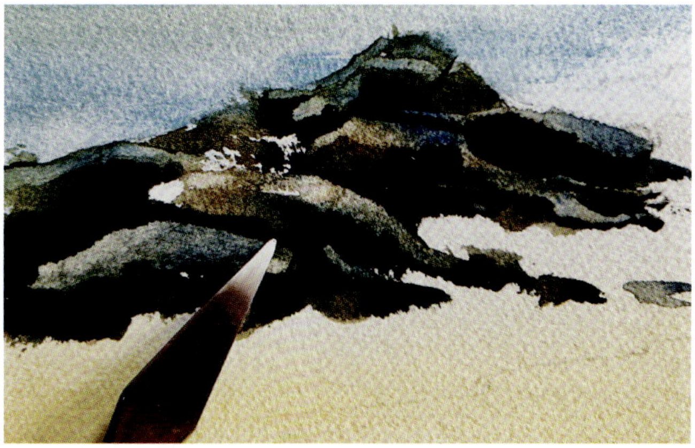

Scraping the dark paint back from the top of the rocks while damp reveals the lighter paint layer below.

Seven Sisters

The iconic Seven Sisters clifftop view always makes a striking and beautiful painting subject. In this scene, the elegant faces of the chalk cliffs almost glow against a diffused winter sky, with drifting clouds promising inclement weather.

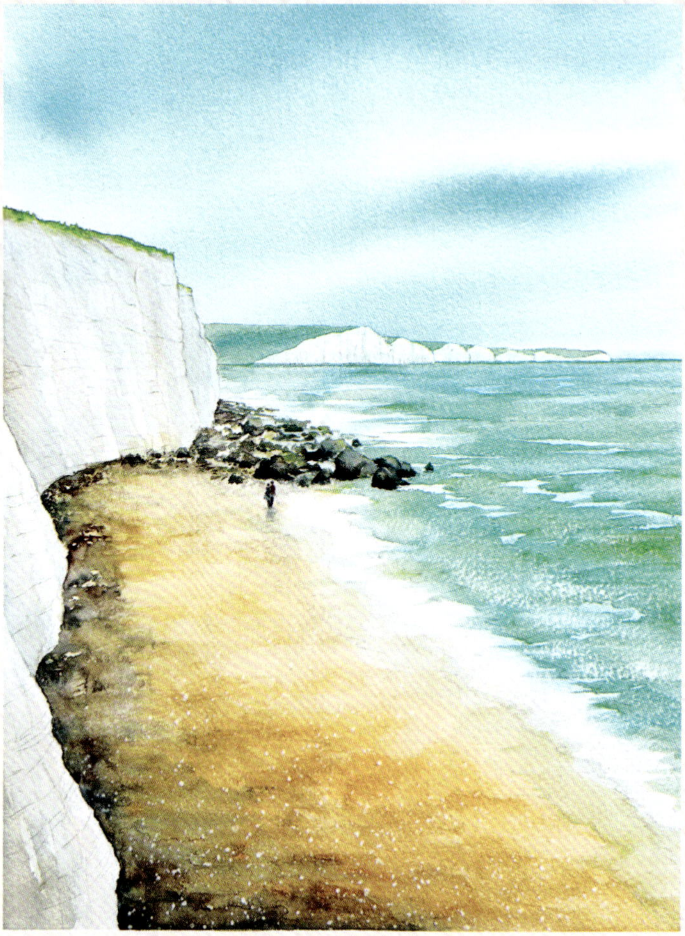

COLOURS NEEDED

Cerulean Blue, Indigo, Raw Sienna, Payne's Grey, Sap Green

Raw Umber, Burnt Sienna, Sepia, White Gouache, Vermilion Hue

Here, I have re-imagined Morgaine's rugged, windswept photo into a calmer scene. Bright winter days on UK shores often come with drifts of pale cloud, soft diffused light and beautiful turquoise seas tipped with white waves. I love the composition of this scene, with the graceful sweep of the Seven Sisters chalk cliffs stretching into the distance. The mid-ground figures, although small, are an important element, as they provide much-needed scale: we immediately realize just how tall and imposing the towering cliffs are in comparison.

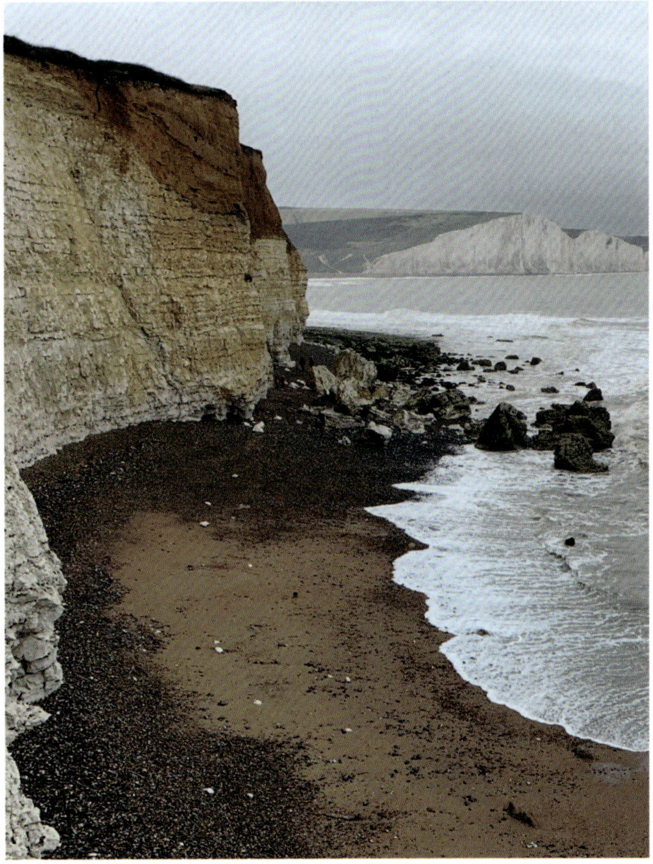

Setting Up

Begin by sketching an outline lightly onto cold pressed watercolour paper using the HB pencil (see page 20). Mask out the distant cliffs using masking fluid and an old small pointed brush (see page 24). Tape your paper to the painting board and lay flat, ready to begin.

YOU WILL NEED

- *140lb (300gsm) cold pressed (NOT) watercolour paper*
- *HB pencil and eraser*
- *Masking fluid and old pointed brush*
- *Painting board and decorator's masking tape*
- *Palette with mixing wells*
- *Kitchen paper*
- *Adhesive eraser*
- *Clean scrap paper*
- *Sandpaper*
- *1½in (38mm) mottler brush*
- *Size 0 round brush*
- *Size 3 round brush*
- *Size 2 quill brush*
- *¾in (20mm) flat brush*
- *Size 2 fan brush*

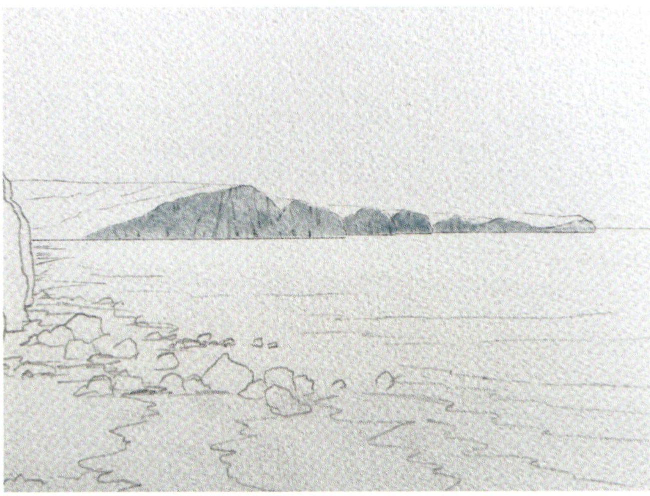

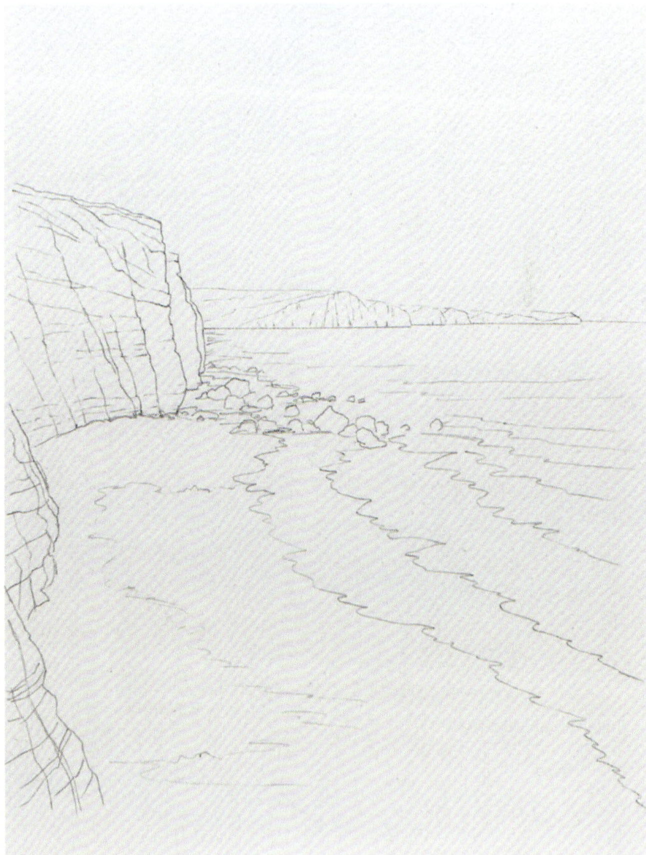

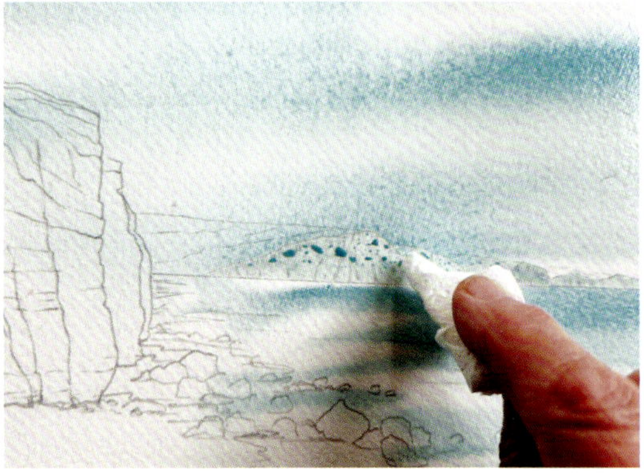

Use a clean piece of kitchen paper to carefully remove paint from the masked-out cliffs.

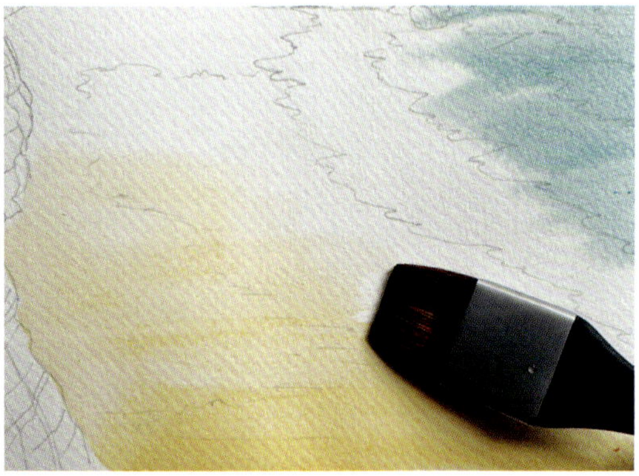

Graduate the Raw Sienna wash on the beach so it is lighter in the middle ground and darker in the foreground.

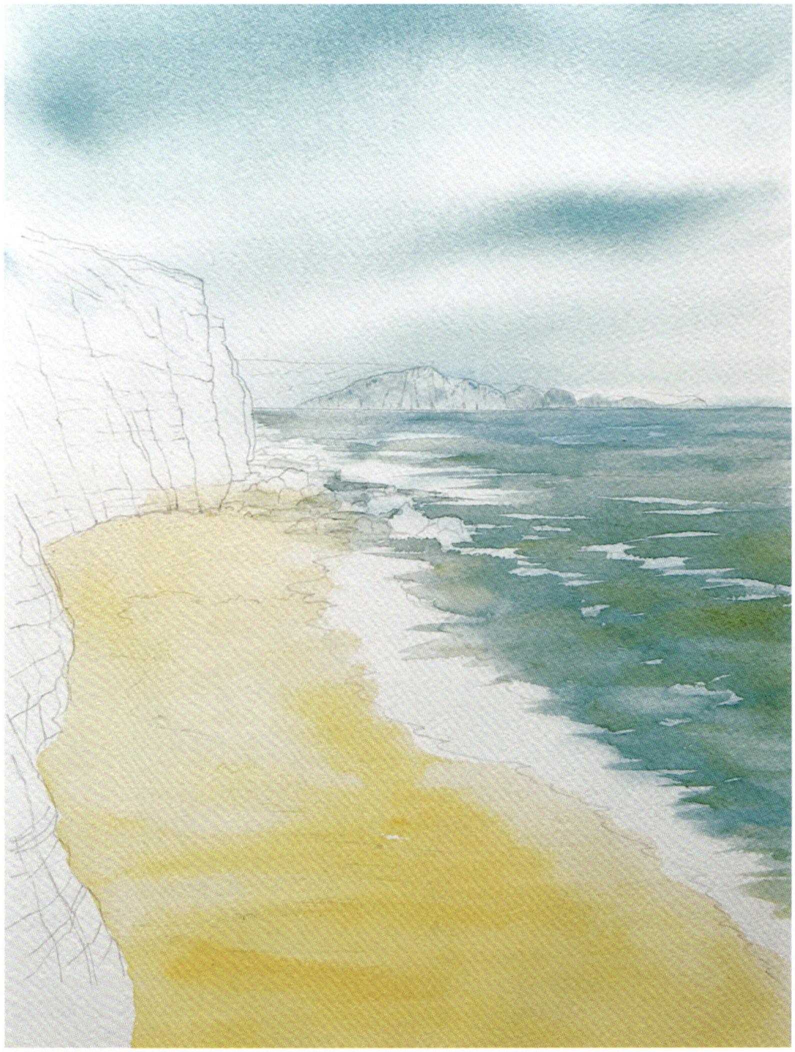

STAGE 1

Mix a large well of mid- to dark-value blue using Cerulean Blue with a little Indigo to desaturate it, and a large well of mid-value Raw Sienna. Wet the sky and sea with clean water using the mottler brush, and wet the beach but leave a band of dry paper at the shoreline. Leave to soak for 30 seconds.

Using the mottler brush, paint the sky with the blue mix using horizontal brushstrokes, keeping the wash darker across the top and becoming lighter towards the horizon. Leave a few narrow unpainted strips for clouds, then paint the wash across the sea, feathering it out at the shore. Rinse the brush, dip it into the sienna and paint the beach. Leave until bone dry.

Add a little Raw Sienna to the sky colour to mix a light-value glaze of greenish-blue, and using the flat brush, glaze over the sea, leaving the underpainting showing through here and there to suggest light on the water. Leave to dry completely.

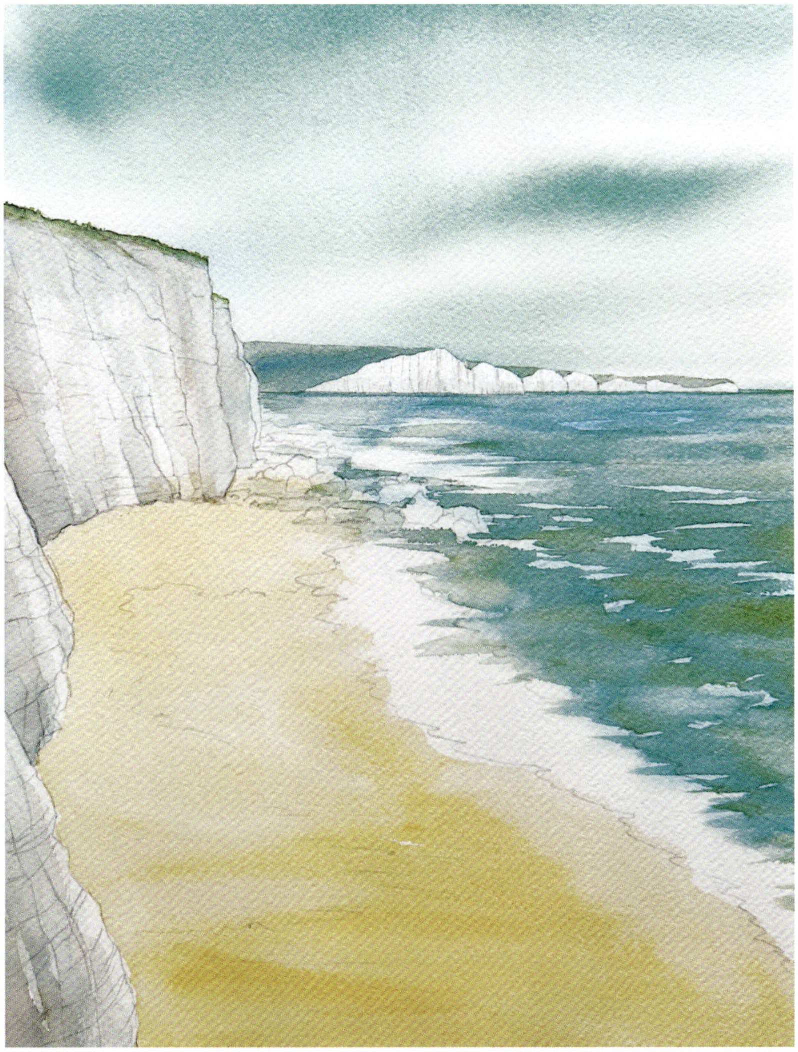

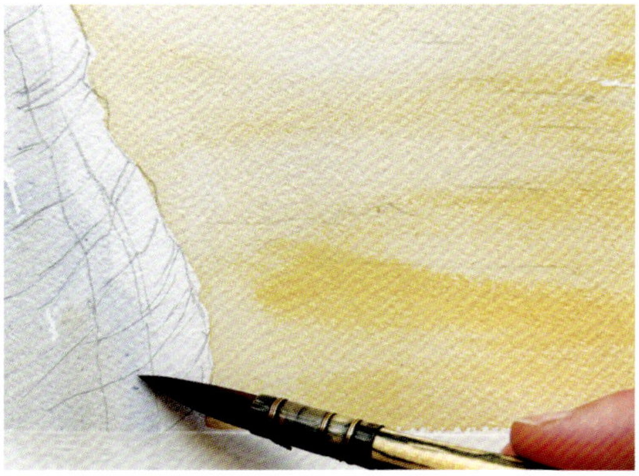

Notice how the light, transparent paint allows the pencil sketch to show through, suggesting strata on the cliff face.

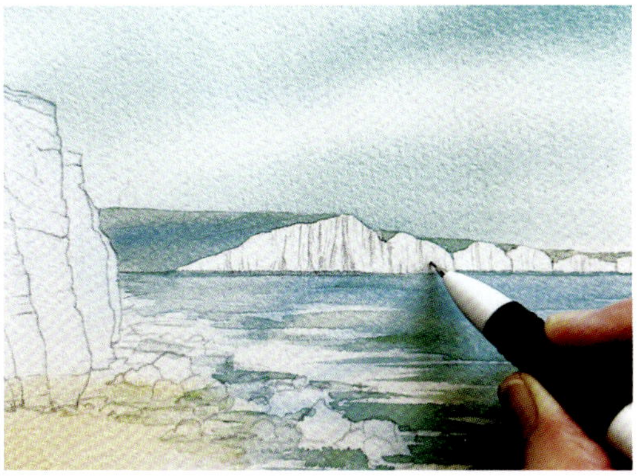

If the strata lines are erased when removing the masking fluid, lightly reinstate them with the HB pencil.

STAGE 2

Use the same colour that you used in Stage 1 for the sea glaze to paint the tops of the distant cliffs with the size 0 round brush. Swap to the size 3 round brush for the hilltop. Leave to dry. Paint a fine line under the cliffs with the same colour, using the size 0 round brush.

Once dry, remove the masking fluid from the cliffs using the adhesive eraser (see page 24).

Mix four small wells of watery, light-value shadow colours: Cerulean Blue with a dab of Payne's Grey, Sap Green, Raw Umber and Burnt Sienna. Using the size 2 quill brush, paint the middle-ground and foreground cliffs using these colours, leaving plenty of white paper for highlights.

While still damp, drop a little more sienna into the shadows here and there. Paint the clifftop grass with the green and umber. Leave to dry.

Tip

If you inadvertently paint over all the white paper on the cliffs, allow them to dry, then add some white with opaque White Gouache.

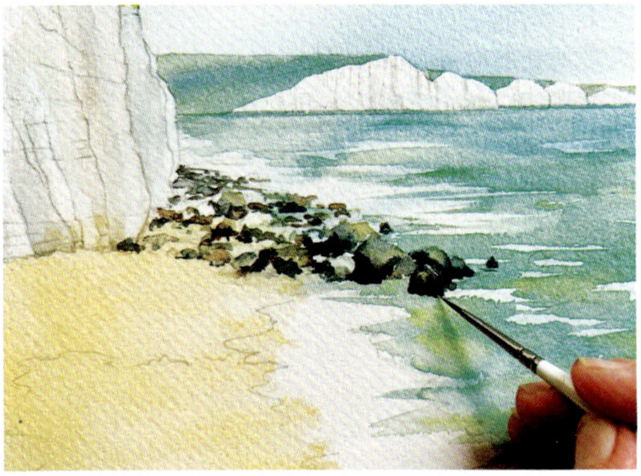

Keep the rocks nice and dark at their bases.

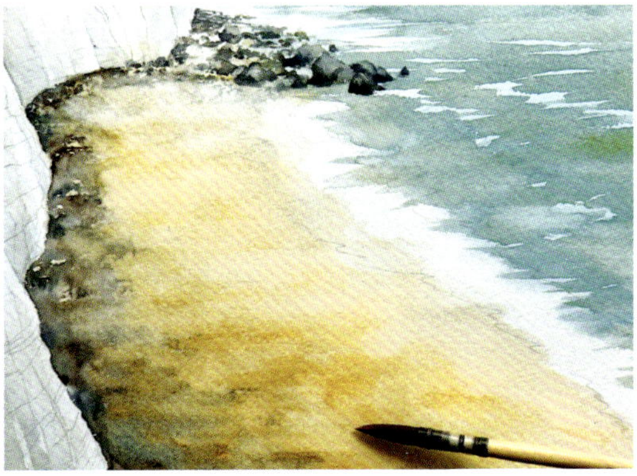

It doesn't matter if the beach ends up looking a little patchy – this will help to add texture to the sand.

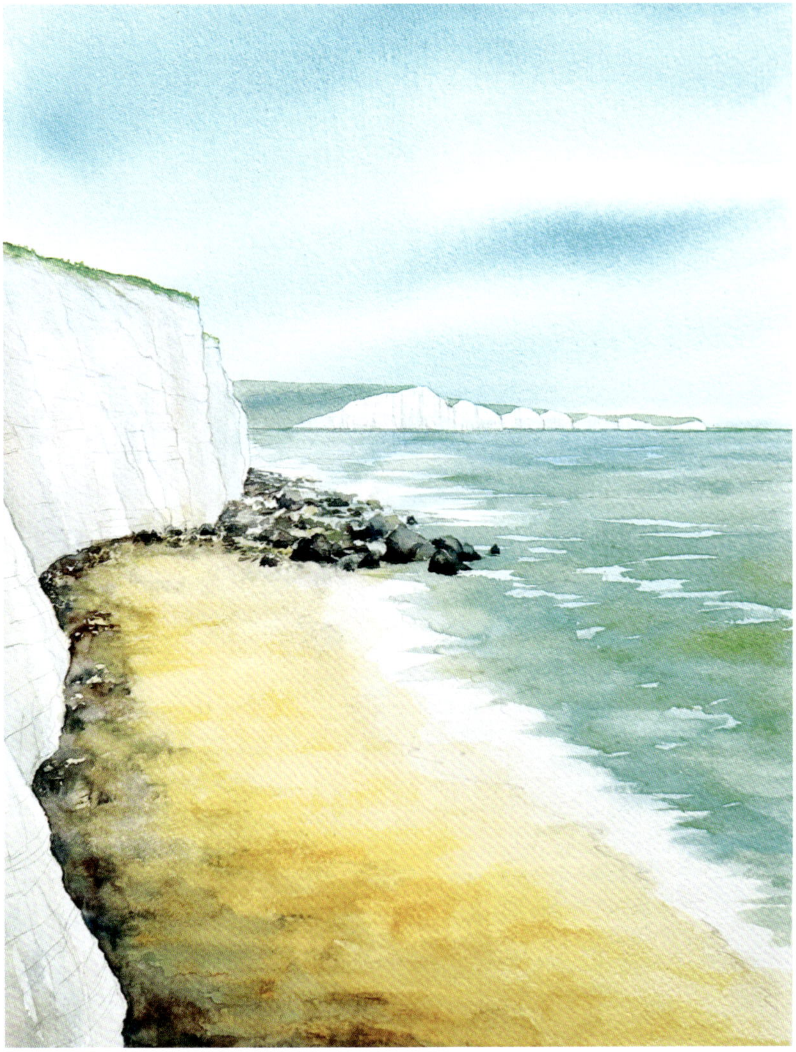

STAGE 3

Mix three wells of mid-value Raw Umber, Indigo and Sepia, and another of dark-value Sepia mixed with Payne's Grey. Starting with the mid-value colours, paint the rocks at the foot of the cliffs in the middle ground, dropping the darker value mix in at the base of the larger ones while wet. Swap between the size 3 round brush and size 0 round brush to do this.

Use the size 2 quill brush to dampen the beach below the rocks and sweep around below the cliffs. Dot and dab all of the shadow colours into this damp area, letting them wet-blend and diffuse on the page to create darker shadows and the suggestion of shingle at the base of the cliffs. Leave a few patches of the underpainting showing through here and there.

Mix a large well of Raw Sienna, and glaze (see page 25) over the beach with the mottler brush to deepen the hue, allowing it to soften and blend with the damp shadow colours. Leave to dry.

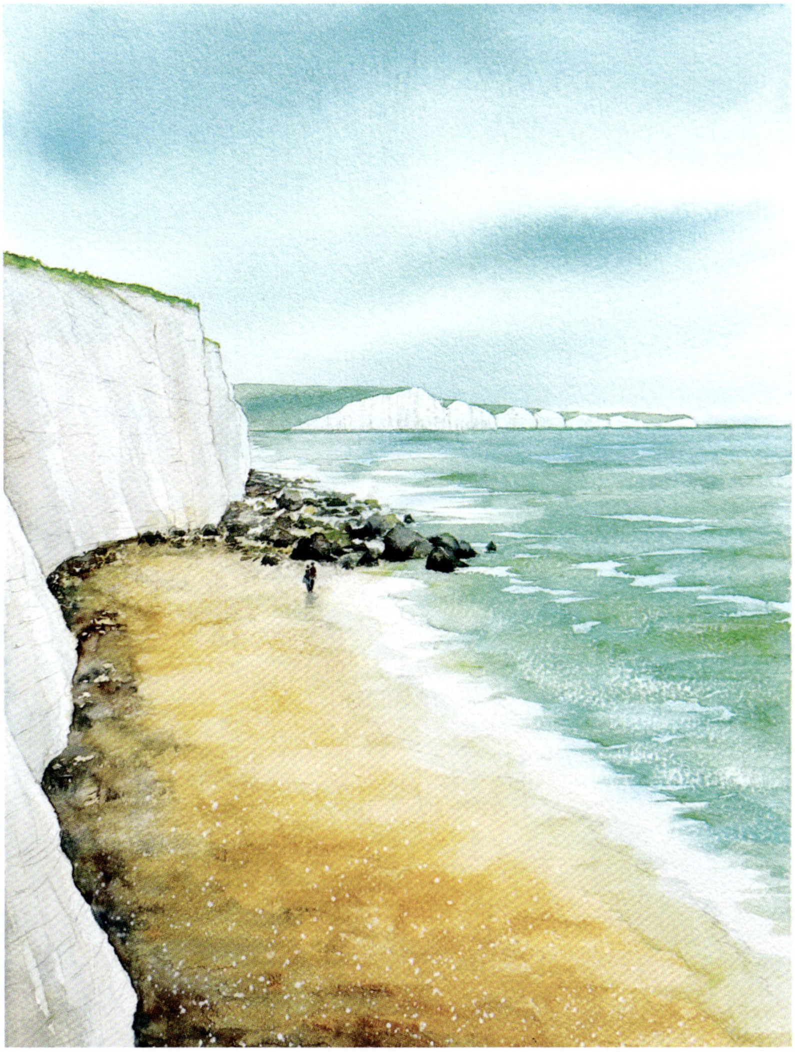

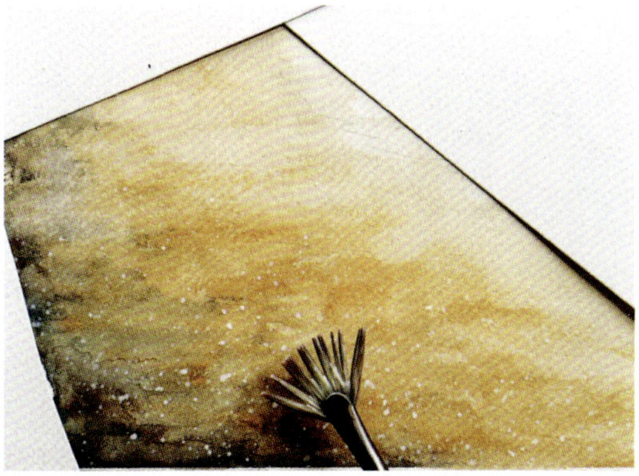

Focus the larger spatter drops in the foreground with smaller drops in the middle ground.

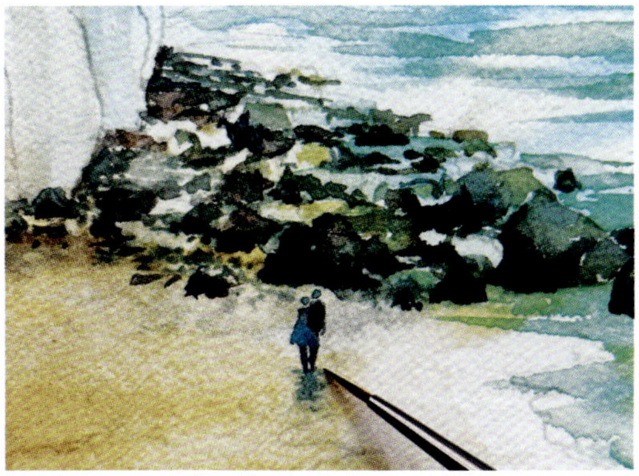

Use a little Payne's Grey to paint a pale shadow beneath the figures.

STAGE 4

Create a 'soft mask' by laying paper over the sea and cliffs to protect them (see page 51). Mix a well of inky consistency White Gouache, and spatter tiny drops across the beach to suggest chalk pebbles using the fan brush.

Mix three small wells: light-value Payne's Grey, mid-value Vermilion Hue and mid-value Cerulean Blue. Use the size 0 round brush to paint two tiny figures in the light-value grey. Dab in a touch of vermilion and the blue while still damp to add a suggestion of clothing.

Mix a very light-value well of Cerulean Blue, and using the size 2 quill brush, glaze over the sand and half of the white shoreline to suggest the wet sand. Leave to dry completely.

Once completely dry, rub the sandpaper gently over the water to create a few highlights.

Tip

When painting the figures, you can simply paint two joined brushstrokes that slightly taper towards the bottom, then add dots at the top for heads.

FOCUS ON *Boats*

I always think there's something romantic about boats. They evoke feelings of adventure and discovery, and can offer us transport to far-off lands. They can weather storms, windswept and wave-tossed; or lie safe and protected in a harbour, waiting for better weather. While this is no doubt an idealized vision, it's one that has inspired artists over the centuries.

Build Your Sketching Skills

Boats are complex structures, coming in so many shapes, sizes and styles, that painting them can certainly seem like a daunting task at first. However, regular sketching practice can help you learn the best way to simplify their shapes, so you can confidently and consistently produce convincing boats in your paintings.

When observing your source material, focus on the angle and position of the vessel in relation to the landscape. This will help you to determine how much you will need to take foreshortening into account (see page 19).

Try sketching the three boats featured here in your sketchbook to familiarize yourself with foreshortening, angles and proportions.

Whether it's fishing boats hoisted up high on the beach, waiting for the tide, ocean-going ships docked in a harbour, or small leisure craft sailing on a river estuary, boats will always bring visual interest, life and movement to a coastal scene.

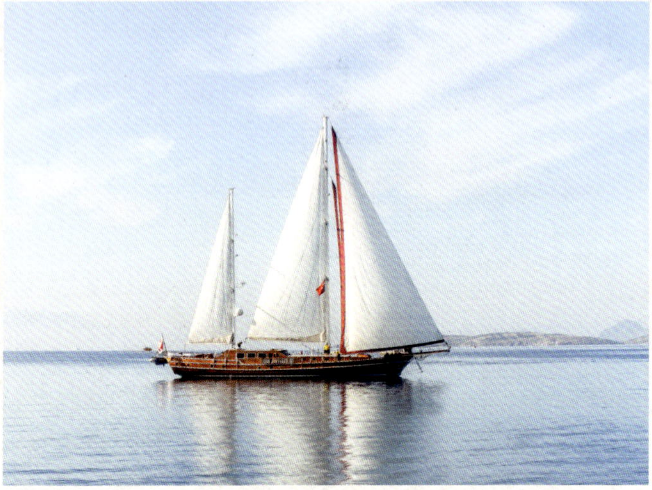

A side view is the perfect place to start, because there is no need to foreshorten the image. Just focus on capturing the simple shapes and proportions of the vessel, and how it sits in the water.

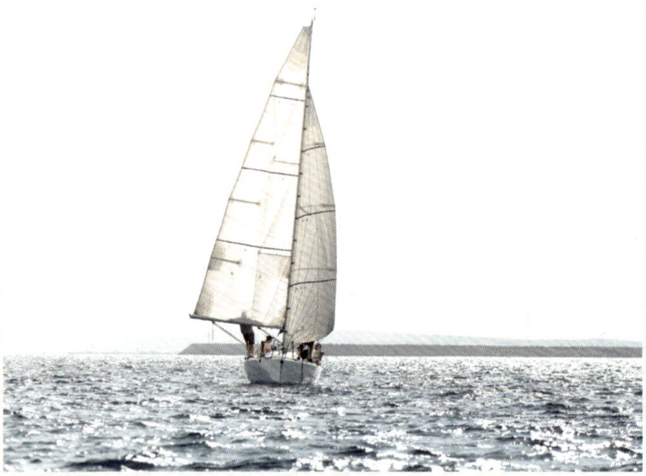

Seen front-on, the hull looks a little like a small shallow bowl or cup. Notice the position and angle of the mast and sails as they catch the wind: replicating that tilt will enable you to add movement and energy to your sketch.

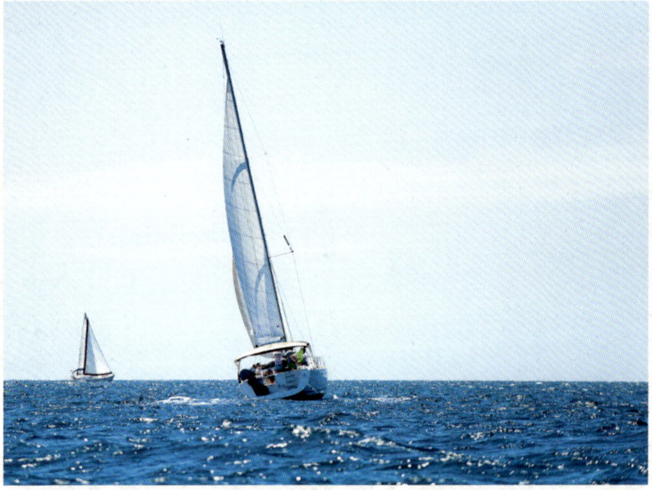

Here, you can see the stern of the boat, and a small amount of the foreshortened hull to the right. Focus on the proportions and angles of these shapes, as well as the angle of the masts and sails.

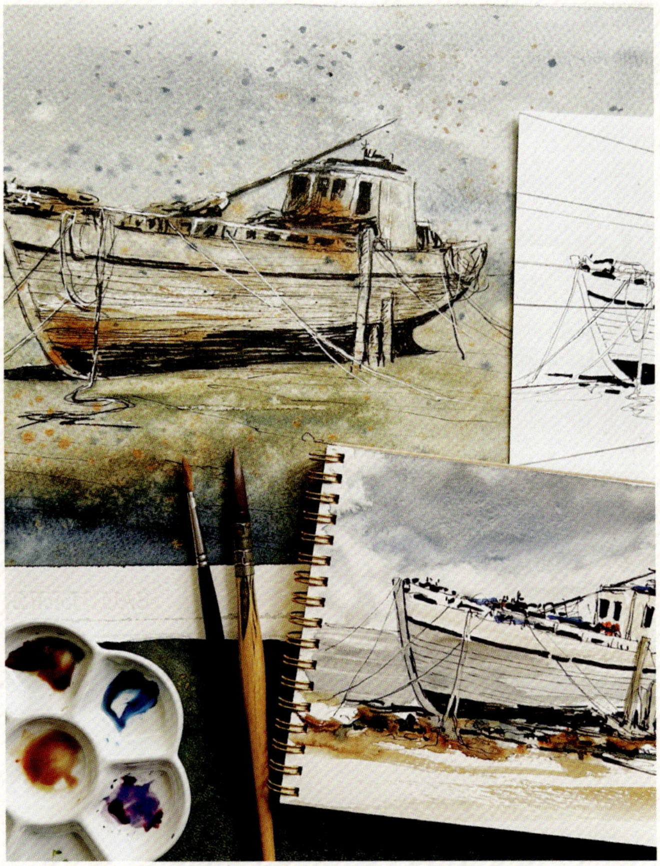

When you visit harbours, boatyards and estuaries, always carry a sketchbook and a pencil with you, and sketch anything that inspires you. Take reference photos, too, so you can work your ideas up into finished paintings.

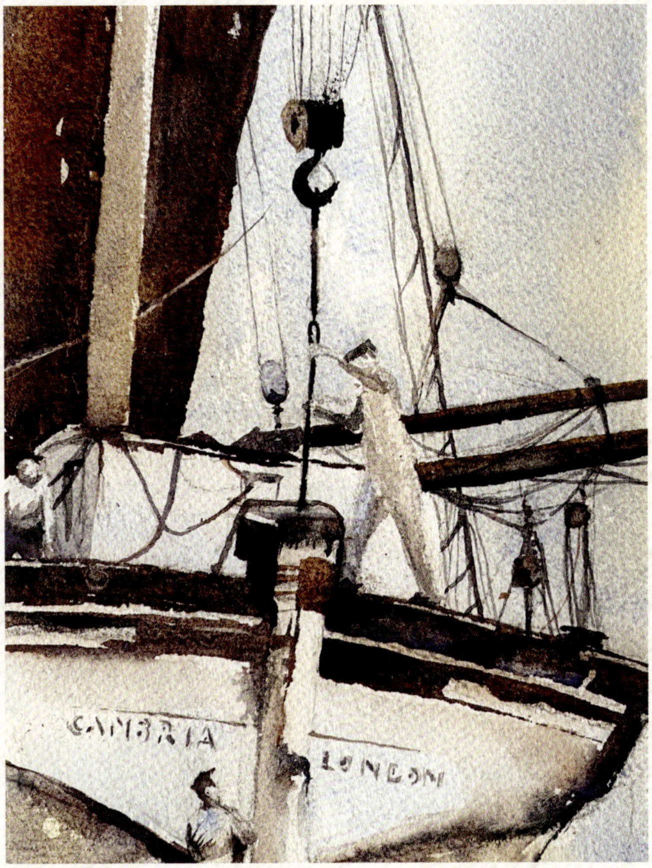

Focusing on close-up scenes and details can create lively and interesting compositions. Here, the figures in this painting are kept very simple so as to convey the movement and energy as the men work together on the boat.

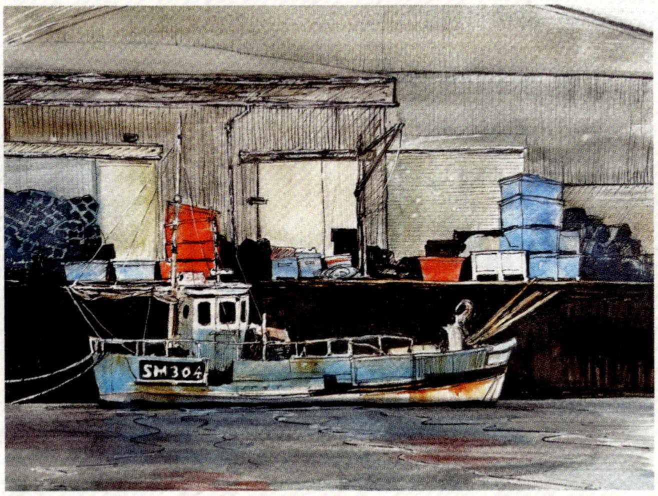

Worn and weathered working boats are fascinating subjects when set against a backdrop of warehouses and industrial buildings, surrounded by colourful crates and lobster pots.

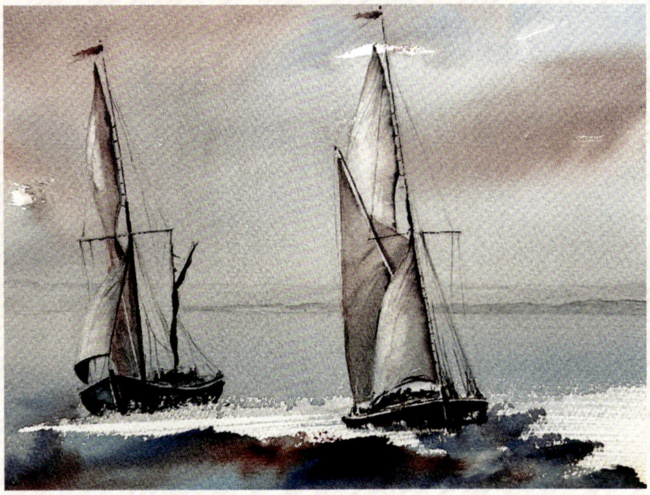

In this painting, the movement of the boats is conveyed by using dynamic angles for the sailing barges, while their passage through the water is suggested with strong tonal contrast and the use of dry-brush technique (see page 38).

Grey Haven

Time seems to stand still in traditional Scottish Highland villages like Plockton. A heavy grey sky is reflected in the still waters of the loch at low tide, and the distant mountains and looming grey clouds add majesty and grandeur to the scene.

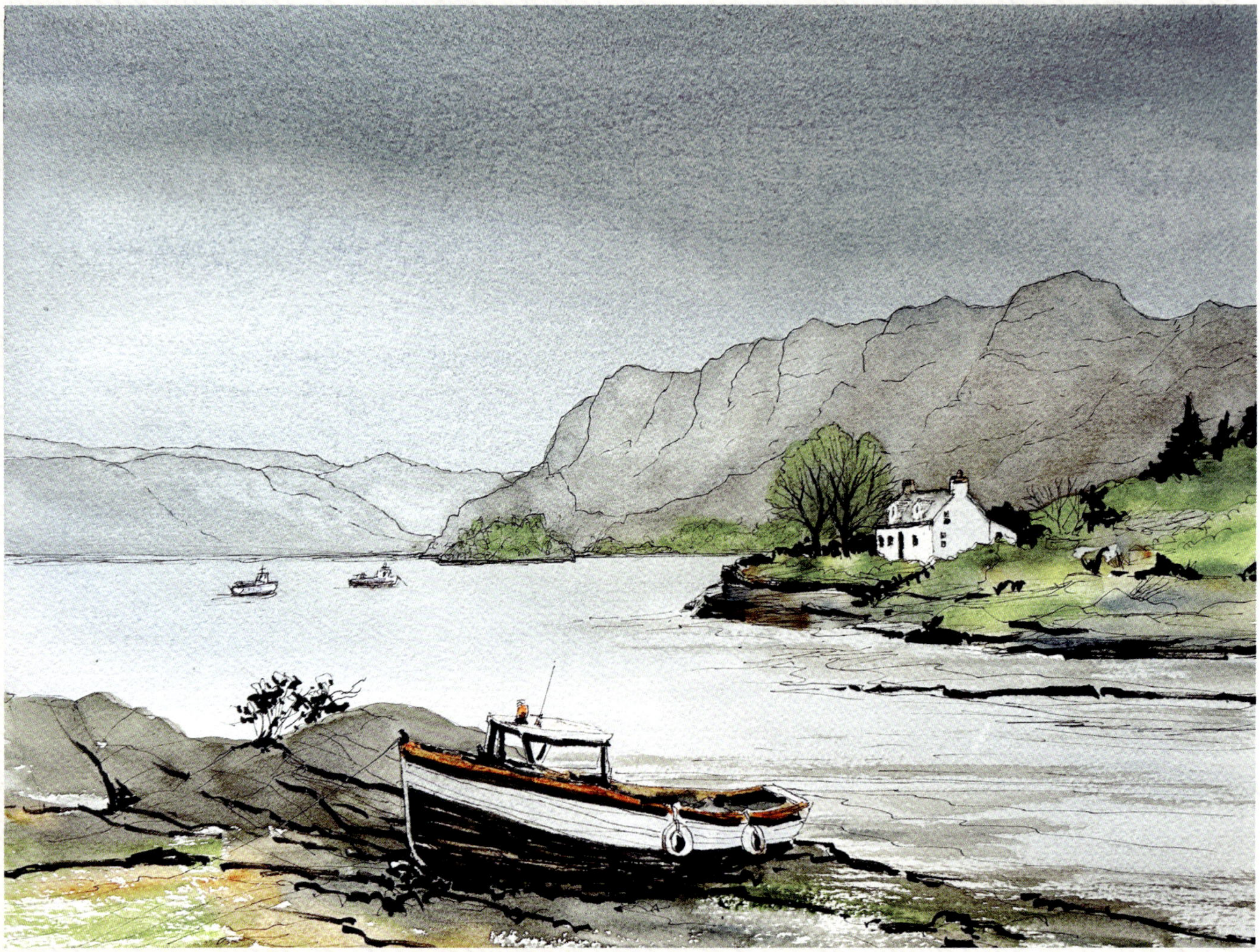

COLOURS NEEDED

Indigo | French Ultramarine | Sepia | Sap Green | Perylene Green | Transparent Yellow | Burnt Sienna

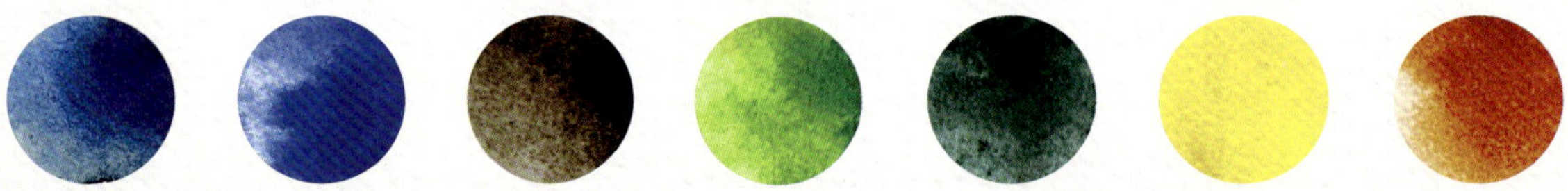

Scottish tidal lochs, with their soaring mountains, old-fashioned rustic cottages, and the water dotted with small sailing boats and fishing craft, provide spectacular subjects for coastal paintings. Small details, such as lichen and seaweed on the rocks, bring bright bursts of colour that contrast beautifully with the atmospheric water and sky.

In this project, the focus is the gleaming white cottage nestled below the mountains in the middle ground. In order to draw the eye to this small area of high contrast, an S- or Z-shaped composition was used at the design stage (see page 18). For this reason, the foreground is painted with simple and suggestive brushwork, while the white areas of the large boat are more subdued than the building – weathered and in shadow, so as to lead the eye towards the idyllic cottage.

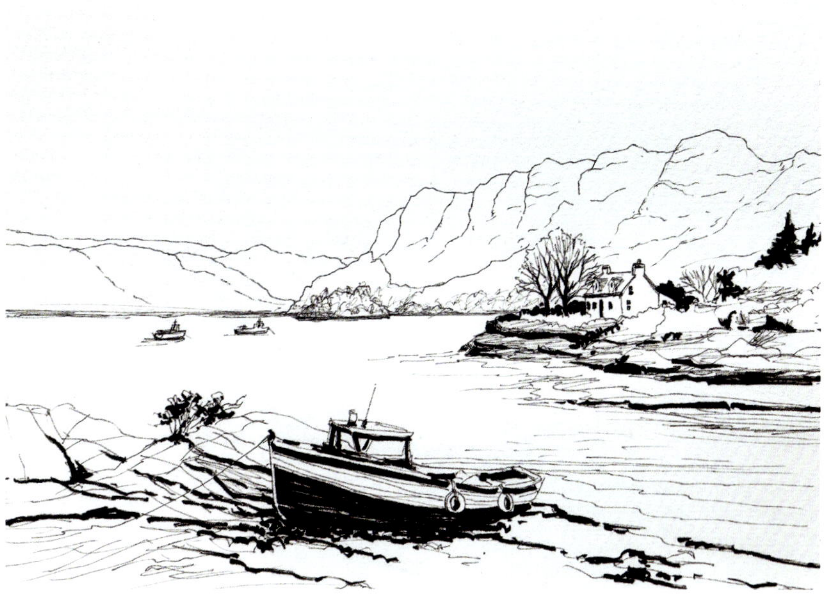

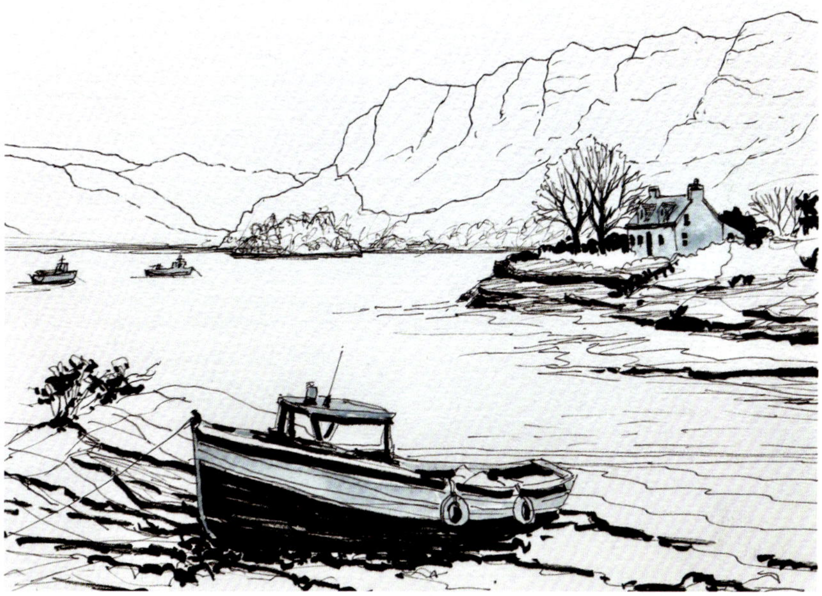

Setting Up

Begin by sketching an outline lightly onto cold pressed watercolour paper using the HB pencil (see page 20). Go over the pencil outline with the black 0.1mm waterproof fine-liner pen to create the line work, followed by the black brush-nib pen to add in darker areas of tone and shadow.

Mask out the cottage, distant boats on the loch and the white parts of the foreground boat with masking fluid and an old small pointed brush (see page 24). Tape your paper to the painting board and lay it flat, ready to begin.

YOU WILL NEED

- *140lb (300gsm) cold pressed (NOT) watercolour paper*
- *HB pencil and eraser*
- *Black 0.1mm and brush-nib waterproof fine-liner pens*
- *Painting board and decorator's masking tape*
- *Masking fluid and old pointed brush*
- *Kitchen paper*
- *Palette with mixing wells*
- *Adhesive eraser*
- *1½in (38mm) mottler brush*
- *Size 2 quill brush*
- *Size 0 round brush*
- *Size 3 round brush*

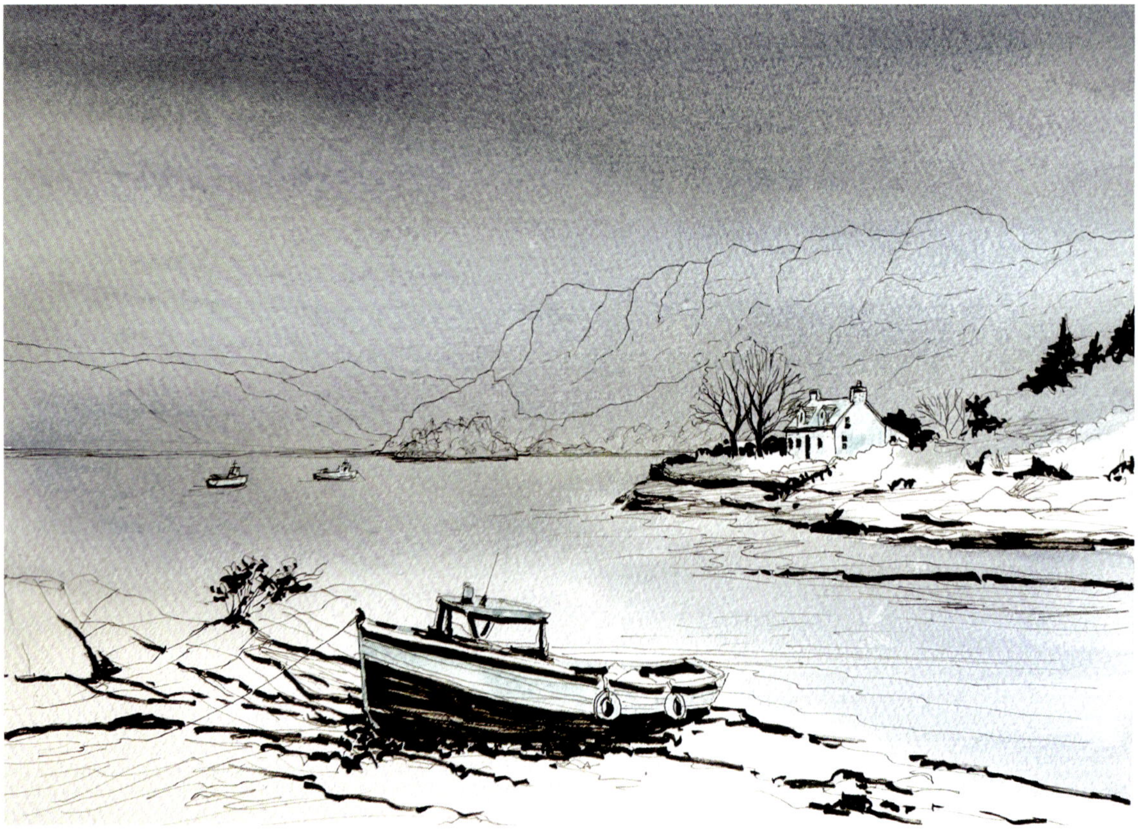

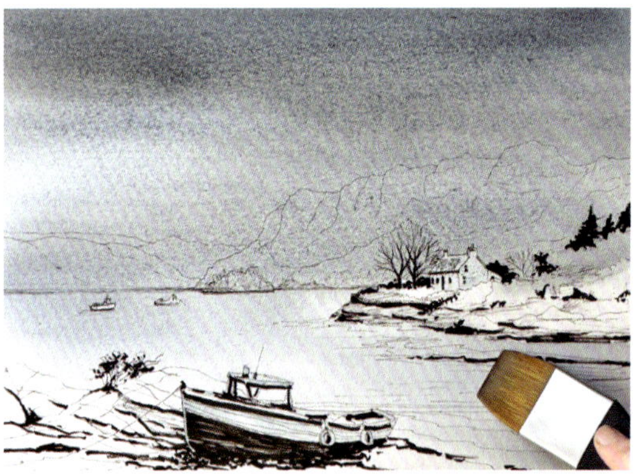

Keeping the brushstrokes horizontal as you paint the loch will help to keep the water looking nice and flat.

STAGE 1

To paint an atmospheric wet-in-wet grey sky, mix a large well of mid- to dark-value blueish-grey using Indigo, French Ultramarine and Sepia.

Wet the sky, mountains and loch with clean water using the mottler brush, working around the headlands and shore, and then leave them to soak for about 30 seconds.

Using the mottler brush and horizontal brushstrokes, paint the sky and mountains with a graduated wash (see page 22); keep the wash dark across the top, adding a little water to the paint so that the wash becomes lighter towards the horizon. Continue to paint the lighter wash across the loch. Leave to dry completely.

Tip

When painting a large wet-in-wet wash like this, use kitchen paper to carefully dab clean the masking tape to ensure that paint doesn't run back from the tape into the painting, creating unwanted marks.

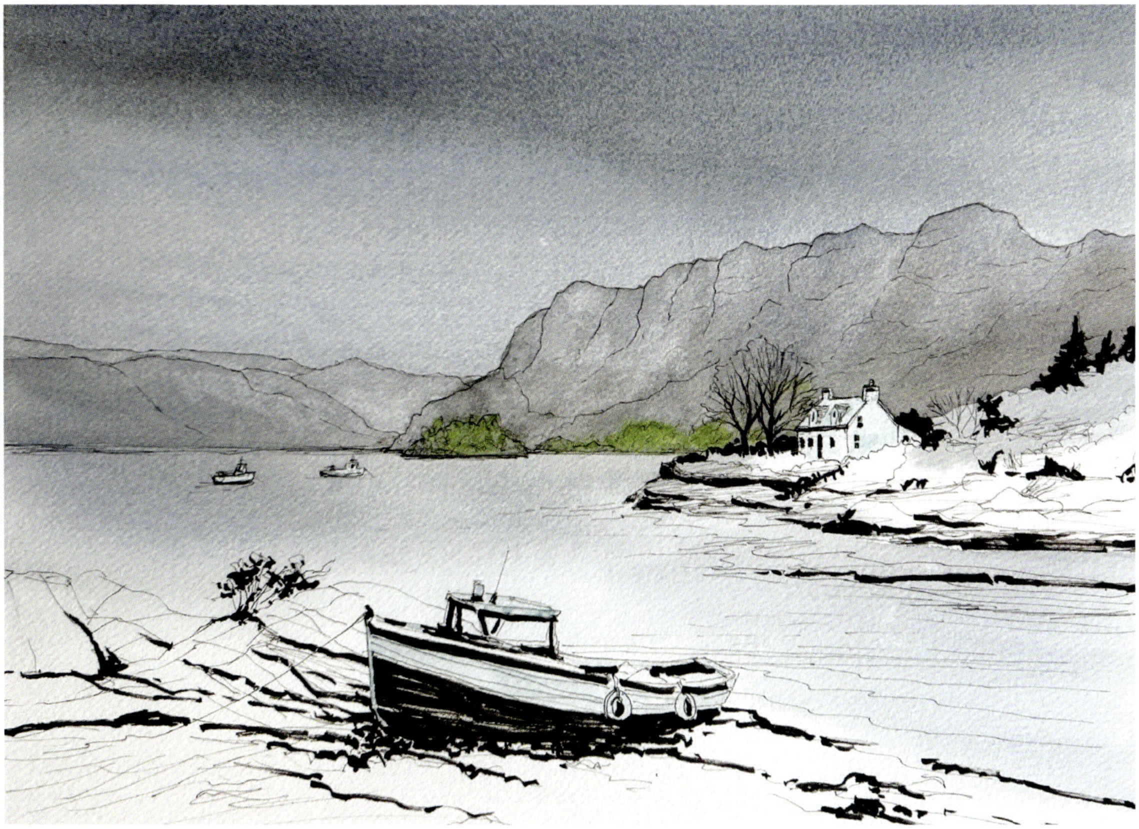

STAGE 2

Mix a well of light-value grey from Indigo, French Ultramarine and Sepia, one of light-value Sepia, plus a third of light-value Sap Green. Glaze the mountains with the grey using the size 2 quill brush, starting from the right (see page 25).

Add a little water to the grey mix as you work along the mountains, so that the glaze becomes paler for the mountains on the left to create aerial perspective as they recede into the distance (see page 19).

While still damp, drop a little of the sepia into the base of the mountains to deepen the tone slightly, and add the green to the island and distant shore behind the cottage to suggest distant trees. Leave to dry.

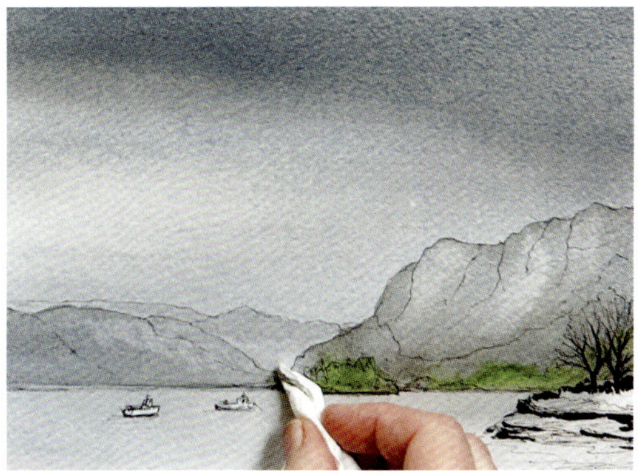

To soften edges in places, gently lift out a little damp paint from the distant mountains with a rolled-up piece of kitchen paper.

Tip

Make sure the painting is bone dry before you glaze the mountains, and work quickly using minimal brushwork so as not to disturb the underpainting.

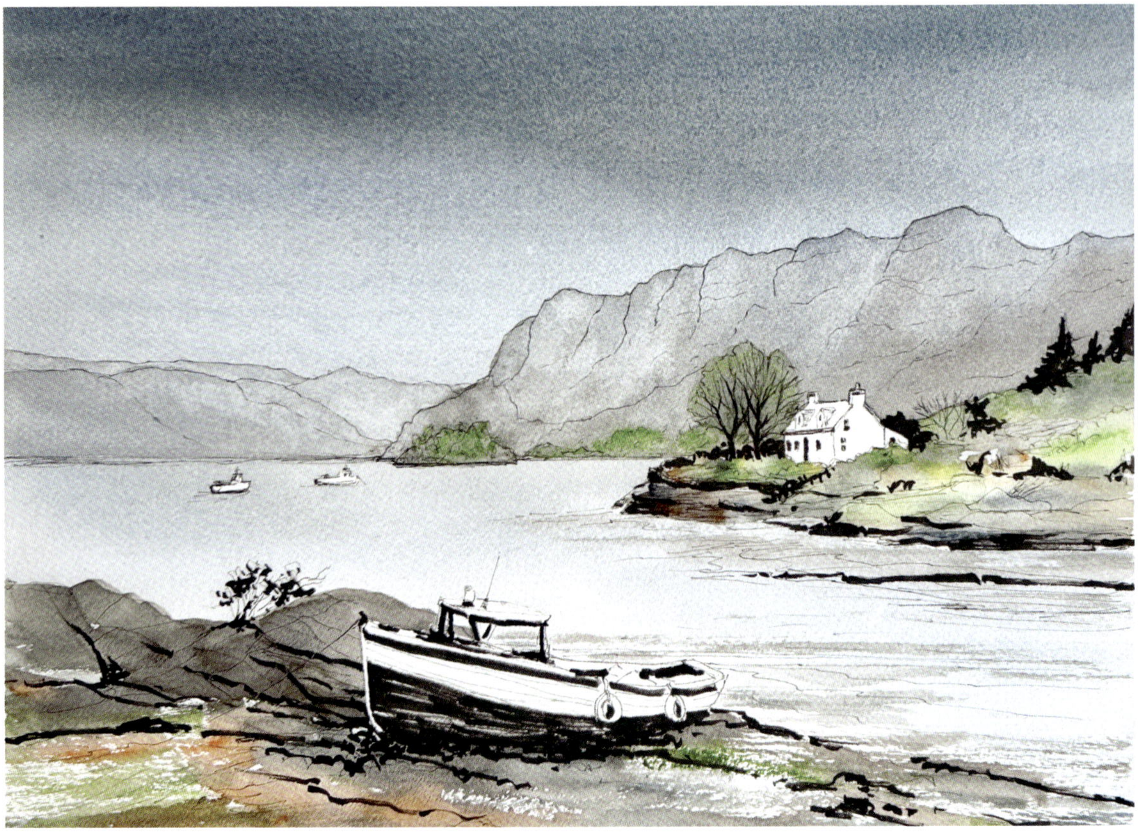

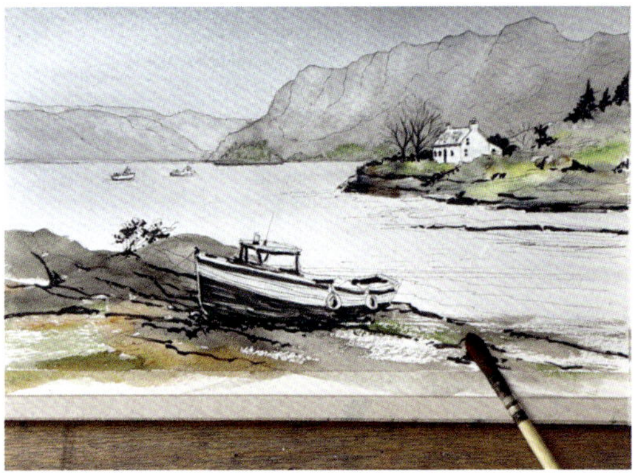

Hold the brush at a narrow angle to the paper to create dry-brush strokes, so the side of the brush skims the surface texture of the paper, leaving the pits as unpainted 'sparkle'.

STAGE 3

To paint the middle-ground headland, mix five wells of mid-value paint: Sap Green, Perylene Green, Transparent Yellow, Burnt Sienna and Indigo.

Using the size 2 quill brush, dampen the headland with clean water, then paint the area with both greens, and drop in a few touches of the yellow for highlights. While still damp, add some sienna and indigo here and there to add a little colour and tone. Allow the colours to softly blend into one another.

Mix a warm, dark grey from Indigo, Sepia, Burnt Sienna and French Ultramarine. Use this grey mix to paint the rocks in the foreground, dragging a little of this colour below the boat and towards the water's edge. Dab the brush on kitchen paper to remove excess water, then use the dry-brush technique to skim Sap Green and the sienna across the shore for the lichen and seaweed (see left).

Once the paint is completely dry, carefully remove the masking fluid with the adhesive eraser.

Tip

Keep it dark around the base of the boat so as to almost lose the edge between the boat and the boggy ground in shadow.

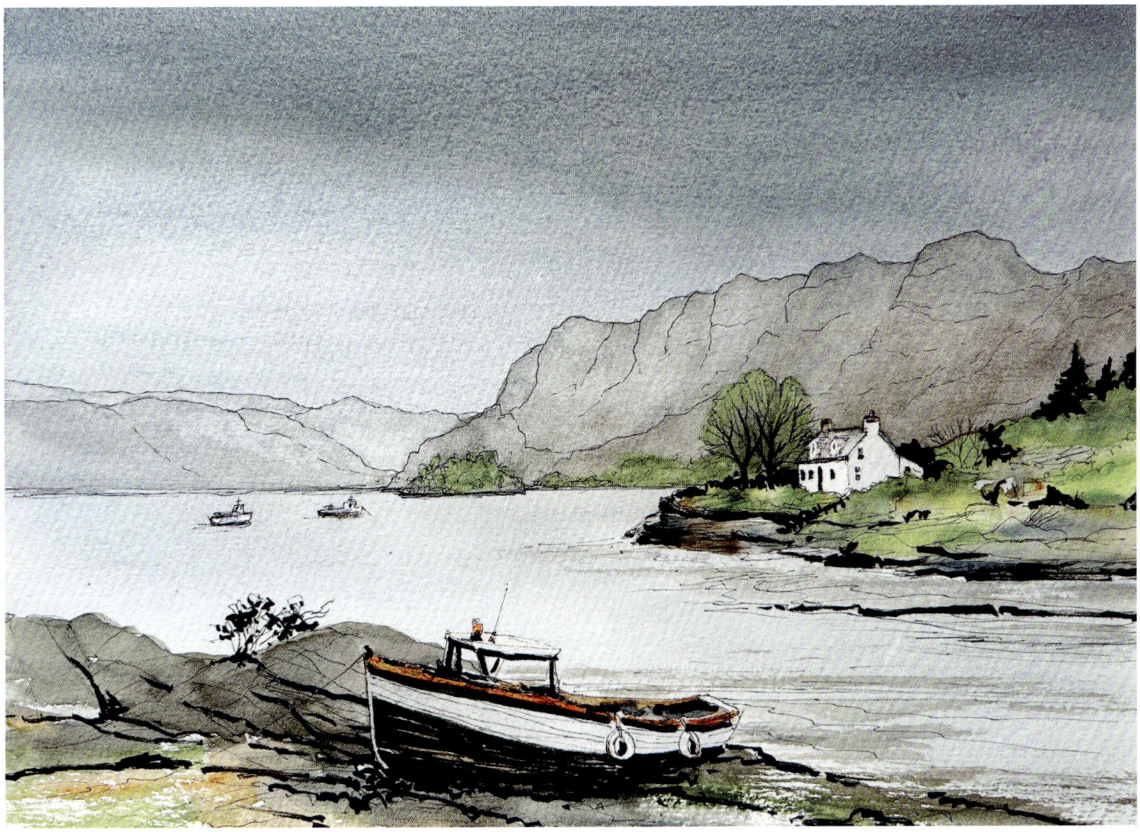

STAGE 4

Mix up a well of very watery, light-value French Ultramarine, and using the size 0 round brush, paint the distant boats to dull the white a little. Paint the gable end of the cottage with this pale blue to add shadow. Dip the round brush into some grey mix from the last stage and paint the roof, working around the little windows, leaving them white. Once the roof is dry, add a dab of Burnt Sienna to each chimney.

Use the light-value ultramarine and the size 2 quill brush to add shadow to the white boards on the foreground boat. Drop in a little grey here and there while the hull is wet to deepen the shadows and suggest weathering. Leave to dry.

Paint a stripe of sienna along the top of the hull using the size 3 round or size 0 round brush, whichever you prefer.

Finally, mix a well of very watery Burnt Sienna and lightly glaze the nearest mountains with the size 2 quill brush. Leave to dry.

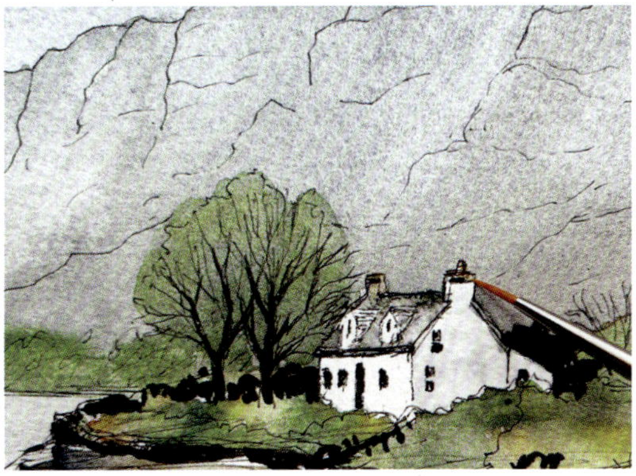

Even very small touches of complementary colour can work wonders to draw the eye to your points of interest.

Tip

The warm Burnt Sienna glaze helps to bring the closer mountain forward a little, as warmer colours tend to come forward in a painting and cooler colours recede.

Red Sails

These iconic working barges, beloved by landscape and maritime artists alike, make wonderful coastal painting features. Their dramatic silhouettes and elegant red sails evoke romantic memories of days long since passed.

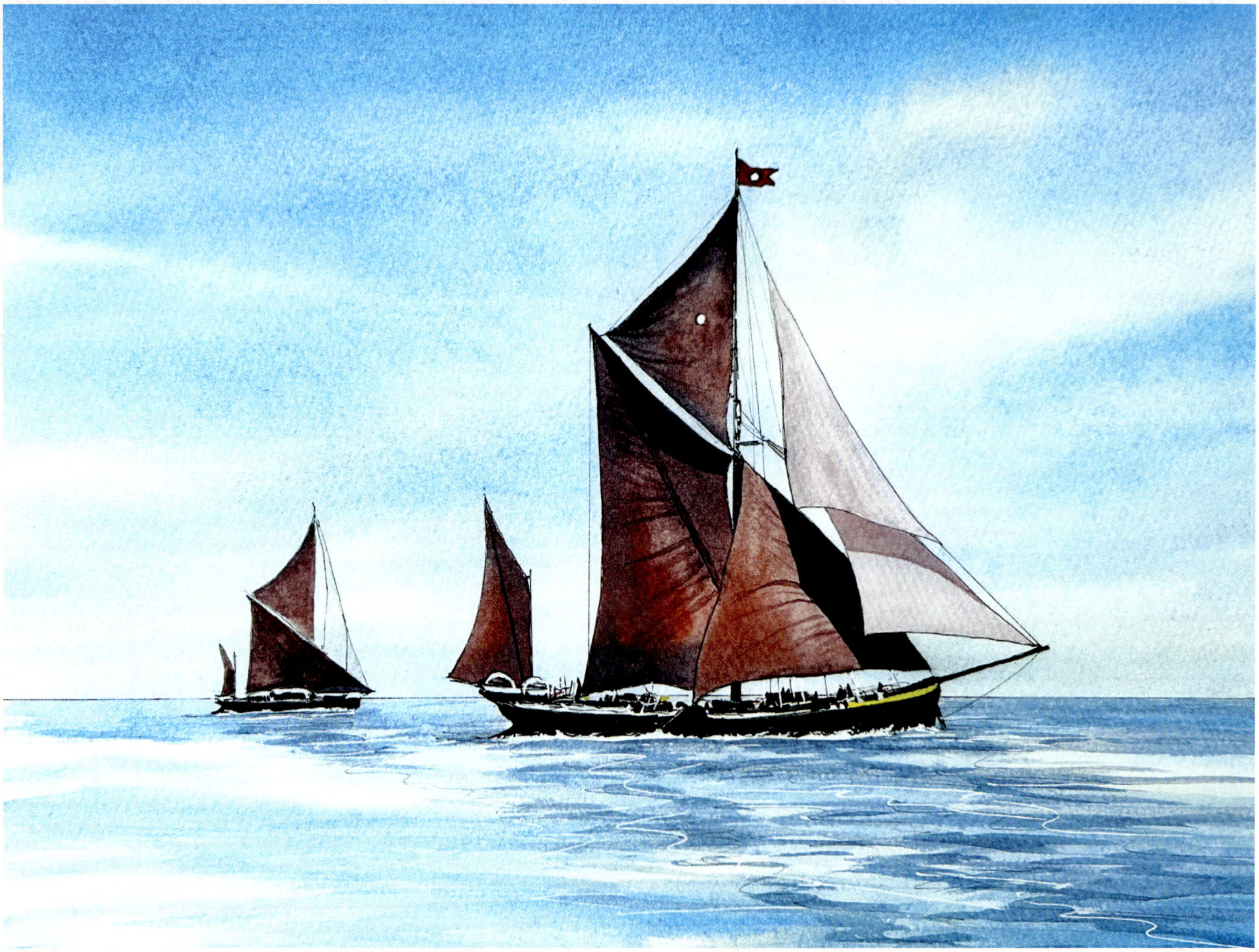

COLOURS NEEDED

- Cerulean Blue
- French Ultramarine
- Raw Sienna
- Venetian Red
- Perylene Violet
- Indigo
- Transparent Yellow
- Pyrrole Red
- Burnt Sienna

The distinctive rusty red colour of the sails on traditional Thames sailing barges comes from the red ochre pigment used to dye them. It helped to protect the sails from sun damage and the elements. These magnificent flat-bottomed boats worked the English rivers, estuaries and coastline around London and Essex for more than 200 years.

There is something visually pleasing about their proportions and shape, and with a little simplification, they can make interesting and very attractive subjects to paint. The diagram below shows the basic configuration of the sails.

Setting Up

Begin by sketching an outline lightly onto cold pressed watercolour paper using the HB pencil (see page 20). Go over the pencil outline with the 0.1mm waterproof black fine-liner pen to create the line work, followed by the brush-nib pen to add darker areas of tone and shadow. Try to keep your outlines as fine as possible, and use a ruler for the masts and any rigging where the ropes are taut. Slightly dotted lines will do a good job of suggesting the creases and curves in the sails. Tape the paper to your board then lay it flat, ready to begin.

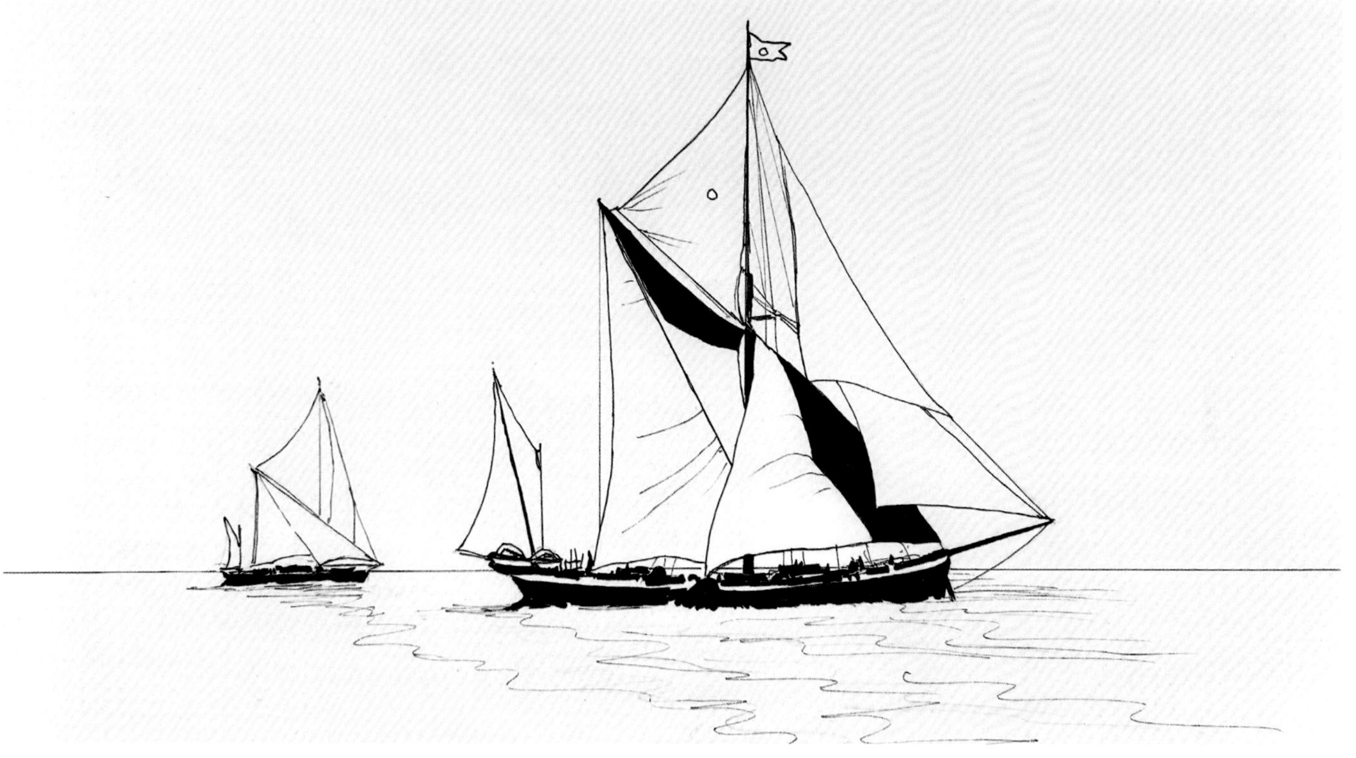

YOU WILL NEED

- *140lb (300gsm) cold pressed (NOT) watercolour paper*
- *HB pencil and eraser*
- *Black 0.1mm and brush-nib waterproof fine-liner pens*
- *Straight-edged ruler*
- *Painting board and decorator's masking tape*
- *Kitchen paper*
- *Palette with mixing wells*
- *White gel pen*
- *1½in (38mm) mottler brush*
- *Size 3 round brush*
- *Size 2 quill brush*
- *Size 0 round brush*
- *¾in (20mm) flat brush*

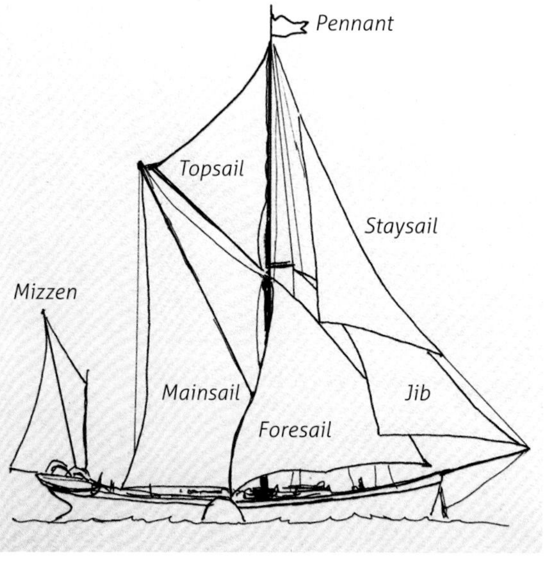

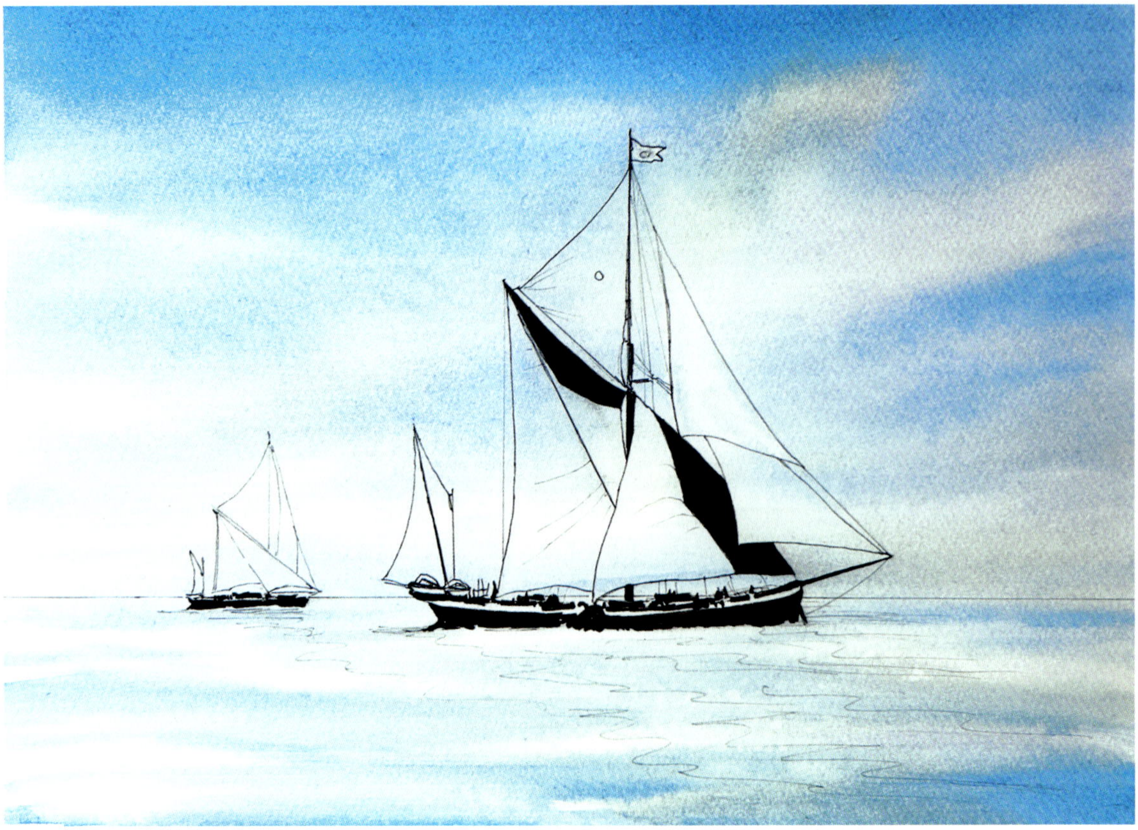

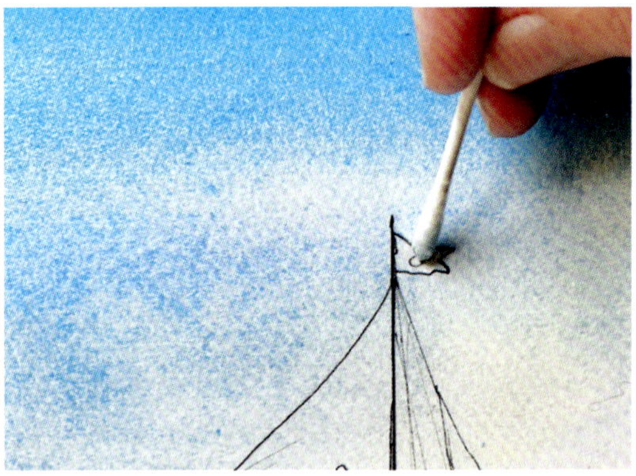

Use a cotton bud/swab to lift off any paint from the pennant, or roll up a tiny piece of kitchen paper to use instead.

STAGE 1

Mix two large wells of mid-value blue from Cerulean Blue and French Ultramarine: a warmer blue with more French Ultramarine, and a cooler blue with more Cerulean Blue. Also mix a small well of light-value Raw Sienna. Wet the sky and sea with clean water using the mottler brush. Leave to soak for about 30 seconds.

Paint a few pale golden streaks across the sky and sea with the sienna, rinse the brush, and dab out excess water on a piece of kitchen paper. Load the brush with the warm blue mix, and starting from the top, begin to paint a variegated wash (see page 22) that is darker across the top for the sky, leaving a few narrow strips of the sienna and unpainted paper. About halfway down, change to the cooler blue and graduate the wash as you approach the horizon by adding a little water.

Next, paint the sea, keeping the brushstrokes horizontal, leaving a few unpainted areas for lighter water. Use kitchen paper to lift out any dark paint from the lighter jib and staysail on the right, but leave the others, as they will be painted dark rusty red in Stage 2. Leave to dry.

Tip

Don't be tempted to fiddle with the sky wash once you have laid it down, or you could end up overworking it. As it dries, it will soften and diffuse and look atmospheric and airy, so it's really important to trust the process!

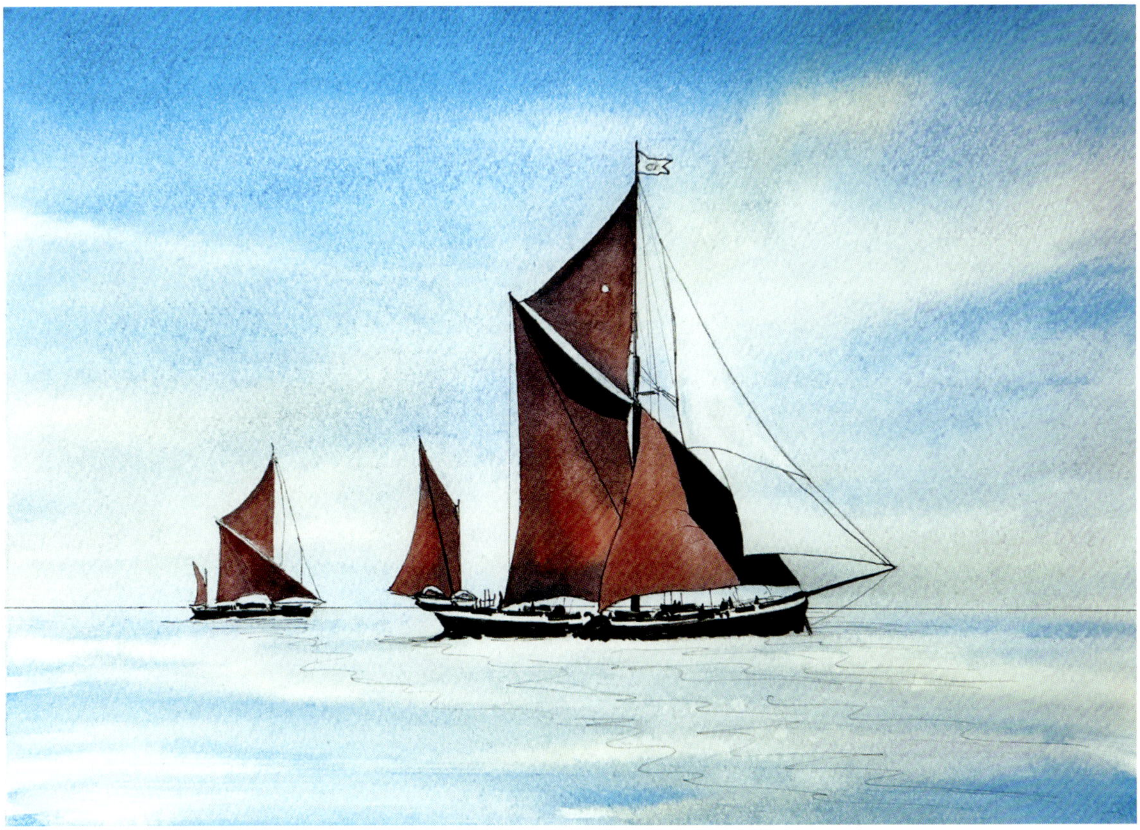

STAGE 2

To paint the red sails, mix two wells of mid-value colour: Venetian Red mixed with Perylene Violet for the rusty red, and Indigo for the shadows.

Paint the sails on the main barge one at a time, starting with the topsail, using this method: first dampen the sail with clean water using the size 3 round brush, then drop the red into the middle, gently coaxing the paint towards the edges with the brush. The paint will softly diffuse into the wet surface of the paper. While still damp, drop a little indigo into the margins to suggest shadows.

Repeat this for the mainsail and mizzen. Omit the indigo shadow stage for the foresail, to keep it slightly paler than the others. This will bring this sail forward nicely.

Swap to the size 0 round brush and repeat the process for the distant barge, keeping it a little paler to add aerial perspective. Leave to dry completely.

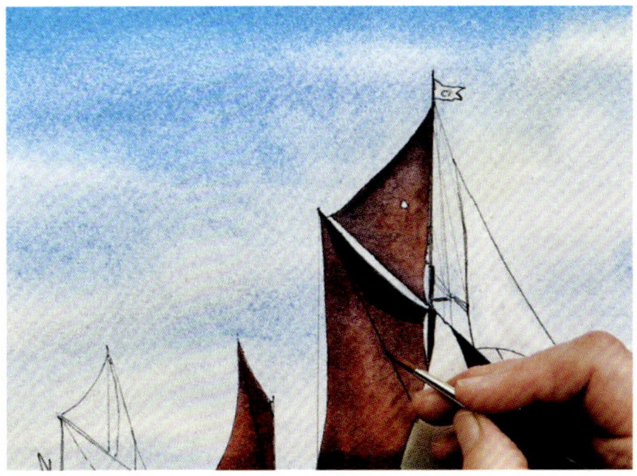

Before it all dries, you can use a damp brush to gently lift a little paint from the middle of the sails to lighten them if necessary.

Tip

Working from top to bottom will help to avoid any unwanted smudging of wet paint as you work across the painting.

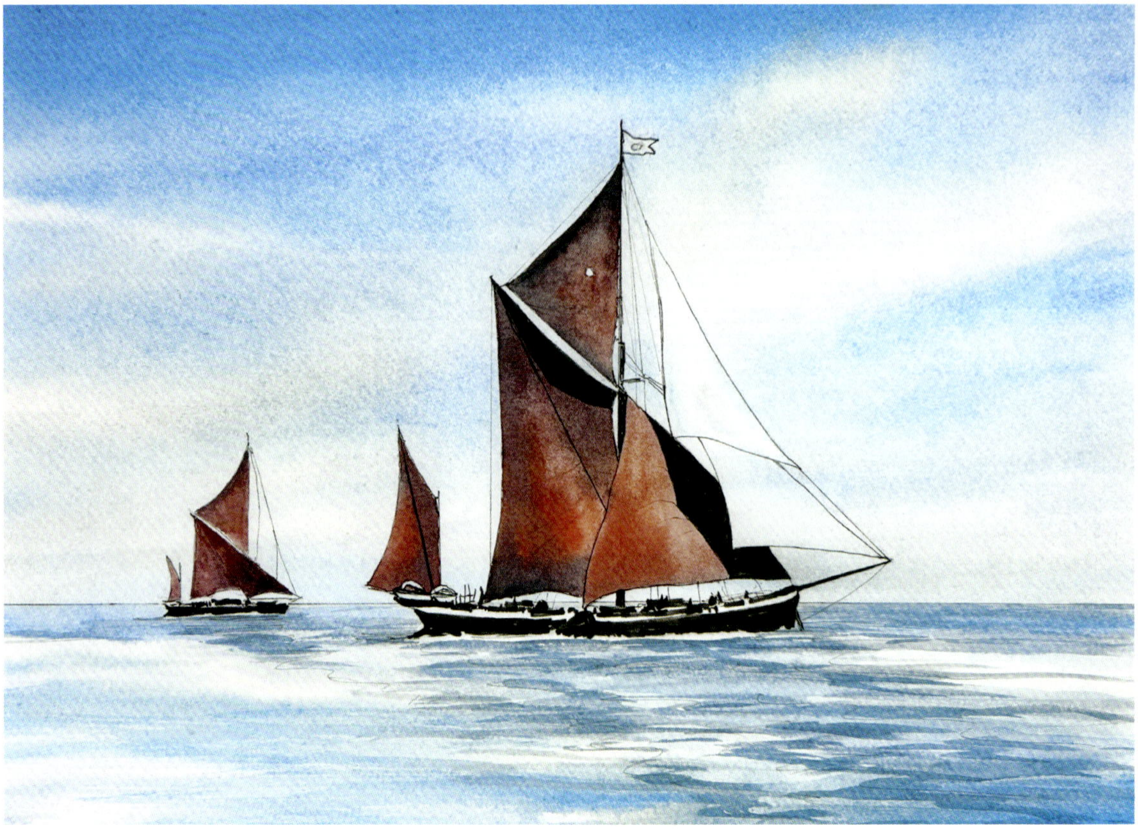

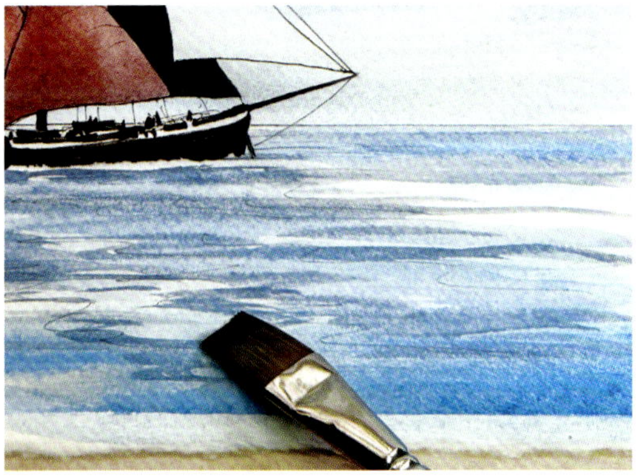

The calligraphic marks made by using the flat brush and a side-to-side motion create a convincing suggestion of movement.

STAGE 3

Mix two wells, one from mid-value Cerulean Blue and French Ultramarine, and another with the same two colours but darkened with a touch of Indigo.

Start with the first mix, and colour the sea below the horizon line with the tips of the flat brush. Continue to add the blues to the rest of the sea using the tips of the brush and side-to-side brushstrokes, working around the underpainting so most of this still shows through.

Change to the darker blue and add some darker brushstrokes below the boats and also between the lighter and brighter areas of water, to create a variety of values in the water. Leave to dry completely.

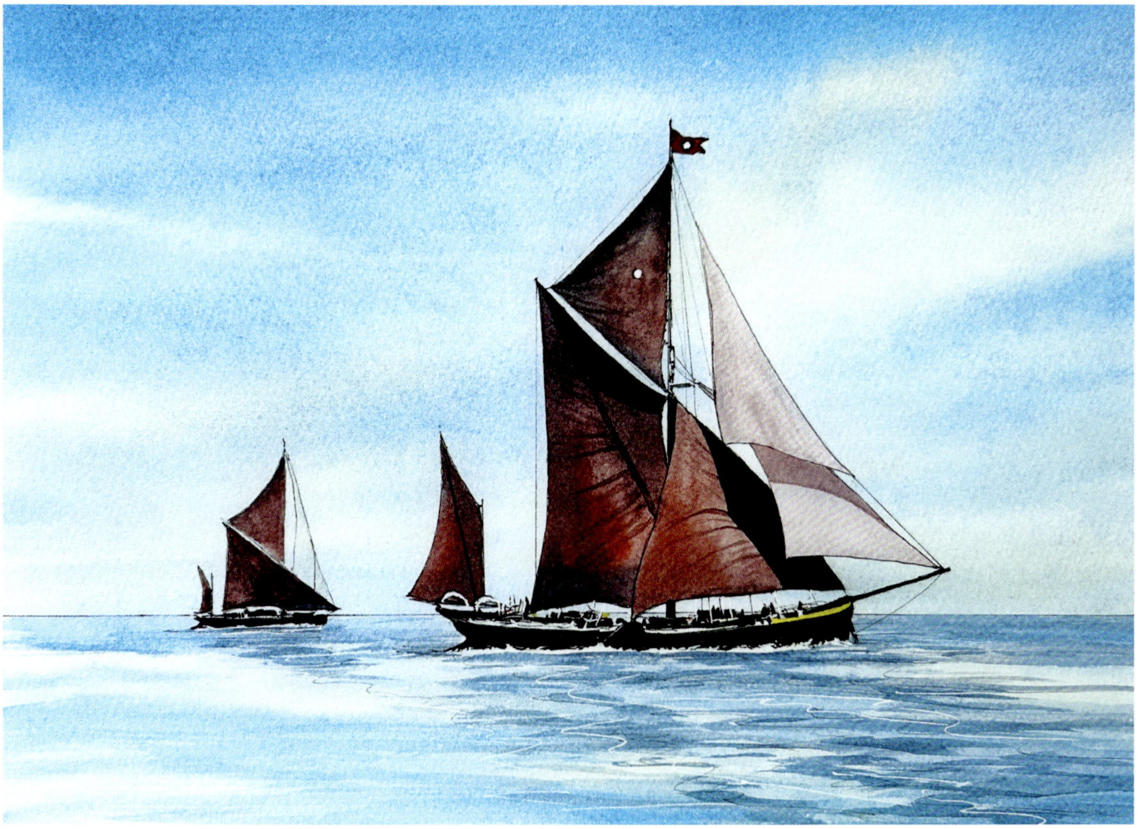

STAGE 4

Take a little of the red mix from Stage 2, and add water to it to make a very pale pinkish red. Dampen the jib and staysail with clean water and then colour them with this paler mix. Repeat for the distant boat. Once dry, add a little more Venetian Red to the mix and paint some shadows on the staysail. Allow this to dry, then add a dab of Indigo to darken the colour, and carefully add in the curved shadow on the jib.

Mix three small wells: Transparent Yellow, Pyrrole Red and Burnt Sienna. Use the size 0 round brush to paint the board on the right of the hull yellow, the pennant red, and a few small dabs of these two colours to the barge here and there to suggest objects on deck. Leave to dry.

Mix a small well of the rusty red sail colour from Venetian Red and Perylene Violet, and using the size 0 round brush, add a few delicate curving lines to suggest some creasing and the curve of the sails as they belly out in the breeze.

Once everything is dry, use a white gel pen to add the white spots to the pennant and mainsail, a few highlights on the rigging, and a little below the boats to suggest a white-water wake. Finally, add some white highlights in the water with the gel pen.

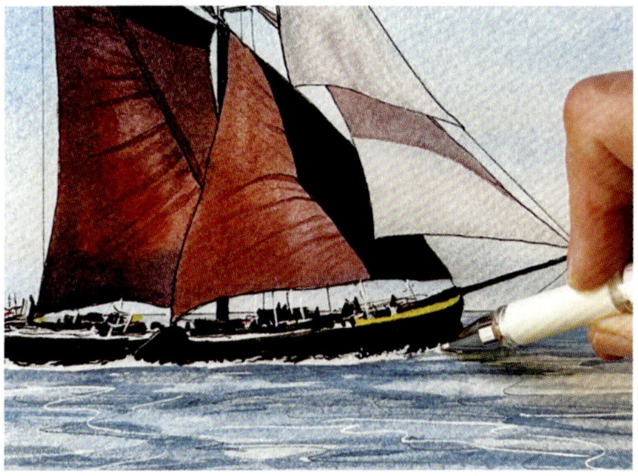

If you have lost your white highlights during the painting process, you can easily add them back with a white gel pen.

Safe Harbour

There is something so evocative about working beaches – wandering between the rows of fishing boats, their weathered hulls heaved high up on the shingle, moored among the ropes, crates, winches and lobster pots, surrounded by the fresh salt tang of the sea and, of course, the cries of the ever-hungry gulls.

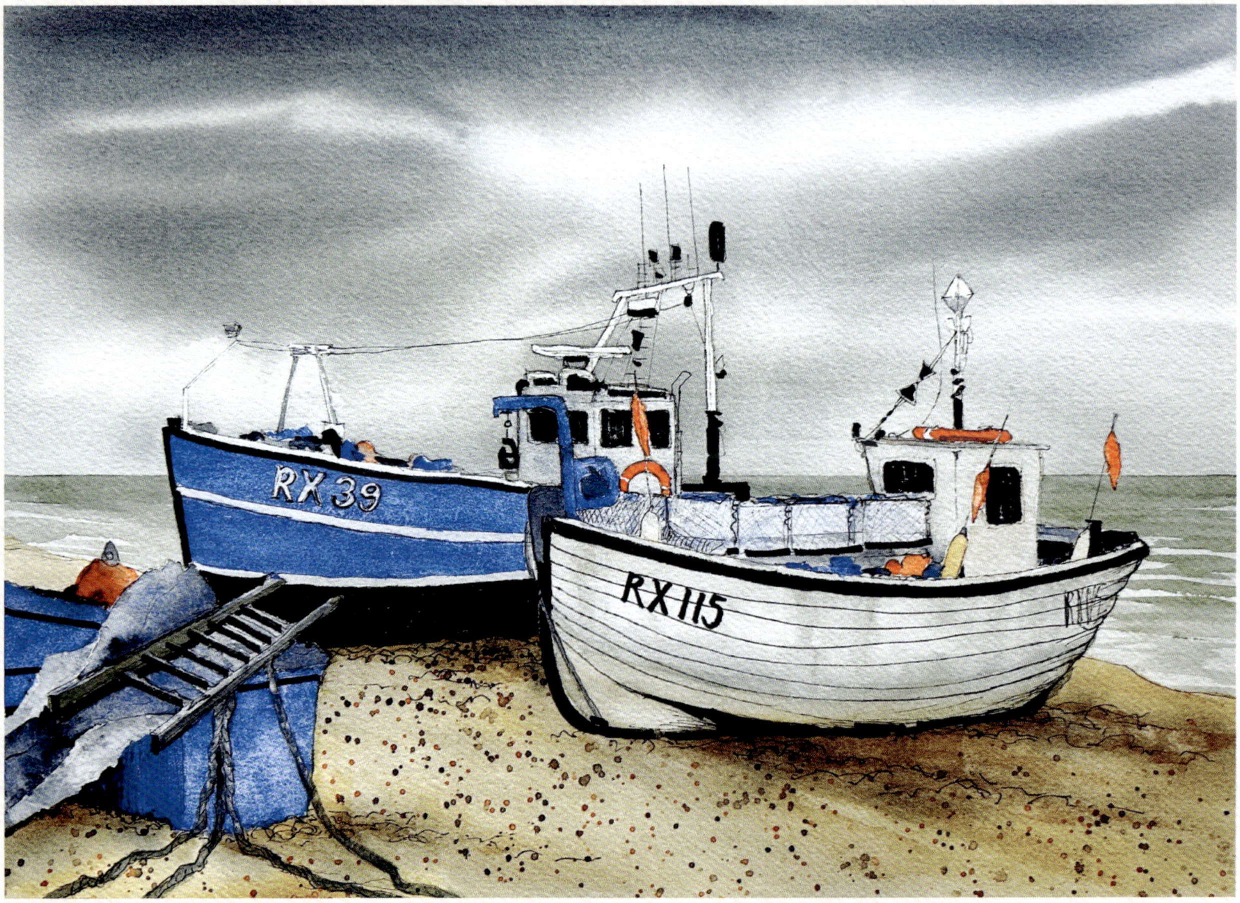

COLOURS NEEDED

Raw Sienna | Payne's Grey | Sepia | French Ultramarine | Cobalt Blue | Vermilion Hue | Transparent Yellow | Burnt Sienna

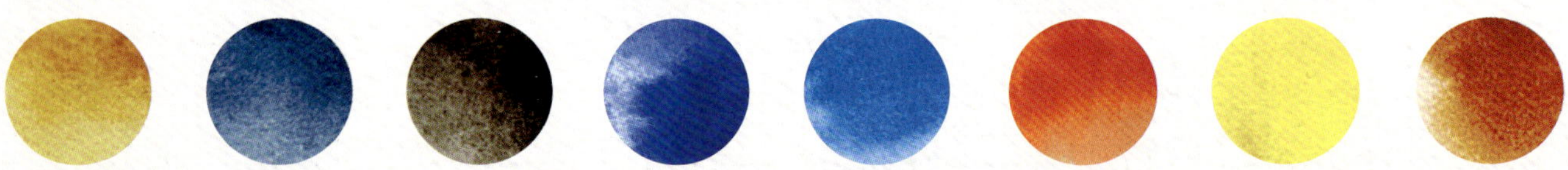

There is something unique about the quality of light on the coast. Sunny days are all very well and good, but when the skies are grey and stormy, the sea is lit with the most wonderful deep, greyish-green hues, and this is what I try to capture in this painting. The use of strong contrasts is key: by juxtaposing the paler areas of sky against the distant storm clouds, we create a dynamic sense of light and shadow. Pops of bright Vermilion Hue serve not only to guide the viewer's eye around the painting, but also to enhance the shades of blue, (see colour theory page 17), helping the details sing against the darker, desaturated background.

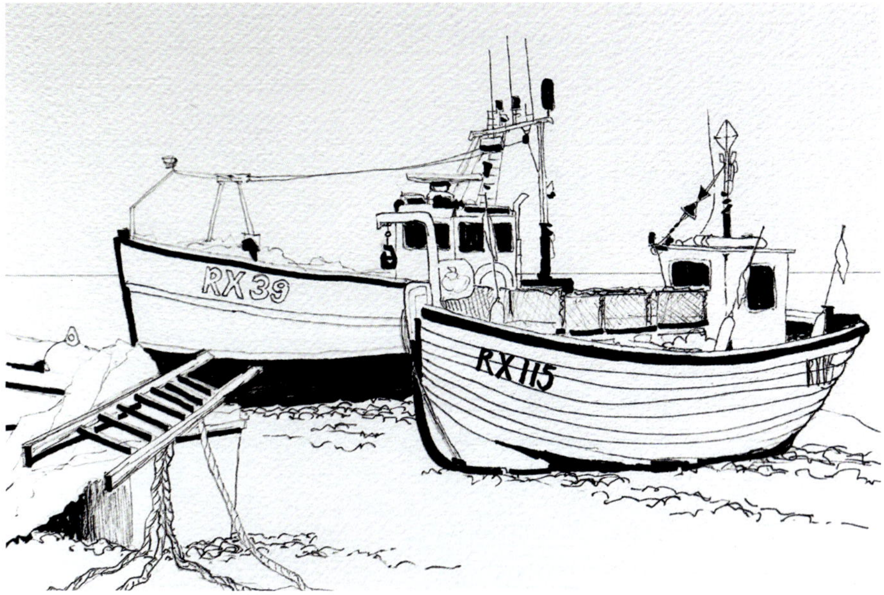

Setting Up

Begin by sketching the outline lightly onto cold pressed watercolour paper using the HB pencil (see page 20). Go over the pencil outline with the black 0.1mm waterproof fine-liner pen to create the line work, followed by the brush-nib pen to add larger areas of tone and shadow.

Mask out the boat cabins, radar infrastructure, lettering and some of the tarpaulins with masking fluid and an old small pointed brush (see page 24). Tape your paper to the painting board and lay it flat, ready to begin.

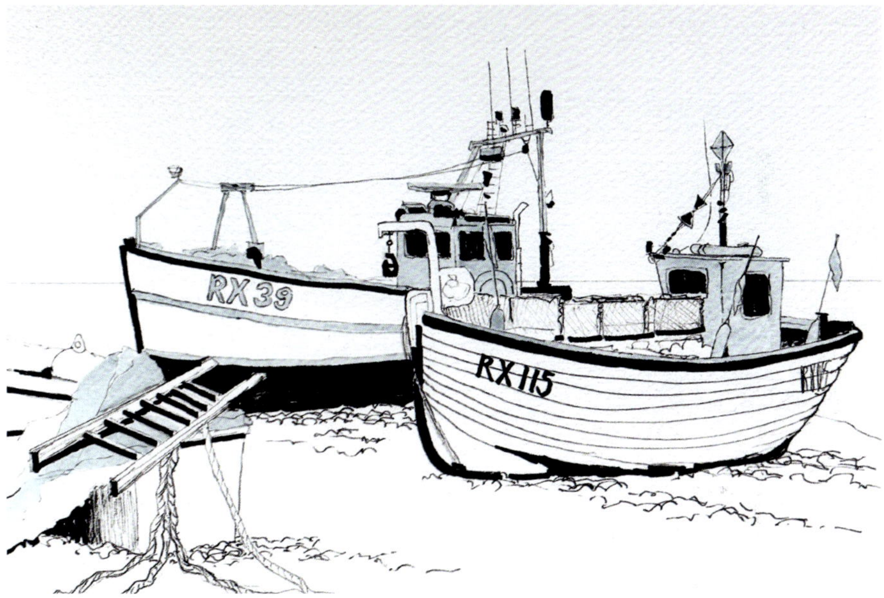

YOU WILL NEED

- *140lb (300gsm) cold pressed (NOT) watercolour paper*
- *HB pencil and eraser*
- *Black 0.1mm and brush-nib waterproof fine-liner pens*
- *Masking fluid and old pointed brush*
- *Painting board and decorator's masking tape*
- *Palette with mixing wells*
- *Kitchen paper*
- *Adhesive eraser*
- *Clean scrap paper*
- *1½in (38mm) mottler brush*
- *Size 2 quill brush*
- *¾in (20mm) flat brush*
- *Size 3 round brush*
- *Size 2 fan brush*

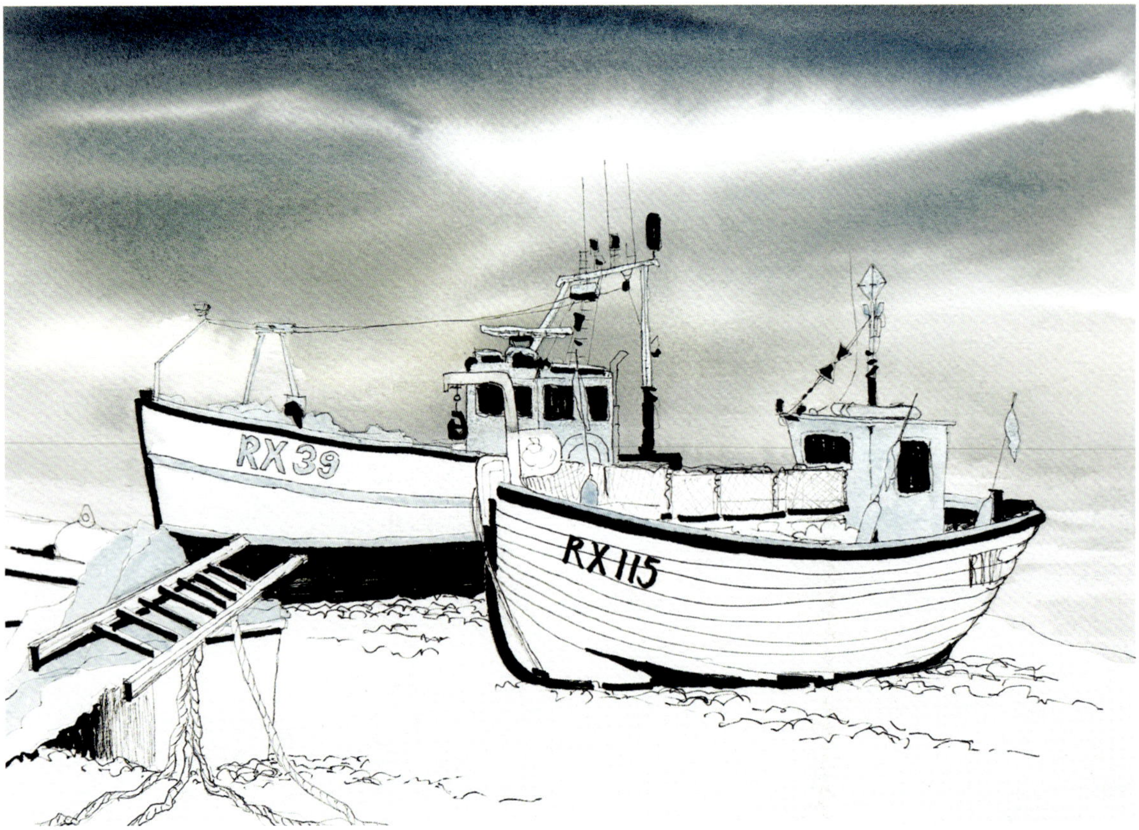

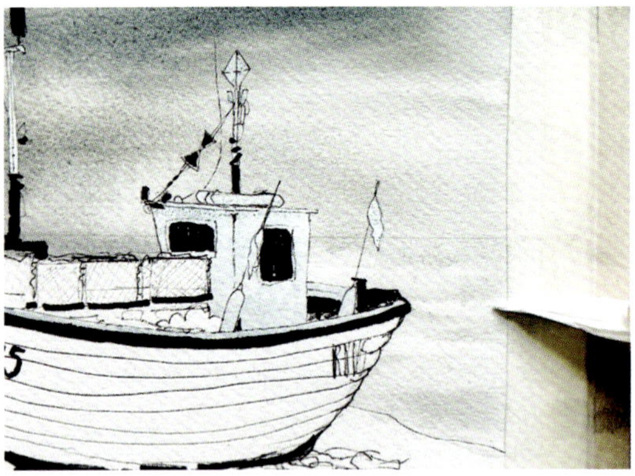

To easily and accurately lift out narrow bands of damp paint from the sea, use a piece of kitchen paper that has been rolled to create a point.

Tip

If you inadvertently get some paint on the boats or beach, wipe it off quickly with kitchen paper before it dries.

STAGE 1

Mix a small well of light-value Raw Sienna and a large well of mid- to dark-value Payne's Grey and Sepia.

Paint an atmospheric wet-in-wet stormy sky (see pages 22–23). Wet the sky and sea with clean water using the mottler brush, working around the boats. Leave to soak for about 30 seconds.

Using the mottler brush, paint a few horizontal streaks of the sienna above the horizon to introduce an underlying subtle glow to the sky.

Without rinsing the brush, load it with plenty of the grey and sepia mix. Starting at the top, sweep the brush across the sky using broad horizontal brushstrokes. Leave some gaps of unpainted paper and sienna between the darker clouds, and allow the paint to run out on the brush as you get closer to the horizon, so the paint becomes lighter. Now paint the sea on either side of the boats.

Lift a little paint from the sea with kitchen paper to create the suggestion of waves and light close to the shore. Leave to dry.

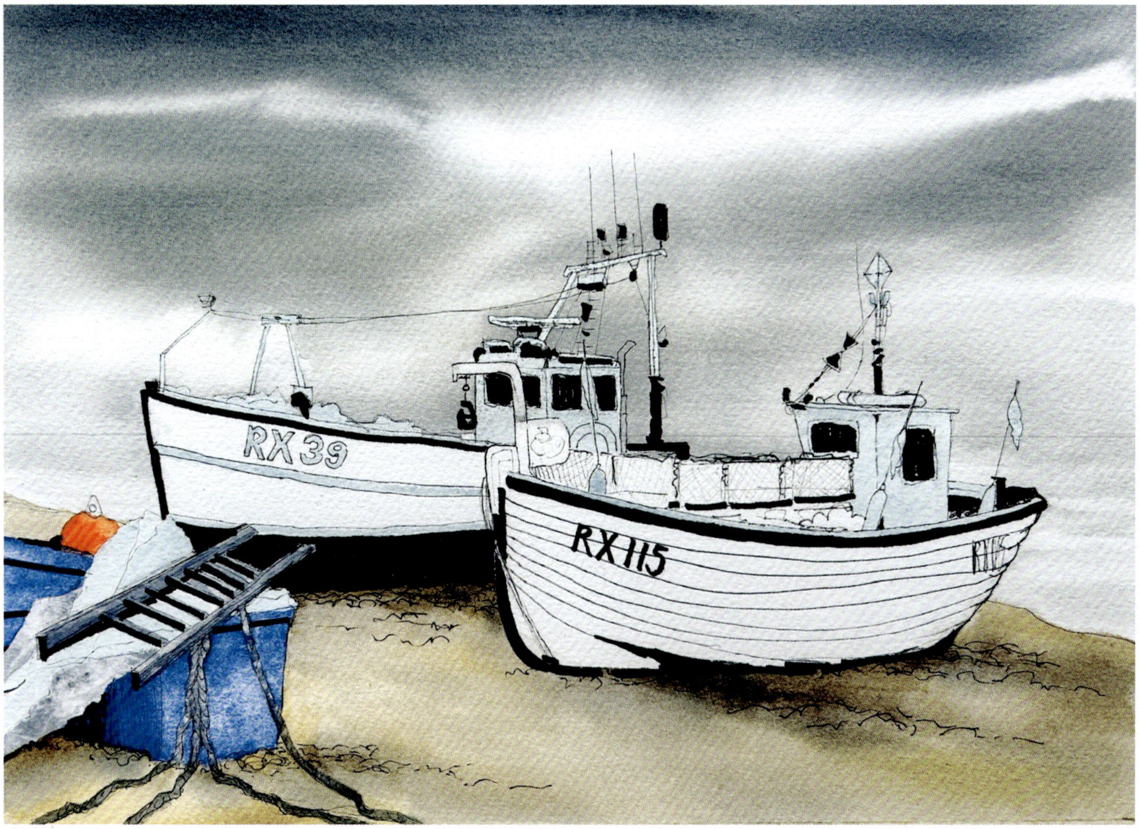

STAGE 2

Mix a well of mid-value Raw Sienna. Also mix two light-value wells: one of Sepia and the other Payne's Grey. Paint the whole beach with the sienna using the size 2 quill brush, and while the paint is still wet, drop in small patches and streaks of the sepia and grey, focusing on the shadows below the boats and allowing the colours to softly diffuse together to create a variegated wash (see page 22).

Once dry, paint the crates, ladder and tarpaulins on the left. Mix a small well of mid-value French Ultramarine and Cobalt Blue, as well as three small wells of Payne's Grey: one light value, one mid value and the third dark value. Also mix a small well of mid-value Vermilion Hue.

Start by painting the crates blue. Once dry, use the different mixes of the grey to paint the ladder, tarpaulins and ropes, varying the tones to show the light sides and shadow sides. Once this has dried, paint the fishing float with the vermilion. Leave to dry completely.

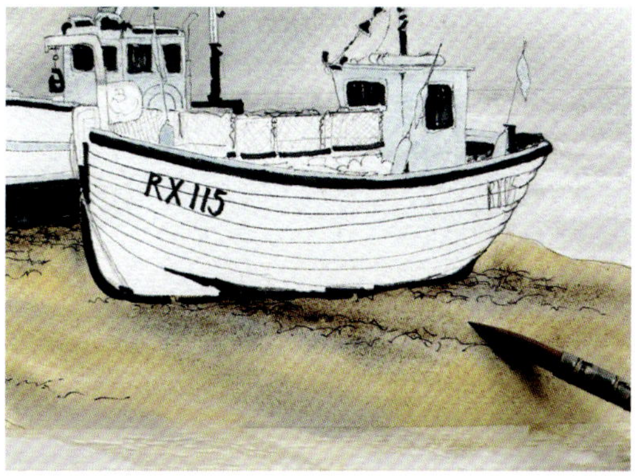

Adding soft shadows beneath the boat hulls helps to 'ground' them on the shingle beach.

Tip

While still damp, dab the tarpaulins lightly with crumpled kitchen paper to lift a little paint and create texture.

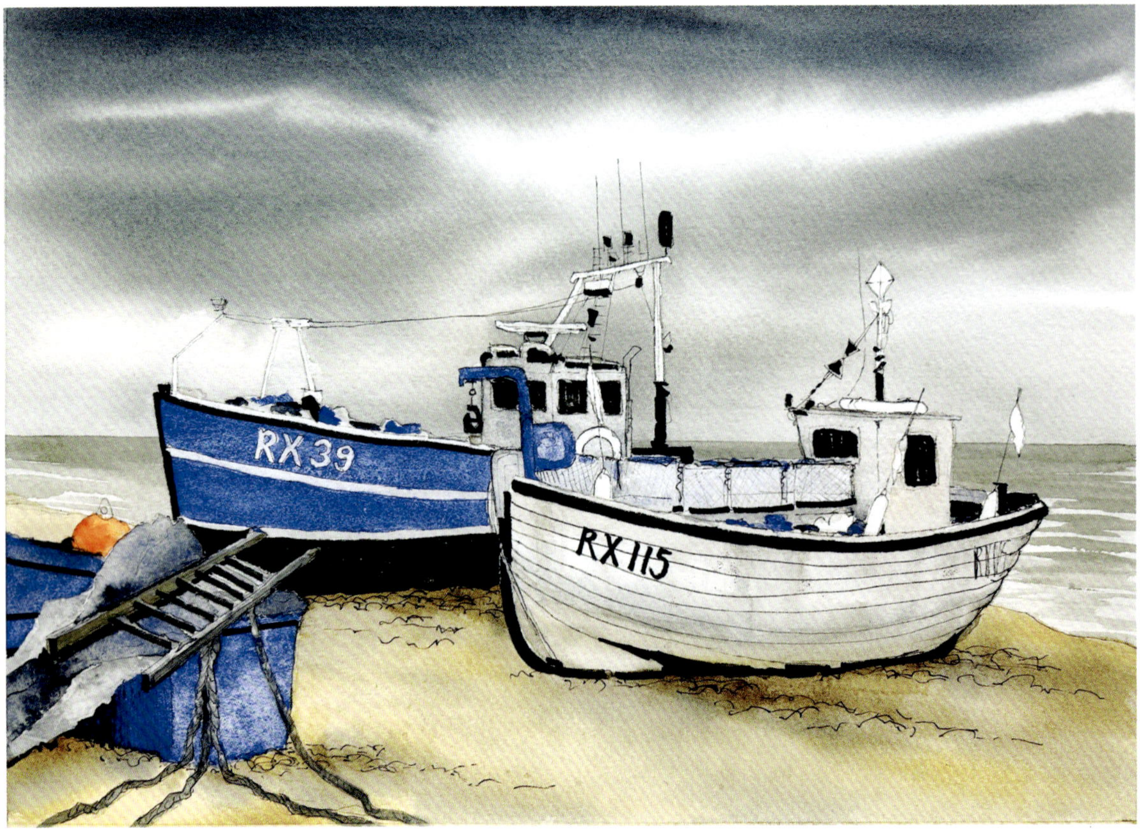

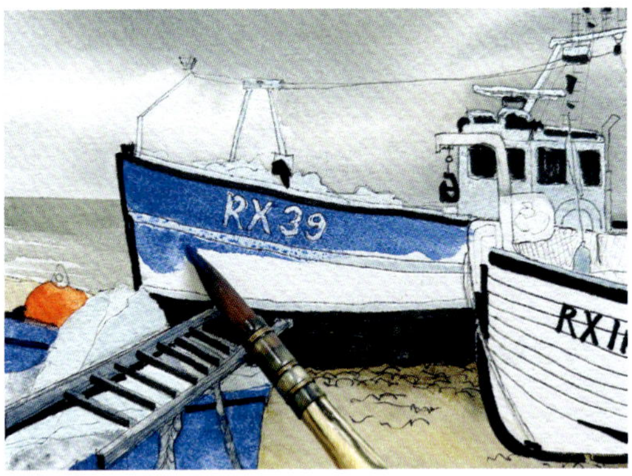

The masking fluid protects the white details on the hull, making it much easier to create an even, flat wash (see page 22).

Tip

Make sure your paint mixes for the cabins and hull of the white boat are barely more than tinted water to ensure subtle weathering effects. If they dry a bit pale, you can always add another light glaze.

STAGE 3

To paint the sea, mix a light-value well of Transparent Yellow, tinted with a little Payne's Grey to create a greyish-green hue. Starting at the horizon, glaze over the sea with the flat brush (see page 25), leaving a few gaps for the grey to show through as you near the beach to suggest waves. Allow to dry.

Mix a well of mid-value French Ultramarine and Cobalt Blue, and using the size 2 quill brush, paint the hull of the left boat, the pot-hauler winch on the front of the white boat, and the glimpses of tarpaulins on the boat decks. Add a little water to lighten the value and paint the tops of the lobster pots on the white boat. Leave to dry completely.

Remove the masking fluid with the adhesive eraser (see page 24). Mix four wells of very light-value paint: French Ultramarine, Payne's Grey, Raw Sienna and Burnt Sienna. Paint the lobster pots with ultramarine with the size 2 quill brush, dropping in a touch of the grey at the base and below the pots while still damp. Rinse the brush and paint the cabins with the light sienna, dropping in small touches of the blue and grey while still wet to give the cabins a weathered effect. Repeat this process on the hull of the white boat. Glaze the crates and tarpaulins on the beach with the grey and blue in a few places to add shadows. Leave to dry.

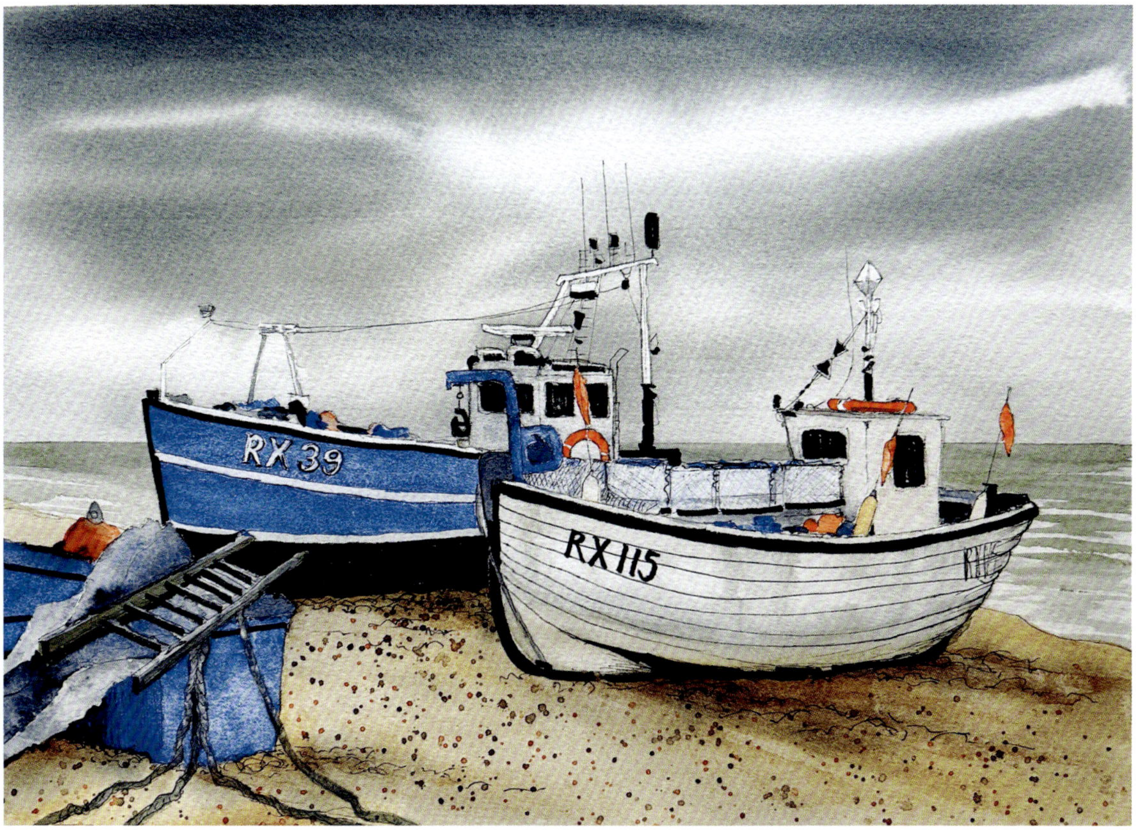

STAGE 4

Paint the slim pot floats on the white boat with the light-value sienna used in Stage 3. Now mix a small well of mid-value Vermilion Hue, and using the size 3 round brush, carefully paint the life rings and pot-float flags. Leave to dry completely.

To create a suggestion of shingle on the beach, mix two small wells of inky consistency Burnt Sienna and Payne's Grey. Lay scraps of paper over the boats, crates and sky to create a 'soft mask' to protect the painting (see right), then use the size 2 fan brush to spatter these colours lightly over the beach (see page 23). Dab off any unwanted large spots with kitchen paper.

When the painting is dry, go over any of the line work that may need a bit more definition with the 0.1mm fine-liner pen, and add a darker outline to the numbers on the blue boat hull.

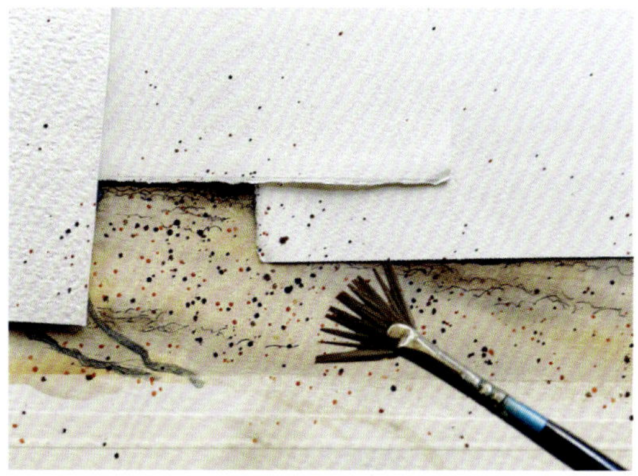

To soft mask elements in the painting to remain free of spattered paint, carefully arrange several pieces of scrap paper to create the best shape for protecting them.

Tip

If the shadows beneath the boats on the beach look a little pale once everything is dry, use the size 2 quill brush to glaze with light-value Sepia mixed with a little Burnt Sienna.

FOCUS ON *Creating Atmospheric Scenes*

Watercolour paints possess unique qualities, such as translucency, luminosity and the way the colours flow and blend on the page, making them an ideal vehicle for creative expression. They come into their own for creating atmospheric paintings that express how you feel about the scene you are painting, as well as what you see.

Choose a Limited Palette

Whether you are looking to express a dramatic landscape or an intimate and tranquil scene, choosing a limited palette can help you create atmospheric and harmonious paintings.

A good place to start with choosing such a palette is with the three primary colours, red, blue and yellow, plus a compatible dark or neutral colour; most colours can be mixed from the three primary colours. The darker colour can desaturate hues, thus providing limitless possibilities by just using four paints. 'Venetian Lagoon' below uses a limited colour palette of Hansa Yellow Deep, Pyrrole Red and Winsor Blue, plus two darks: Neutral Tint and Payne's Grey.

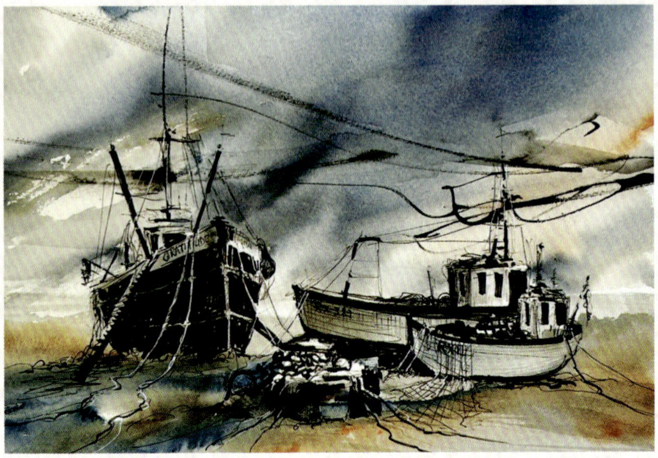

The loose brushwork and limited colour palette create an atmospheric and dynamic painting.

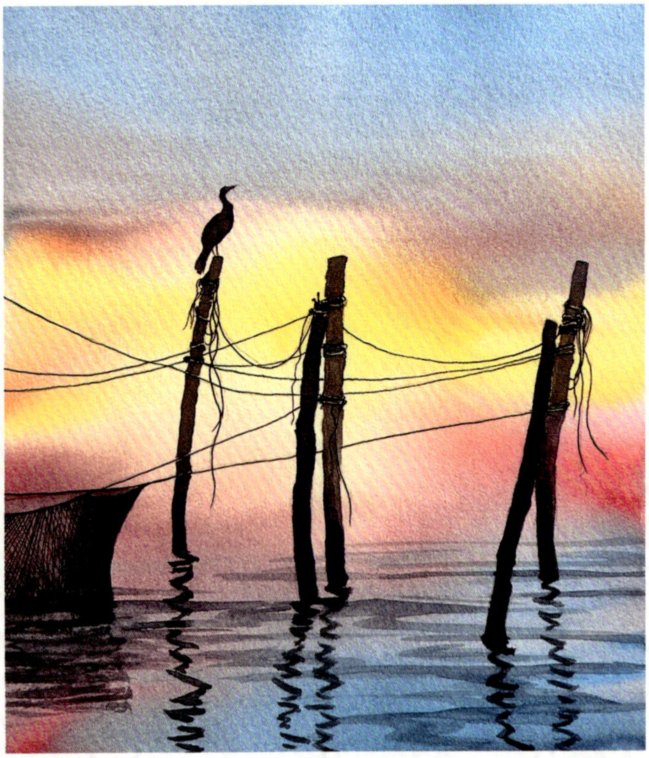

In this example, three primary colours plus the addition of Neutral Tint work together to produce a wide variety of colours that contrast beautifully with the dark silhouettes.

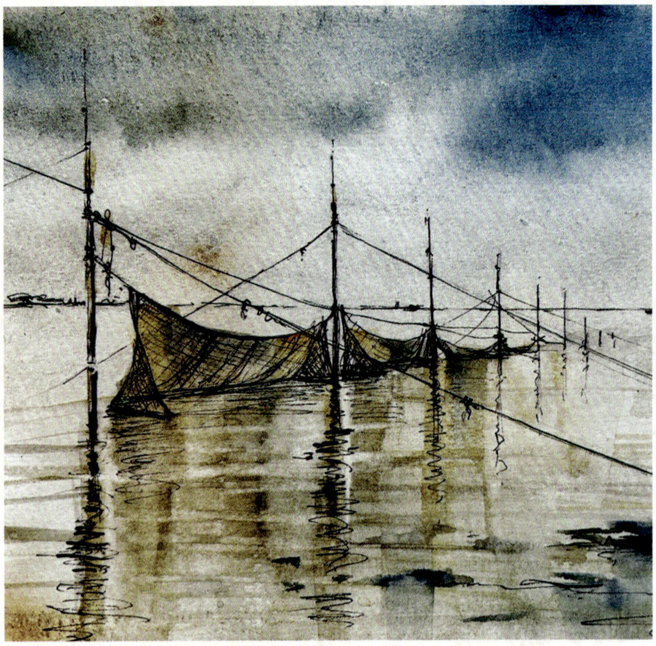

Here, a simple limited palette of Indigo, Sepia and Payne's Grey enabled the mixing of soft, yet strong washes of colour to create an atmospheric painting.

Use a Loose Painting Style

Choosing to paint in a loose painting style can help you create an impression of the scene rather than painting every detail. By focusing on tonal values and contrast rather than colour, you can create effective and expressive paintings.

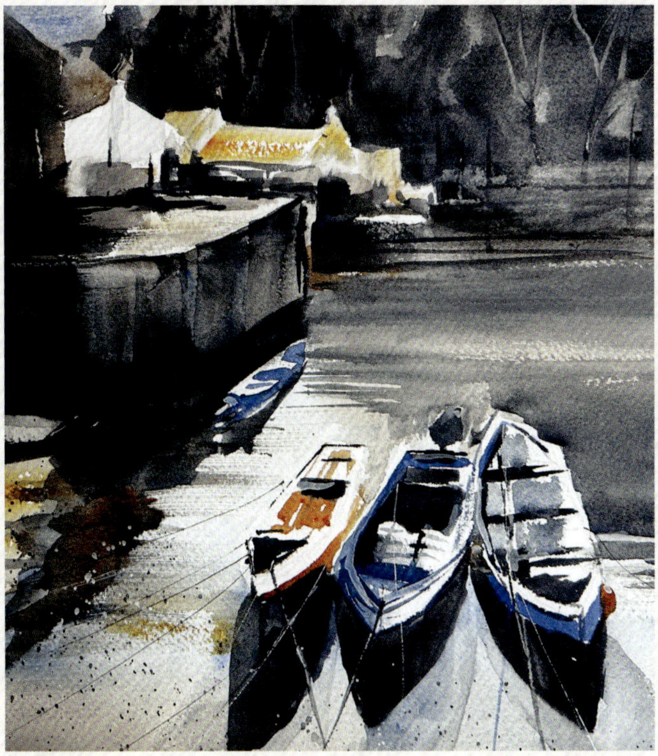

The loosely painted harbour, trees and buildings provide an effective framing device for the areas of greatest contrast between the light and shadows.

Experiment with Alternative Tools

While paintbrushes are perfect for watercolour painting, a little lateral thinking can help to create something expressive and very different. Applying paint with alternative tools such as a palette knife or flexible plastic store card can create really different marks and expressive passages of paint. You can also use items such as sponges and kitchen paper to add, lift and spread colour. The possibilities are endless!

Tip

You can consider colour theory (see page 17) when choosing a limited palette, but the best way to find interesting and expressive colour combinations is to spend a little time experimenting with different colours, to discover combinations that appeal to you – and more importantly those that don't!

Toned Paper and Mixed Media Approach

A great alternative to traditional white watercolour paper, toned paper provides a mid-toned base for painting on. This paper is available at art supply shops in many colours, such as buff, grey, blue and brown. You can add white highlights in pastel or ink, which will really stand out on toned paper!

If you wish to create your own toned paper, start by painting a flat wash (see page 22) in a neutral colour over the paper and allowing it to dry, then work into it with fine-liner pens, watercolour and other media, such as coloured pencils and soft pastels. Take care not to overwork the media on top of the wash with too much water, or it could cause the watercolour background to lift.

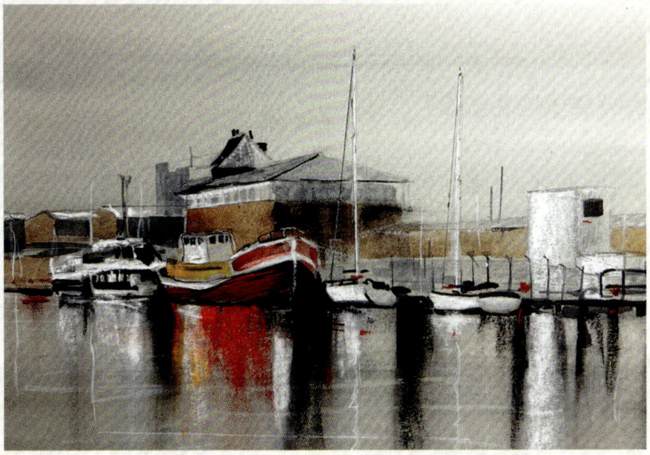

This painting uses watercolour, pastels and ink. The red ship and reflections contrast well with the toned paper, and the white pastel highlights really pop against the background.

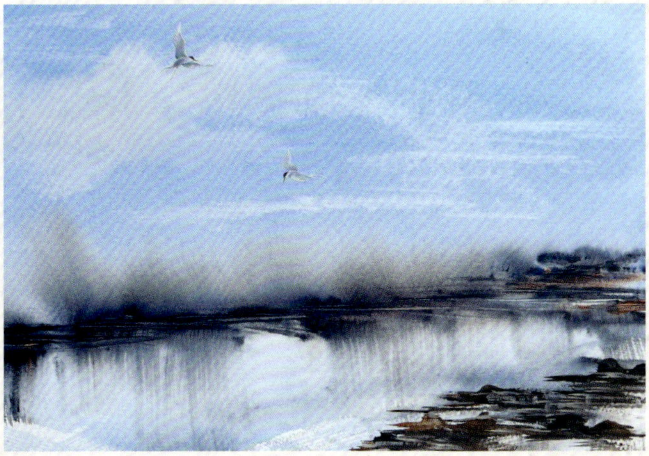

Using a palette knife to apply the beach textures has given this painting a unique quality that would be difficult to reproduce using only paintbrushes.

A Quiet Sunset

Sometimes, stillness is just as worthy a subject for painting as activity. I wanted to capture a sense of serenity in this composition, inspired by the crystalline reflection found in calm, unbroken waters.

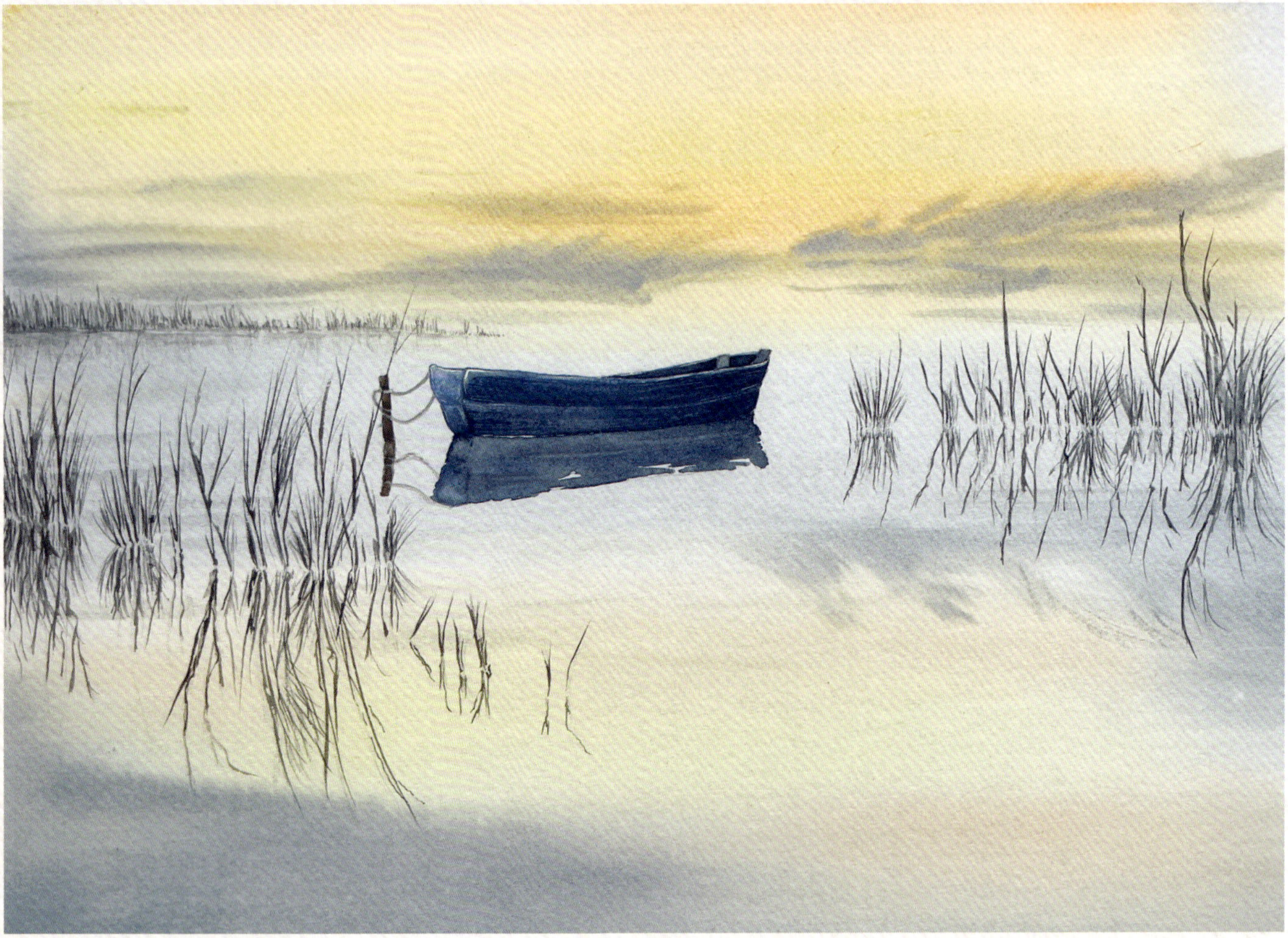

COLOURS NEEDED

Transparent Yellow, Indigo, Transparent Orange, Payne's Grey, White Gouache, Lavender, Burnt Sienna

For this painting, I worked from a reference photograph that I found inspiring. I loved the relative simplicity of the overall composition, with the little boat moored among the reeds and rushes, and the quiet reflections in the water, without even a breath of wind to disturb its surface. I wanted to maintain this sense of serenity while still creating a dynamic painting, so I chose to enhance the light in the sky, using vibrant yellow and orange to transform this gentle light at dusk into a simple yet effective sunset.

Making this change to the overall colour and tone of the painting meant that I also needed to adjust the colour of the boat; the original red felt a little too brash and bright for the scene that I was creating. I opted to paint the boat using cool blue tones instead, utilizing Lavender and Indigo to harmonize with the colours in the sky.

When working with reference photographs such as these, it's important not to feel too bound by them. It's all too easy to fall into the trap of feeling 'under pressure' to recreate a picture-perfect version of the photo; but that's not what art is about. Painting can capture a sense of place, a sense of emotion, a feeling: a thing that is entirely different to what may be captured in a photograph. Adjusting the colours in a simple composition is a simple way to enhance what is already present and turn it into something new.

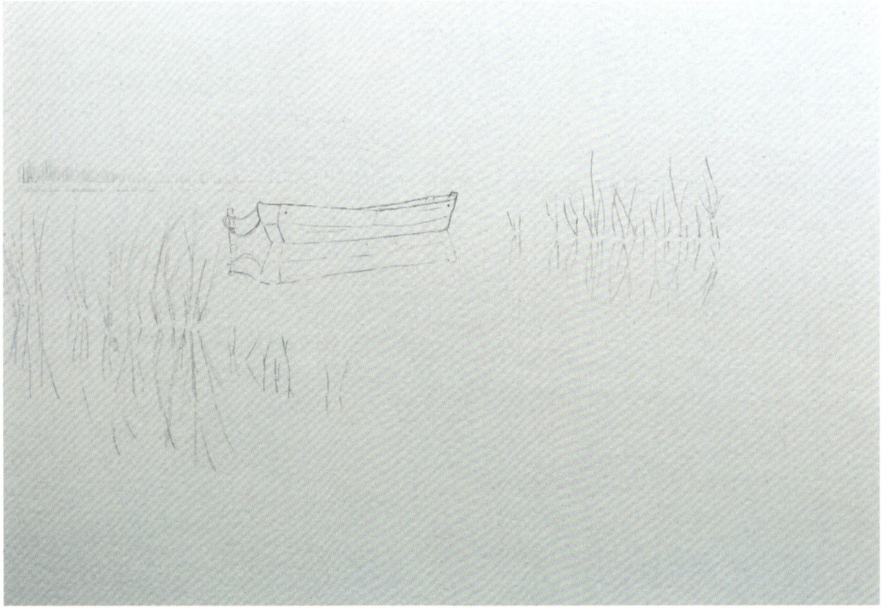

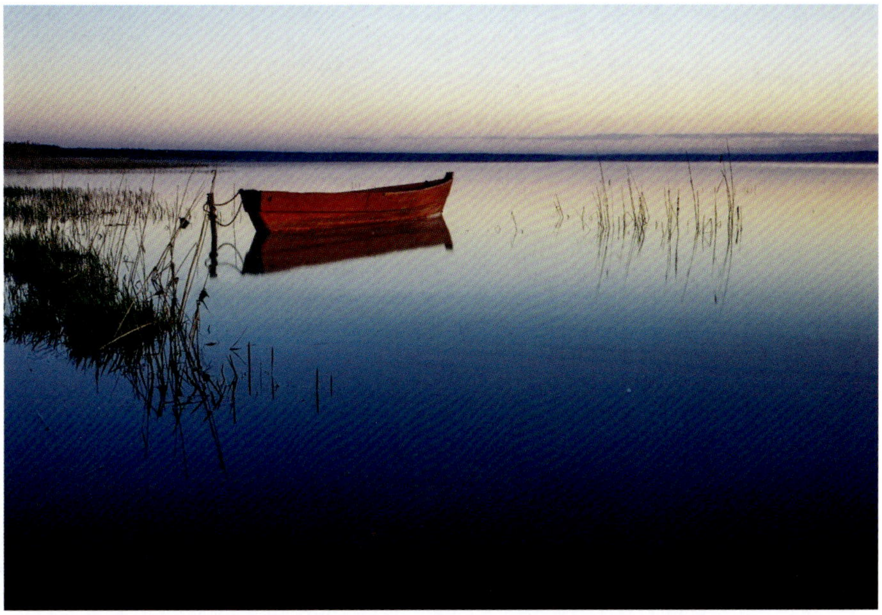

Setting Up

Begin by sketching an outline lightly onto hot press watercolour paper using the HB pencil (see page 20). Tape your paper to the painting board and lay it flat, ready to begin painting.

YOU WILL NEED

- *140gsm/300lb hot press watercolour paper*
- *HB pencil and eraser*
- *Painting board and decorator's masking tape*
- *Sponge or kitchen paper*
- *Palette with mixing wells*
- *1½in (38mm) mottler brush*
- *Size 20 mop brush*
- *Size 10 mop brush*
- *Size 3 round brush*
- *Size 0 round brush*
- *Small sword liner brush*

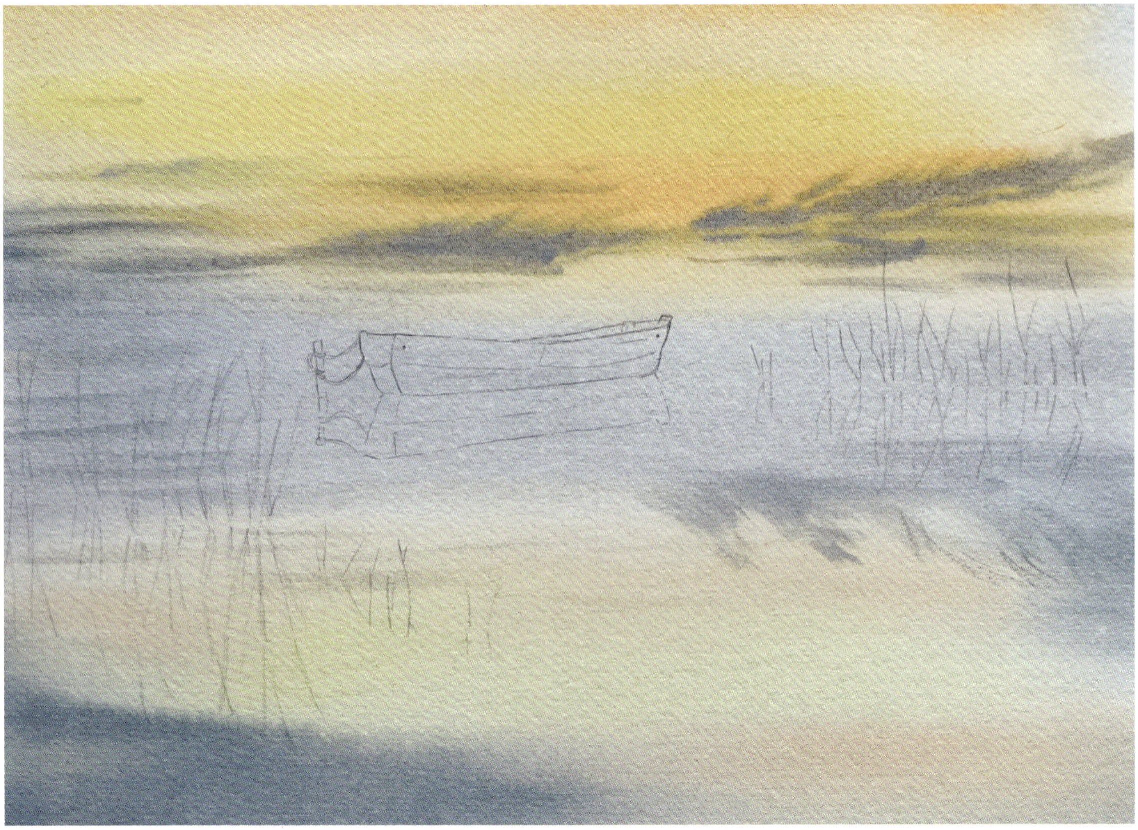

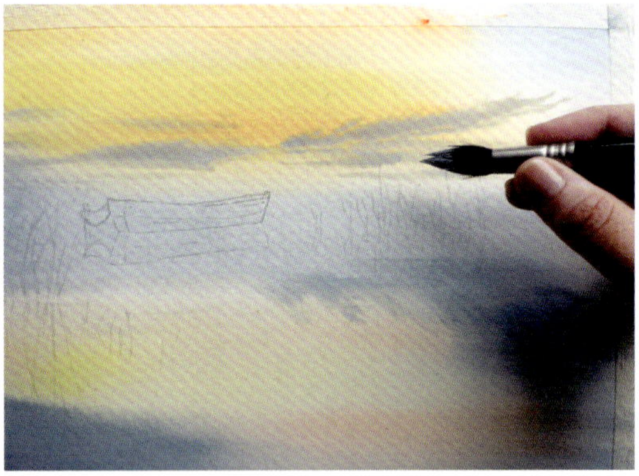

Keeping the gouache mix quite thick and 'dry' (i.e. using very little extra water) will help the cloud patterns stand up against the watercolour sky when added to a wet wash. If your mix is too thin, the colour will simply disperse into the wash and turn it muddy.

STAGE 1

Prepare three wells of colour for the sunset: Transparent Yellow, Indigo and Transparent Orange. These are all bold colours, so keep them mid-value to maintain a soft natural-looking scene. Wet the entire paper all over with clean water using the mottler brush and allow to rest for 30 seconds.

Switch to the size 20 mop brush to add your colours in a wash (see page 22). Begin by sweeping a little yellow from the top left corner, bringing it down and across the top third of the page. Dip it into the orange, and combine with the yellow on the paper, so that the colours soften beautifully together. Add a little more yellow and orange along the lower third of the paper, mirroring the shapes you just created; this will be your reflective water. Now dip the mottler brush into the indigo. Use horizontal sweeping motions to bring the colour up from the lower edge of the paper, working the brush around the sunset colours and filling in the gaps to create a soft, dusky sky that is reflected in the still water below.

While this wash is still wet, mix a touch of Payne's Grey into some White Gouache to create an opaque pale grey. Use this and the size 10 mop brush to dab some cloud patterns across the sky; doing this while the paper is still damp will give the clouds soft, diffused edges. Loosely mirror the patterns you've just painted in the water below. Leave to dry.

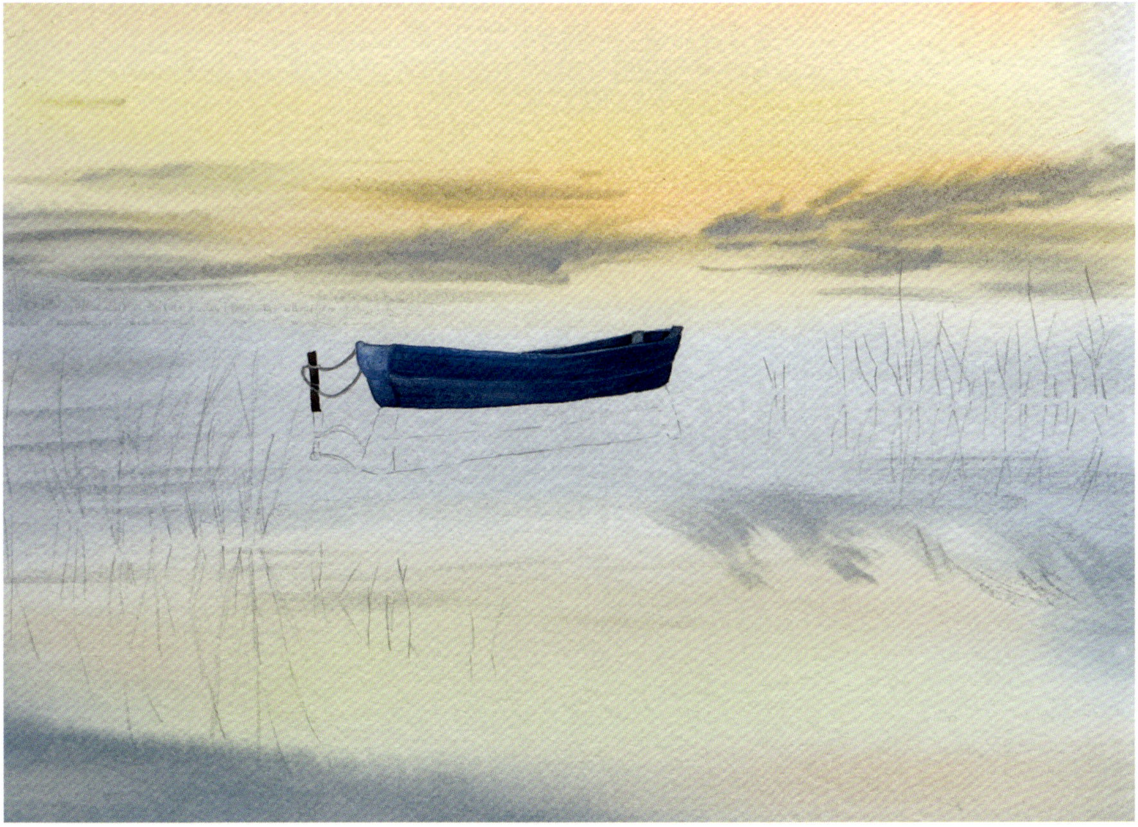

STAGE 2

Once dry, paint the small boat, following the pencil outline that should still be visible through the wash. Prepare two wells, one with mid-value Lavender and the other with mid-value Indigo.

Using the size 3 round brush, begin by placing the lavender in the areas that need to be paler, then gradually add the indigo to shade the darker areas. Tidy up any fiddly areas using the size 0 round brush.

Add a little Indigo to a separate area of your palette and add a touch of Burnt Sienna to create a cool greyish-brown hue. Use this and the size 0 brush to paint the post and the ropes.

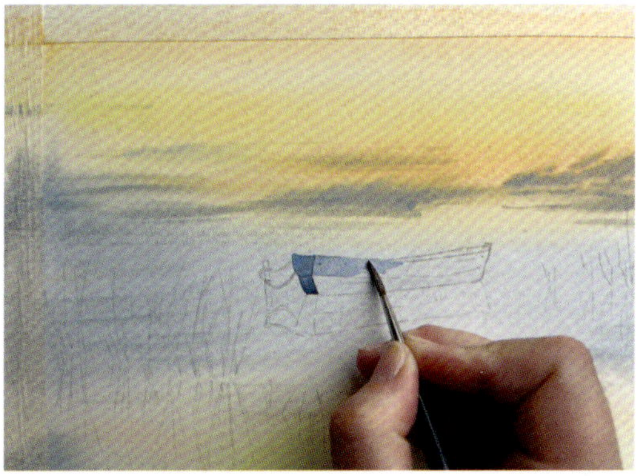

I find the simplest way to paint something like this is to start very light, then work my way down to the right level of dark. It's much easier to add colour than it is to take it away!

Tip

If you are struggling to see your pencil outlines through the watercolour wash, go over them again carefully with the HB pencil. Don't press too hard, or you may create indents in the paper's delicate surface.

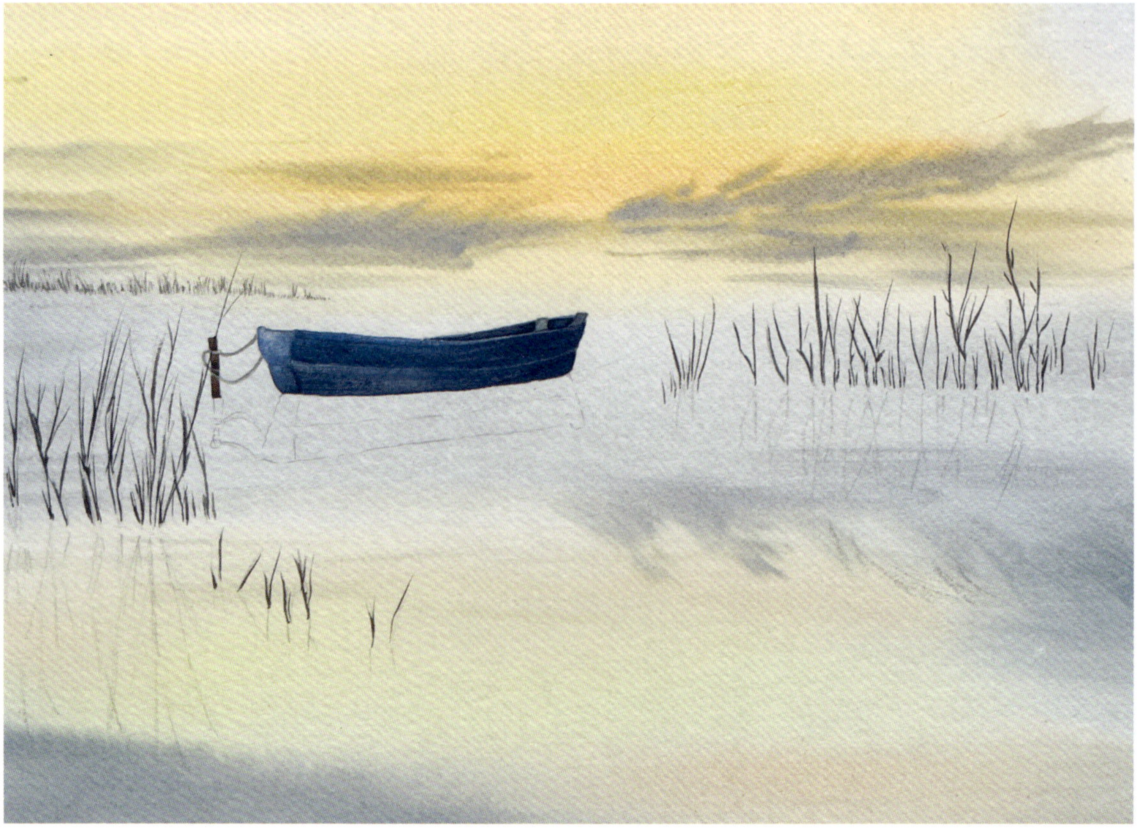

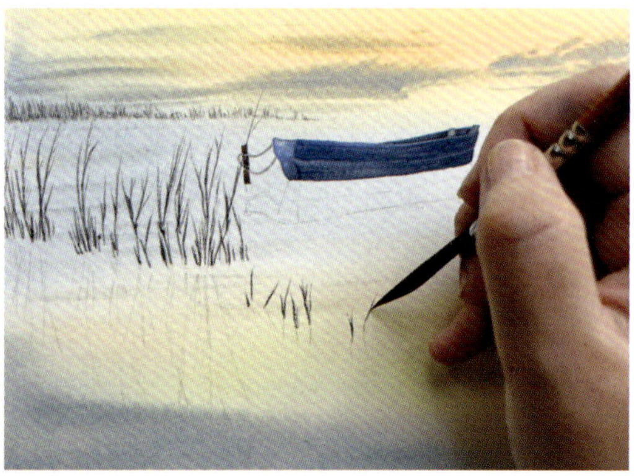

STAGE 3

Use the same grey-brown mixture in Stage 2 to add colour to the reeds (mix more paint if required). To do this, use the small sword liner brush to create loose, flicky lines (see page 23), roughly following the pencil guides. A good way to make the marks appear natural is to begin at the base of the reed, then flick the brush confidently upwards to create an angled, vertical line. Use a bold darker colour for the reeds closer to the foreground, and thin paler lines for the reeds in the far distance.

Use the fine tip of the sword liner's hairs to loosely follow the pencilled outlines; but don't worry if your marks aren't neat and wobble a bit; this will help them to look more natural and organic.

Tip

If you are concerned that your reeds are going in too dark, use a clean piece of kitchen paper to quickly dab out excess strong colour.

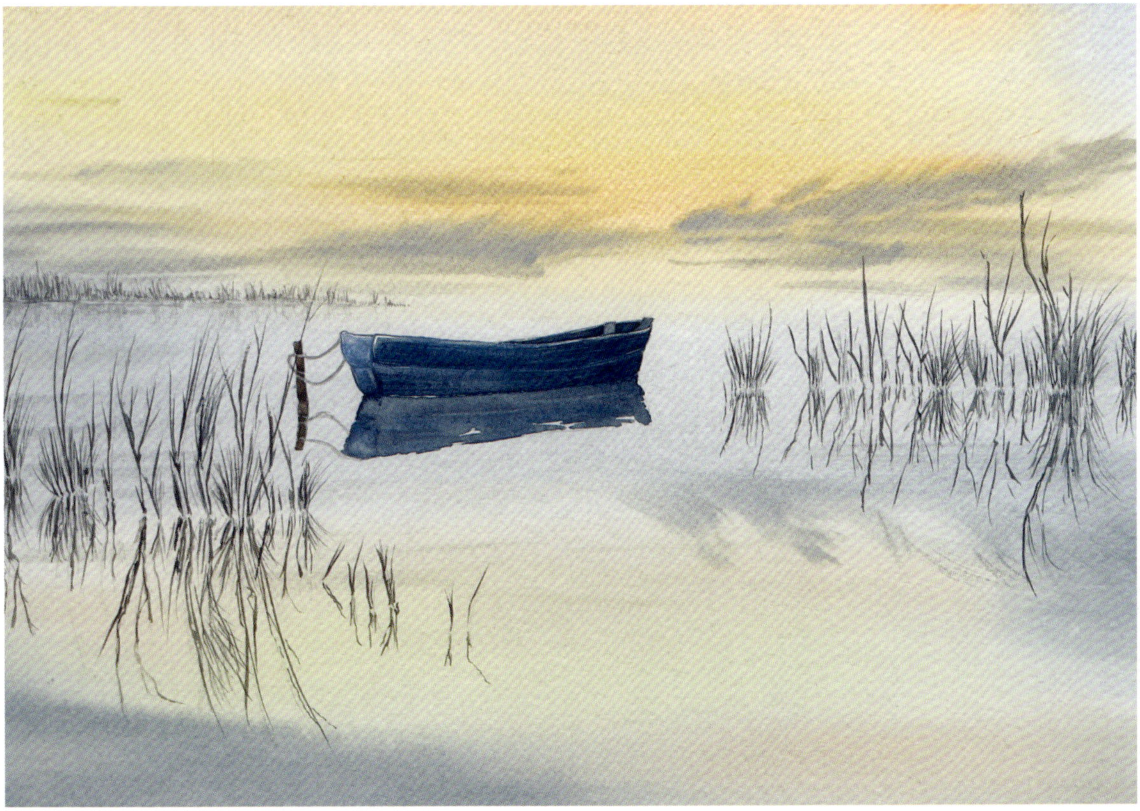

STAGE 4

Time to add the reflections! Use slightly paler, watered-down versions of the same colours used previously for each feature, such as watered-down indigo and lavender to loosely paint the reflection of the fishing boat, again using the size 3 round brush. Follow your pencil guidelines to create a series of mirror images reflected in the still waters. Use the sword liner brush to repeat the pattern of reeds you have just created, filling them out in places where necessary, and adding the corresponding reflections below.

Finally, tint a little white gouache with the yellow paint, and use it to add a couple of subtle highlights along the top edge of the boat, using the size 0 round brush.

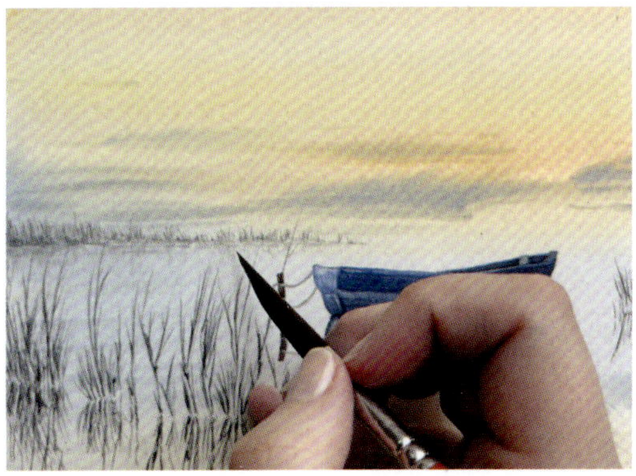

For these very distant reeds, don't worry overly about the individual lines too much; all that's necessary is that the general shapes of the reflections correspond loosely with what you've already painted.

Coastal Beacon

Lighthouses are often seen as romantic symbols of reassurance and safety; these tall beacons of light warn sailors of hazards, allowing them to navigate past unseen dangers during extreme weather conditions and the darkest nights.

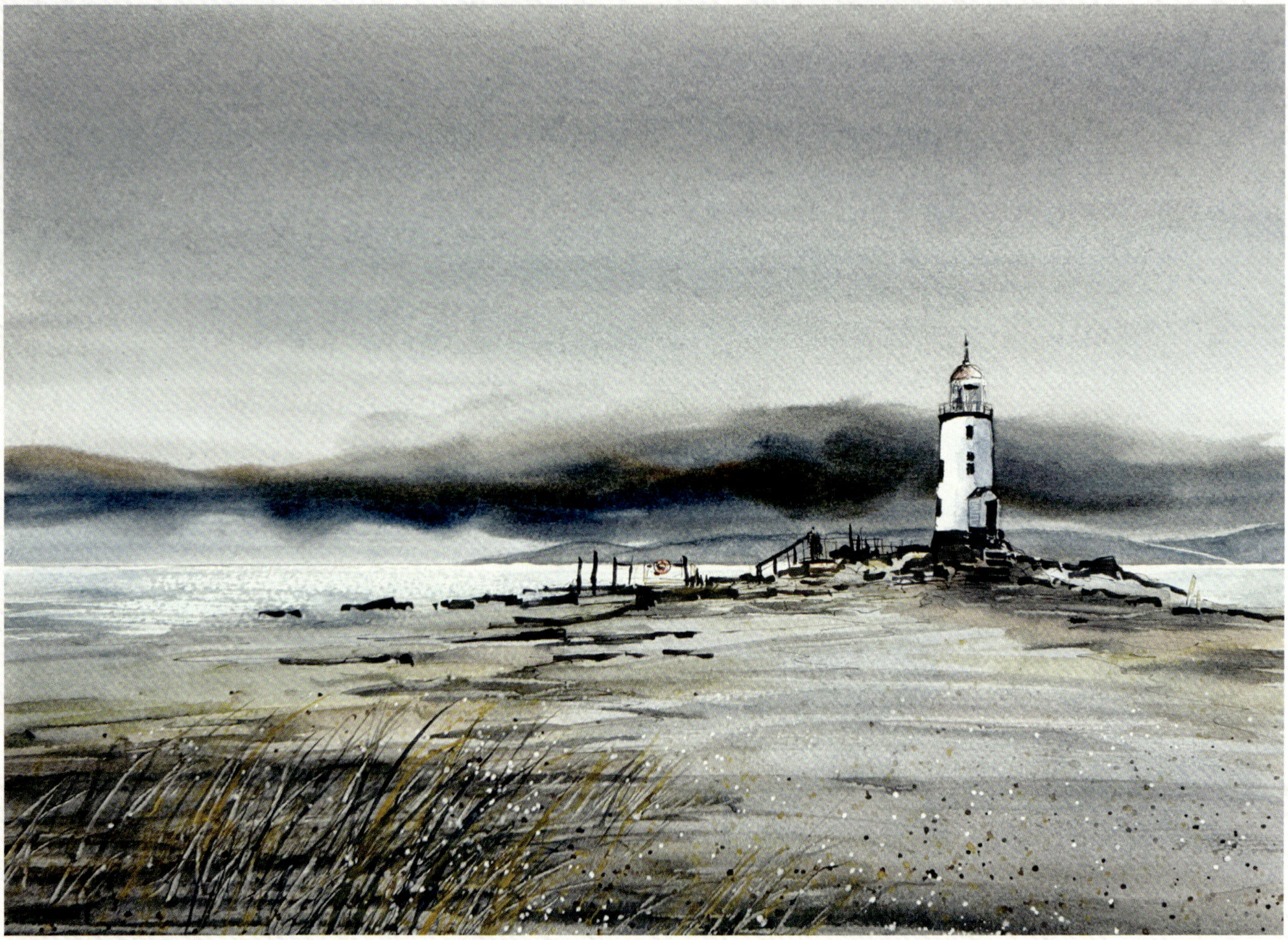

COLOURS NEEDED

Indigo

Sepia

Burnt Sienna

Payne's Grey

Yellow Ochre

White Gouache

Winsor Blue

The gleaming white lighthouse, or coastal beacon, creates a very strong contrast with the low, brooding bank of dark cloud in the background. To achieve this bright white, it is important to protect the white paper with masking fluid (see page 14) around the lighthouse and bay, so that the background washes can be painted freely over these areas.

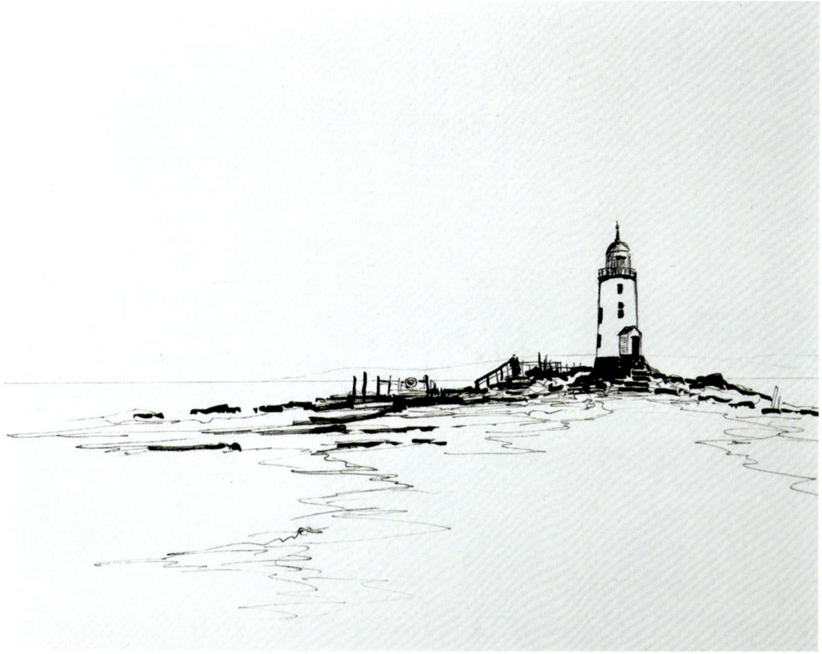

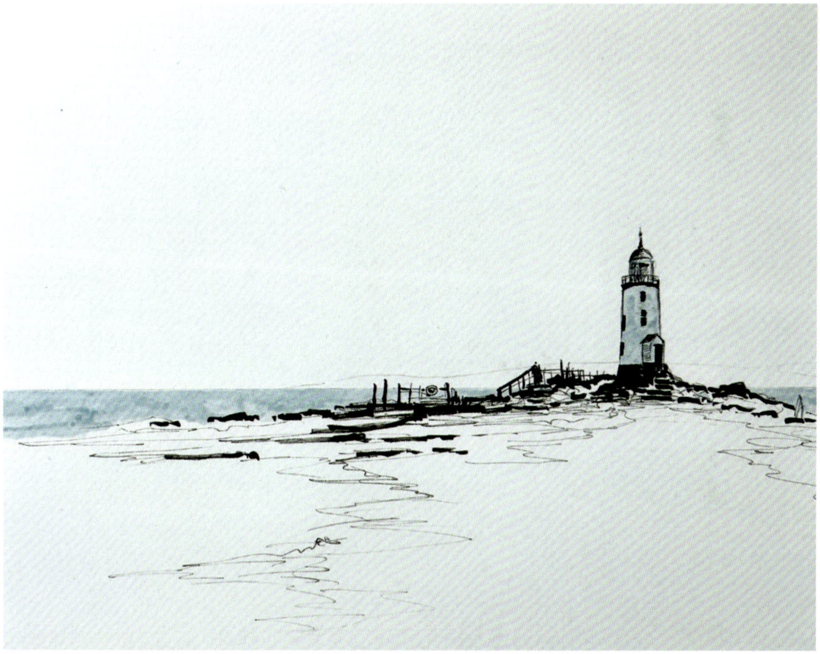

Setting Up

Begin by sketching an outline lightly onto hot press watercolour paper using the HB pencil (see page 20). Go over the pencil outline with the black 0.1mm waterproof fine-liner pen to create the line work, followed by the brush-nib pen to add some heavier lines and areas of tone and shadow. To increase the contrast, try to ensure that your shadows are dark enough in the rocks around the base of the lighthouse.

Mask out the lighthouse and sea with masking fluid and an old small pointed brush (see page 24). Tape your paper to the painting board and lay it flat, ready to begin.

YOU WILL NEED

- *140lb (300gsm) hot press watercolour paper*
- *HB pencil and eraser*
- *Black 0.1mm and brush-nib waterproof fine-liners*
- *Masking fluid and old pointed brush*
- *Painting board and decorator's masking tape*
- *Palette with mixing wells*
- *Kitchen paper*
- *Adhesive eraser*
- *Palette knife*
- *1½in (38mm) mottler brush*
- *Size 2 quill brush*
- *¾in (20mm) flat brush*
- *Size 3 round brush*
- *Size 2 fan brush*

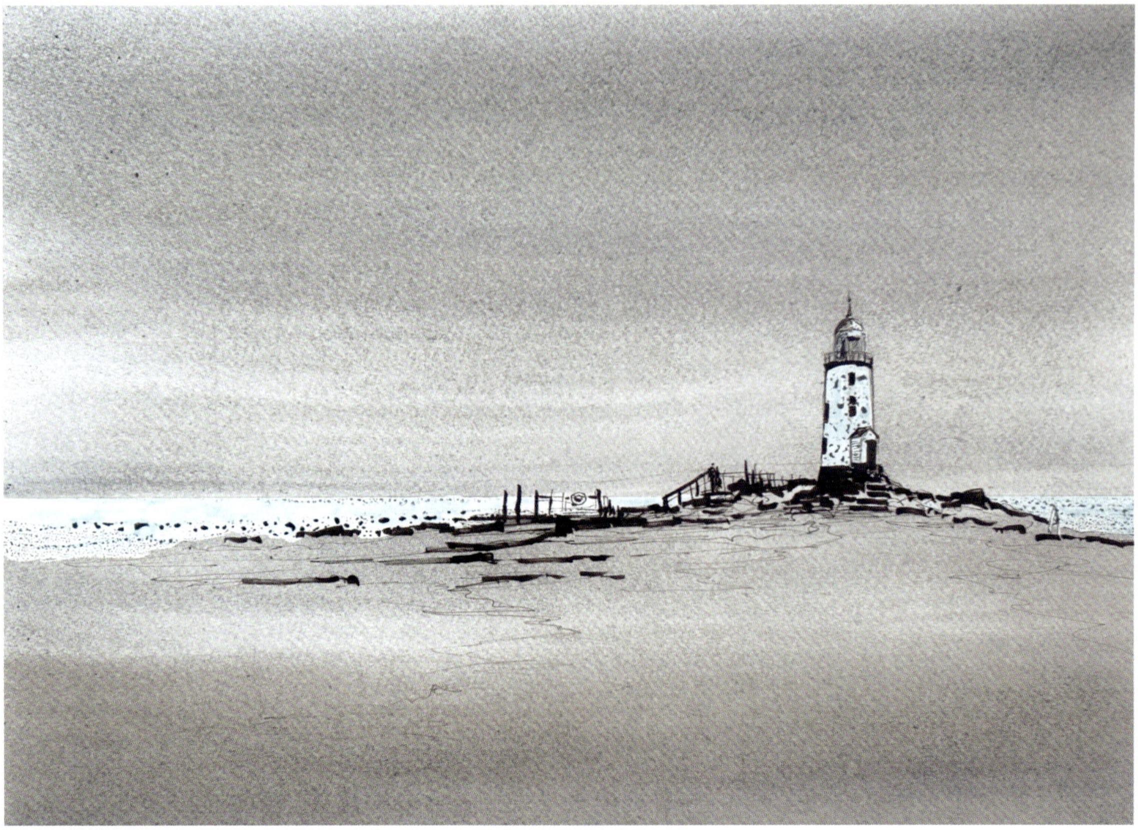

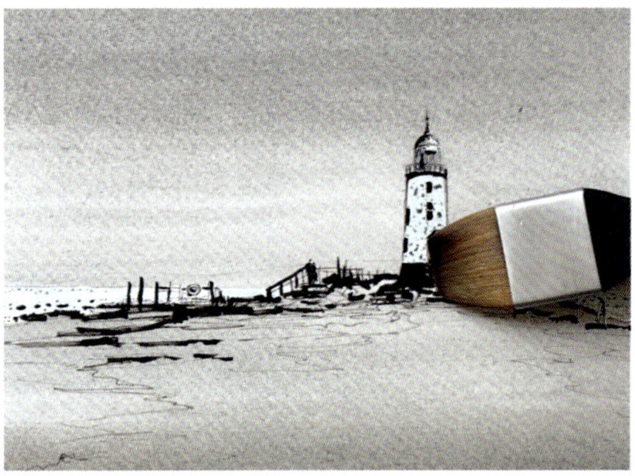

Paint straight over the masked areas, keeping the brushstrokes horizontal.

STAGE 1

Stages 1 and 2 are painted one after the other while still wet, so mix up enough paints for both stages before you start.

Mix a large well of mid-value grey using Indigo, Sepia, Burnt Sienna and Payne's Grey for Stage 1, and four wells of dark-value paint ready for Stage 2: Sepia, Indigo, Burnt Sienna and Payne's Grey. Make sure these four mixes are quite thick and creamy.

Wet the whole page with clean water using the mottler brush. Leave it to soak for about 10 seconds. Then using horizontal brushstrokes, paint the sky with the warm grey, continuing down across the land to create a soft, gently graduated wash (see page 22).

Tip

Keeping all brushstrokes for this wash horizontal will help to deliver an even layer of paint, which will create a soft sky.

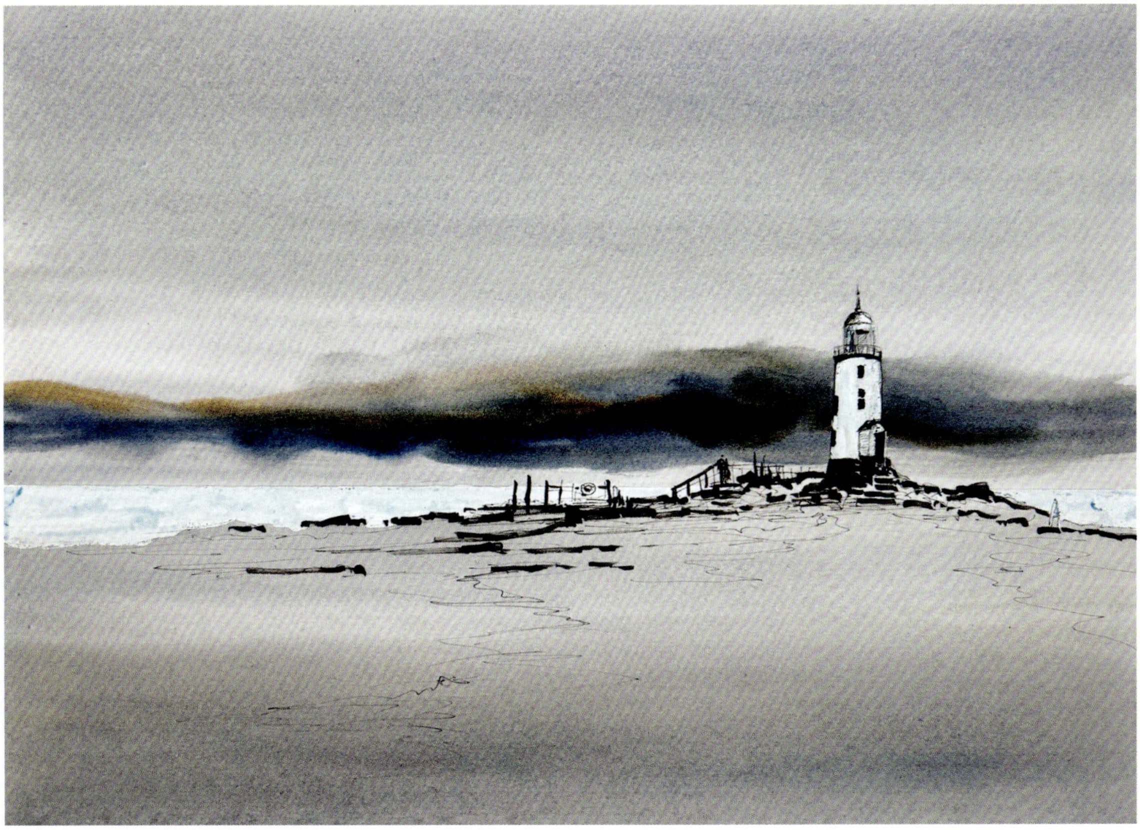

STAGE 2

Working quickly while the wash is still damp, and without rinsing the mottler brush, dip into each of the creamy dark-value mixes so you have all four colours on the brush, ready to create a mixed colour brushstroke (see page 23). Paint a dark cloud just above the horizon, turning the brush slightly as you go to ensure that all four colours blend on the page together, but that there is some variation in tone and hue, which will add shape and form to the low cloud.

Carefully clean the paint from the masking tape and masking fluid surfaces with kitchen paper. Leave to dry completely.

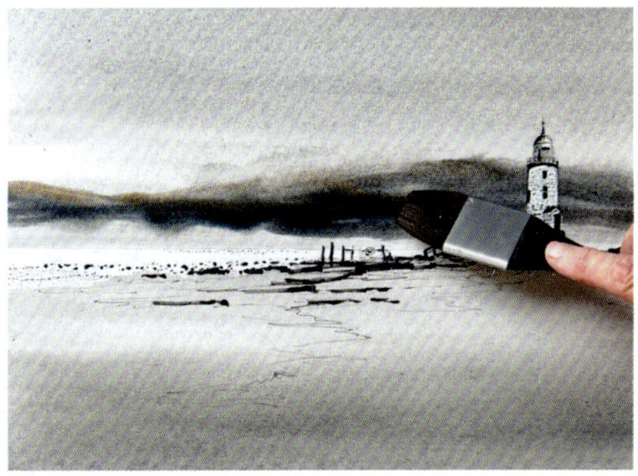

Ensuring that the low cloud is especially dark behind the lighthouse will help to create the maximum contrast.

Tip

Make sure your cloud paint mixes are rich and creamy; in this way the paint will stay in place as a dark mass of cloud with softly diffused edges. Too much water and you run the risk of creating unwanted runbacks (see page 23), or the cloud blending in with the background.

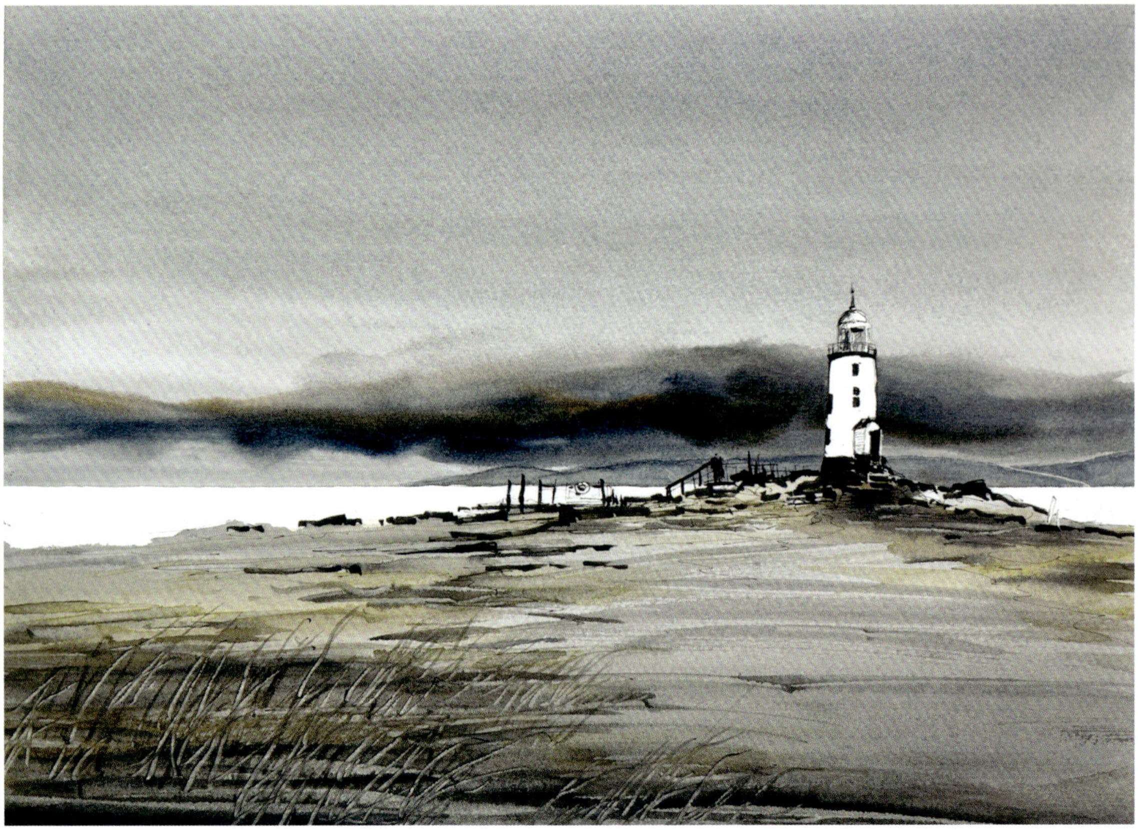

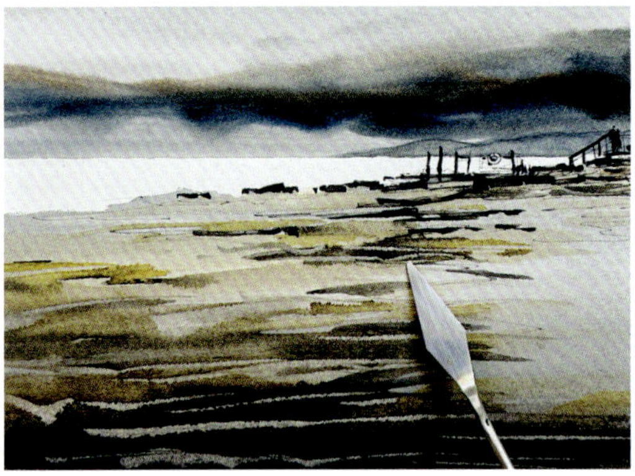

Make sure your palette knife marks work in harmony with the painted brushstrokes to create a textural impression of the wild marshy ground.

Tip

Always ensure the painting is bone dry before removing the masking fluid. Damp paper can easily tear as you try to remove the mask.

STAGE 3

Mix a small well of mid-value grey from Indigo with a dab of Sepia, and paint the headland below the cloud with the size 2 quill brush. Once this is dry, gently remove the masking fluid using the adhesive eraser (see page 24).

Mix five paints: light-value Yellow Ochre and light-value Sepia, and mid-value wells of the same colours, plus a dark-value Sepia with a little Payne's Grey. Use the flat brush to glaze the beach with the light-value yellow ochre, swapping to the stronger, mid-value mix as you near the foreground, Leave the underpainting showing through the centre to suggest a path or causeway.

Repeat with the light-value sepia working around the yellow ochre brushstrokes and again, changing to the mid-value sepia as you reach the foreground. Touch in a little of the dark sepia and grey mix here and there to deepen some shadows.

While still damp, scrape horizontal marks through the paint with the palette knife, then change the direction of your marks to create more organic, gently curving diagonal marks across the left foreground to suggest reeds and grasses. Leave to dry completely.

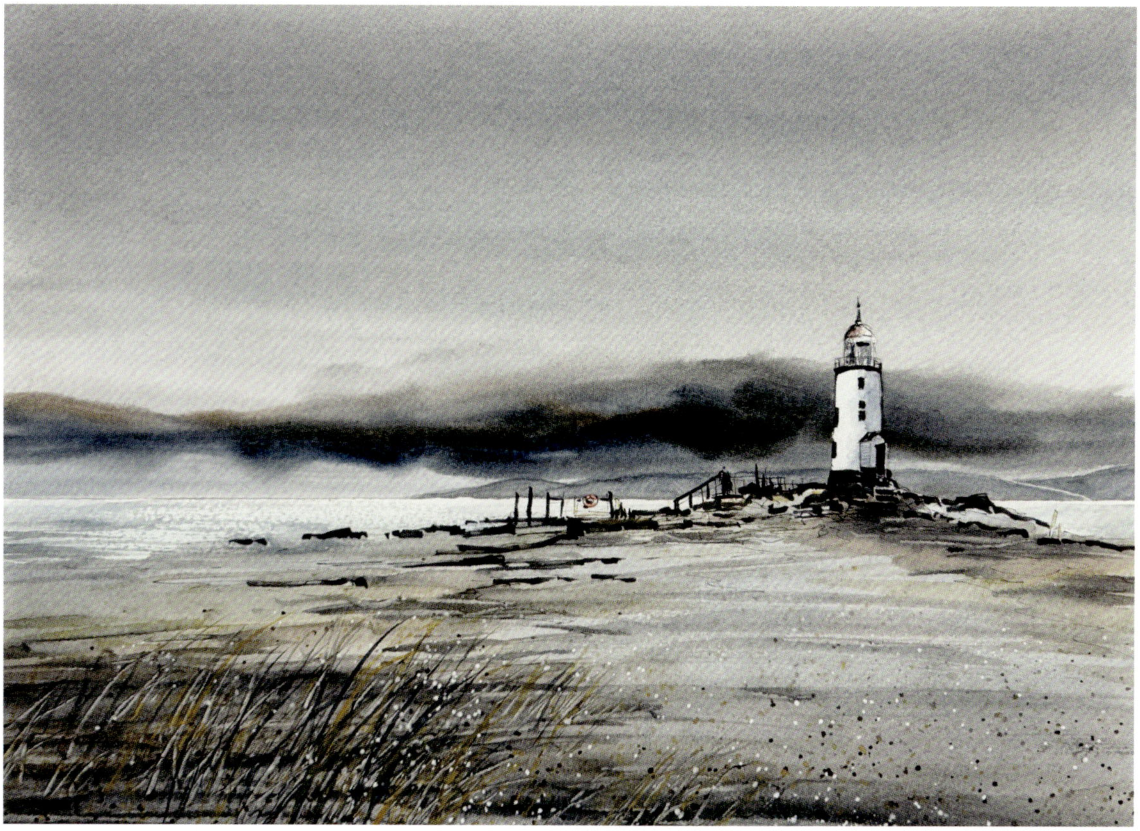

STAGE 4

Mix two wells of very pale Yellow Ochre and Indigo, and use the yellow ochre to paint the sea with the size 3 round brush. Rinse the brush and paint the right side of the lighthouse with indigo to create a shadow side. Leave to dry.

Mix three dark-value paints: inky consistency Yellow Ochre, Sepia, and Payne's Grey, and one of creamy White Gouache. Place a sheet of clean paper over the sea and sky to protect it, and spatter dots of all four colours across the foreground with the fan brush to add texture.

Mix a very watery light-value Winsor Blue, and using the flat brush, glaze the sea and beach on either side of the path to add a tint of blue to it. Leave to dry.

Wait until the sea is dry, then create a dry-brush stroke (see page 38) across the sea using the side of the quill brush and a little light-value Indigo, allowing the underpainting to show through. Leave to dry.

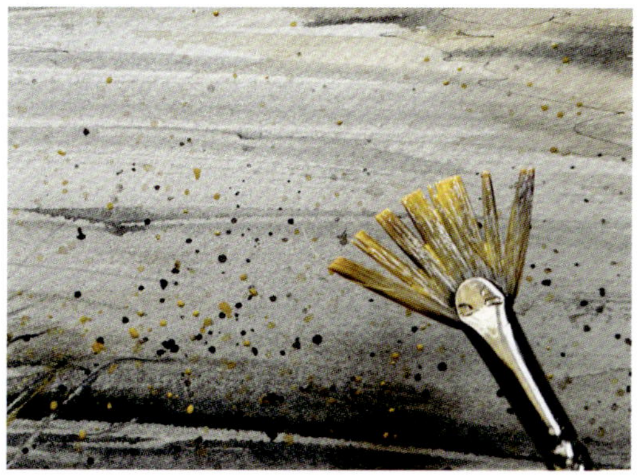

Start with the darker colours when creating the spatter patterns, ending with yellow ochre and white gouache to create subtle highlights as well as texture.

Tip

When painting a dry-brush stroke, after adding paint to the brush, blot it on a piece of kitchen paper to remove all excess moisture. Test on a scrap of paper first to check that the paint is dry enough to create the dry-brush effect.

Hidden Cove

A coastal walk can lead us to unexpected, but delightful, discoveries – a handful of ripe blackberries to eat on your morning stroll, or a secret cove, deserted, pristine and hidden. In such a peaceful place, your only companions will be the quiet calls of distant shore birds, and the gentle sound of waves lapping at a tranquil shore.

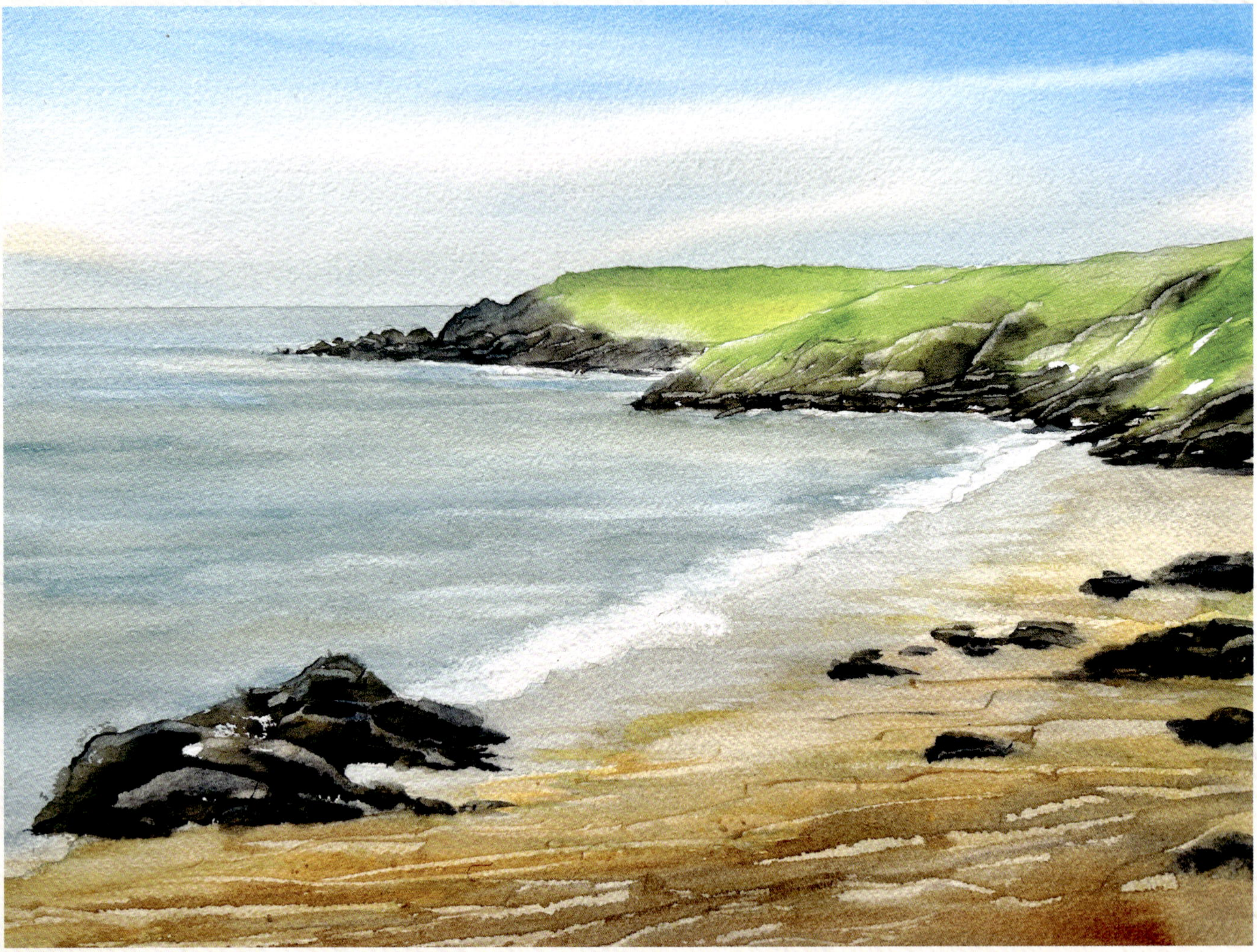

COLOURS NEEDED

Cerulean Blue | French Ultramarine | Raw Sienna | Venetian Red | Sap Green | Transparent Yellow | Payne's Grey | Raw Umber | Burnt Sienna

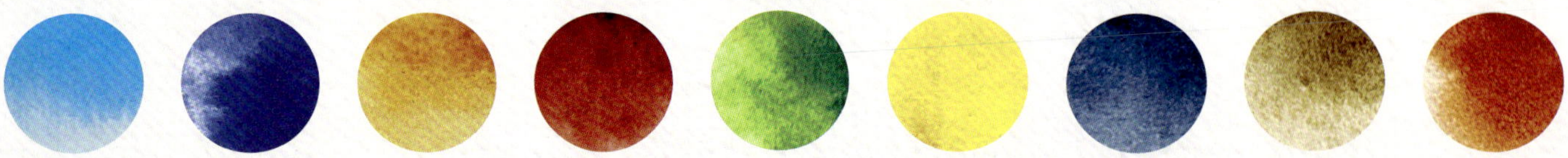

This scene is based on a photograph of Durness Beach, in Scotland; however, for this project, I have 'reversed' this well-known scene using my editing suite, turning it into a new and exciting challenge. This is a great way to approach scenes that you feel are giving you difficulty or to break through a creative block.

This project positions the viewer on a hillside, looking downwards into a peaceful deserted cove. The beach is cradled by the curved sweep of the headland, and the sea beyond, while the summer sun lights up the grassy clifftops, throwing deeper shadows on the rocks and headland. A soft, cerulean sky with a wisp or two of passing cloud offers pleasing contrast against the greenish tint of an inviting, turquoise-coloured sea.

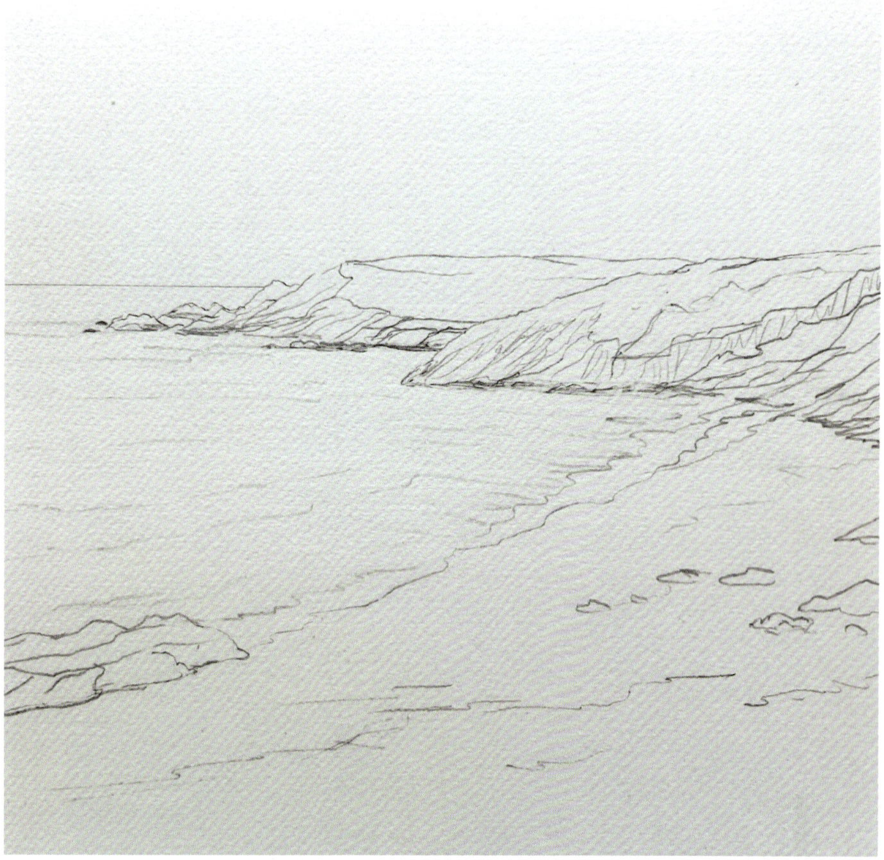

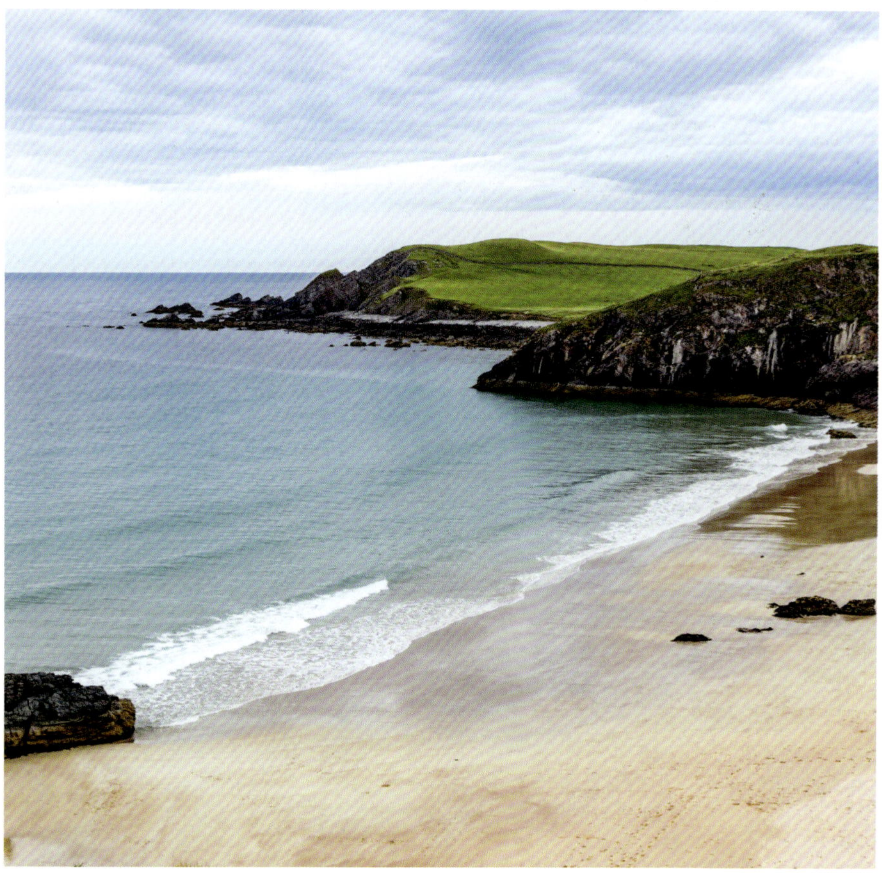

Setting Up

Begin by sketching the outline lightly onto cold pressed watercolour paper using the HB pencil (see page 20). Tape your paper to the painting board and lay it flat, ready to begin.

YOU WILL NEED

- *140lb (300gsm) cold pressed (NOT) watercolour paper*
- *HB pencil and eraser*
- *Painting board and decorator's masking tape*
- *Palette with mixing wells*
- *Kitchen paper*
- *Palette knife*
- *1½in (38mm) mottler brush*
- *¾in (20mm) flat brush*
- *Size 2 quill brush*
- *Size 3 round brush*
- *Size 0 round brush*

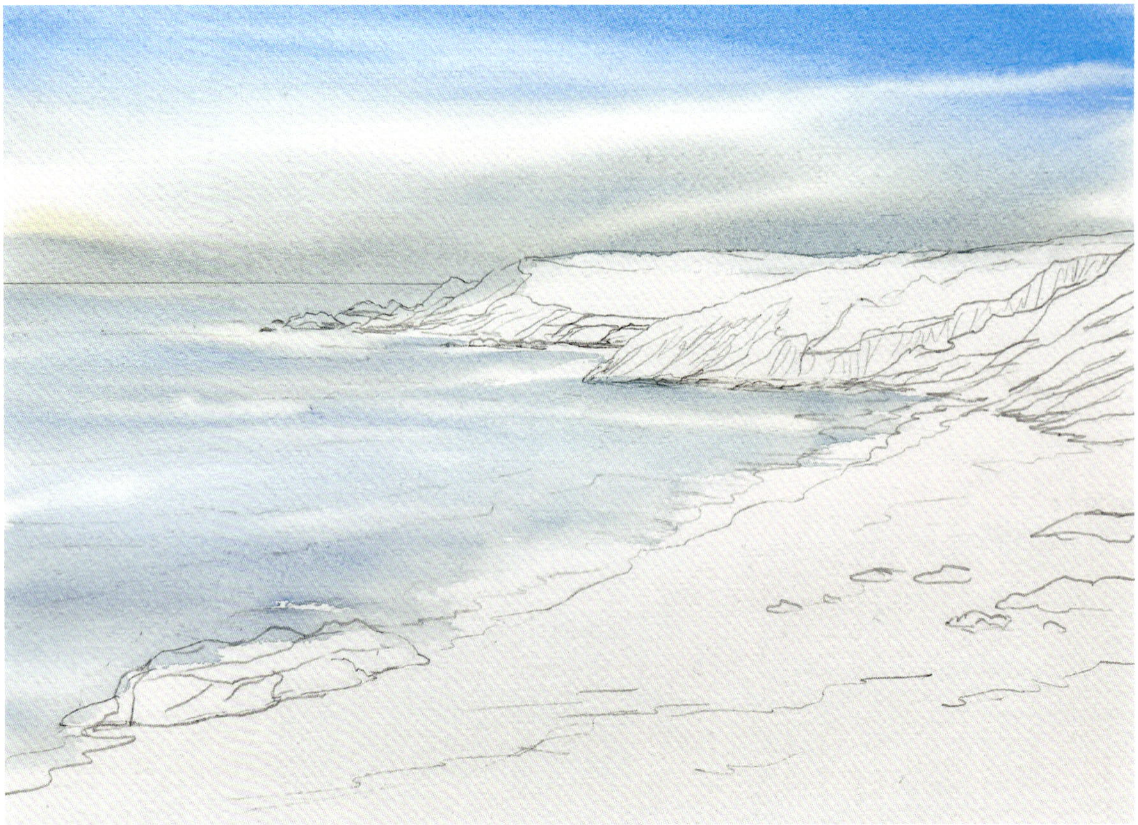

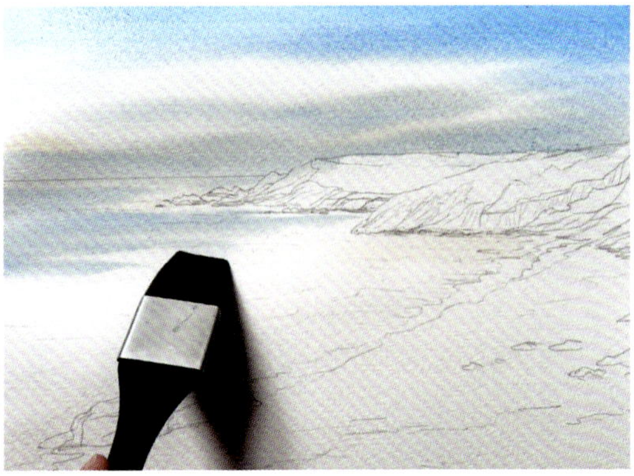

Notice how I use the tip of the brush to sweep the sea colour across the page, leaving some white areas to represent wave crests.

STAGE 1

Mix a large well of mid-value blue using Cerulean Blue with a touch of French Ultramarine, and also mix a small well of light-value Raw Sienna. Wet the sky and sea with clean water using the mottler brush, and work around the headlands, leaving these areas and the beach dry. Leave to soak for about 30 seconds.

Using the mottler brush, paint some pale golden streaks across the sky near the horizon with the sienna.

Rinse the brush and paint a variegated wash (see page 22) for the sky with the blue mix, using horizontal brushstrokes. Leave a few narrow strips of the sienna and unpainted paper as you paint to suggest a sunny glow and clouds. Keep the wash darker across the top, becoming a little paler towards the horizon.

Continue to paint the paler wash over the sea, leaving a few unpainted areas. Leave to dry.

Tip

Be sure to properly dry your brush when rinsing it off between colours to avoid accidentally diluting your paint mix – dab it onto a piece of kitchen paper or sponge to sop up the excess water.

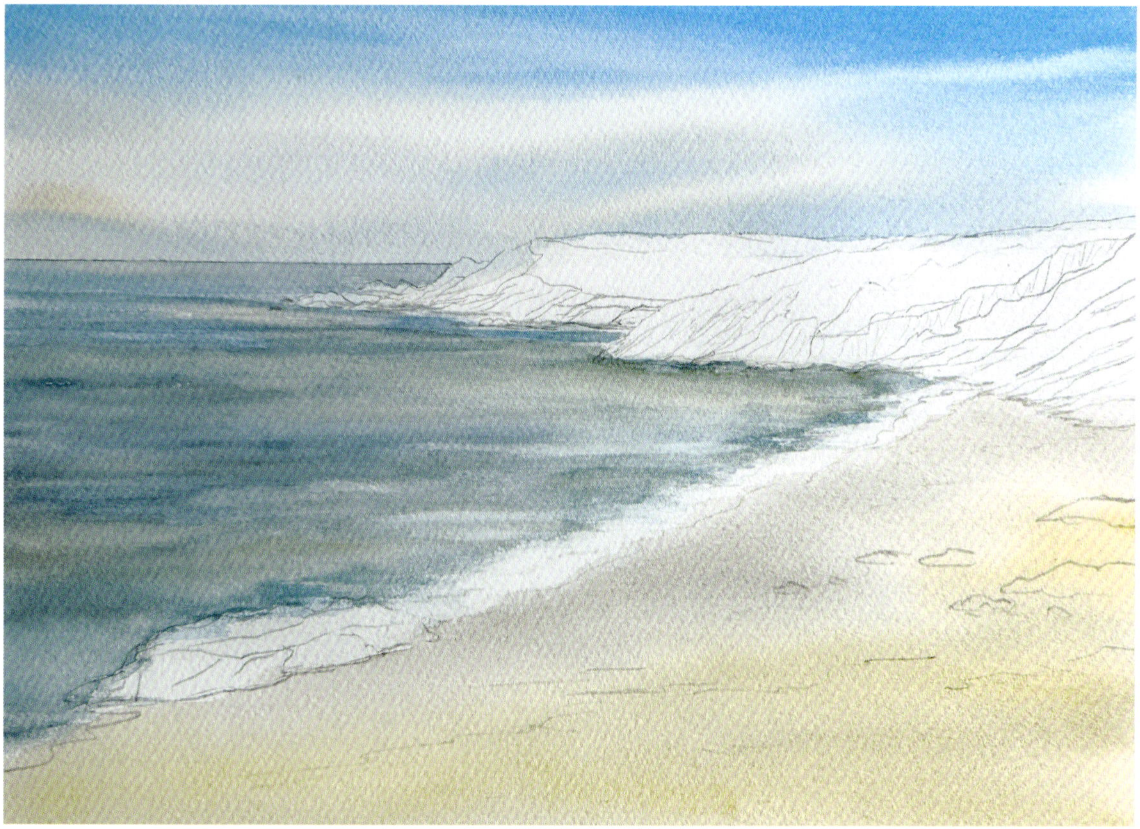

STAGE 2

Mix a mid-value well of Raw Sienna and a light-value grey from Cerulean Blue, Raw Sienna and a dab of Venetian Red. Wet the whole beach lightly with clean water using the mottler brush, and starting from the bottom of the paper with the sienna, paint the beach with a variegated wash. As you get close to the shoreline, dip the brush into the grey to indicate wet sand. Leave a band of unpainted paper between the beach and sea for sea foam. Leave the beach to dry.

Mix a light-value glaze of greenish blue from Cerulean Blue and a touch of Raw Sienna, and glaze over the sea with the flat brush (see page 25). Use the same technique with the tips of the brush and horizontal sweeps, as you did for the sea in Stage 1, leaving the underpainting showing through here and there to suggest light on the water. Leave to dry.

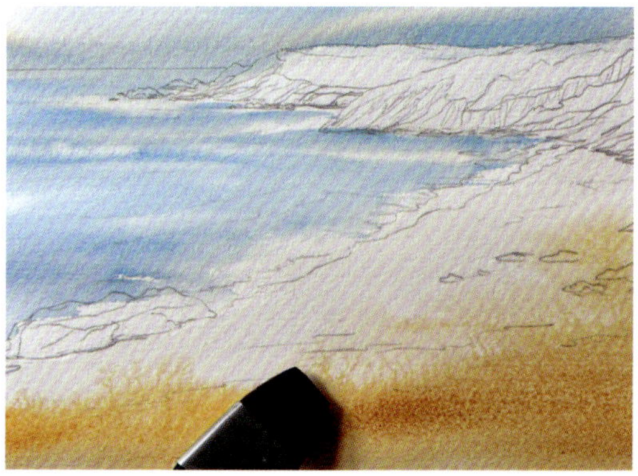

Sweeping your brushstrokes across the tape as you paint rather than trying to fit them within the paper edges gives a fresher, more lively paint application.

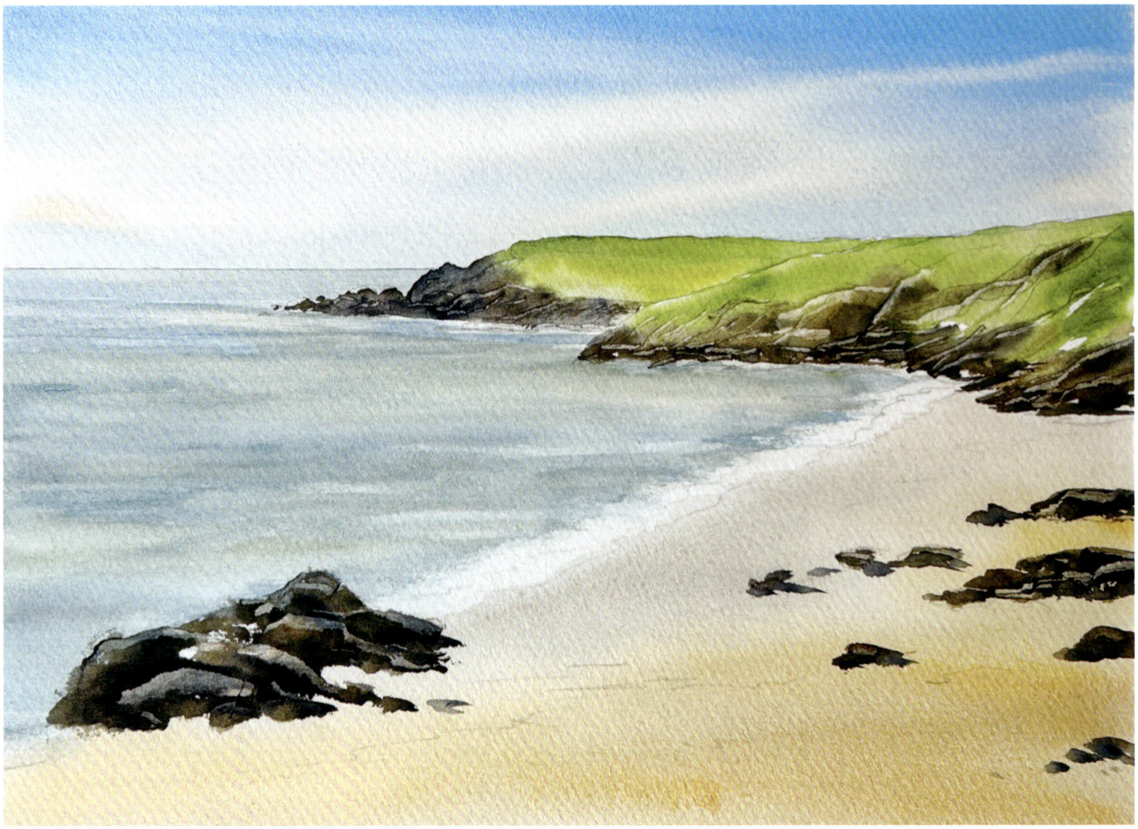

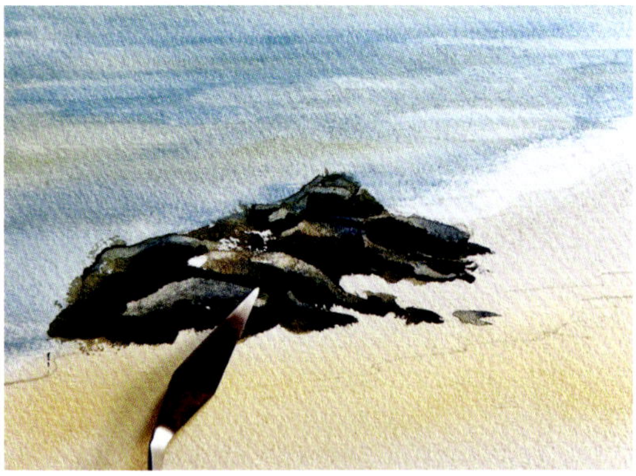

Using the palette knife to scrape away a little of the dark paint on the top of the rocks creates a subtle highlight.

STAGE 3

Mix two mid-value wells of Sap Green and Transparent Yellow, and two dark-value wells of Payne's Grey and Raw Umber. Using the size 2 quill brush, dampen the grassy hilltops and rock faces with clean water, and then drop some green into the grassy hilltop, adding a little yellow into the wet wash to brighten it where it catches the sun. Repeat for the closer clifftop.

Rinse the brush, and paint the rocky slopes, dipping the brush into both the dark-value colours. Follow the direction of the pencil outline, changing from one colour to the other to create dark grey and brown rocks. While the paint is still damp, scrape some strata lines through the rocks with the palette knife.

Repeat this process for the rocks on the beach. Leave to dry.

Tip

If you don't have a palette knife, the rounded corner of a flexible plastic card (such as a reward card from a shop) will work well to create the same set of effects.

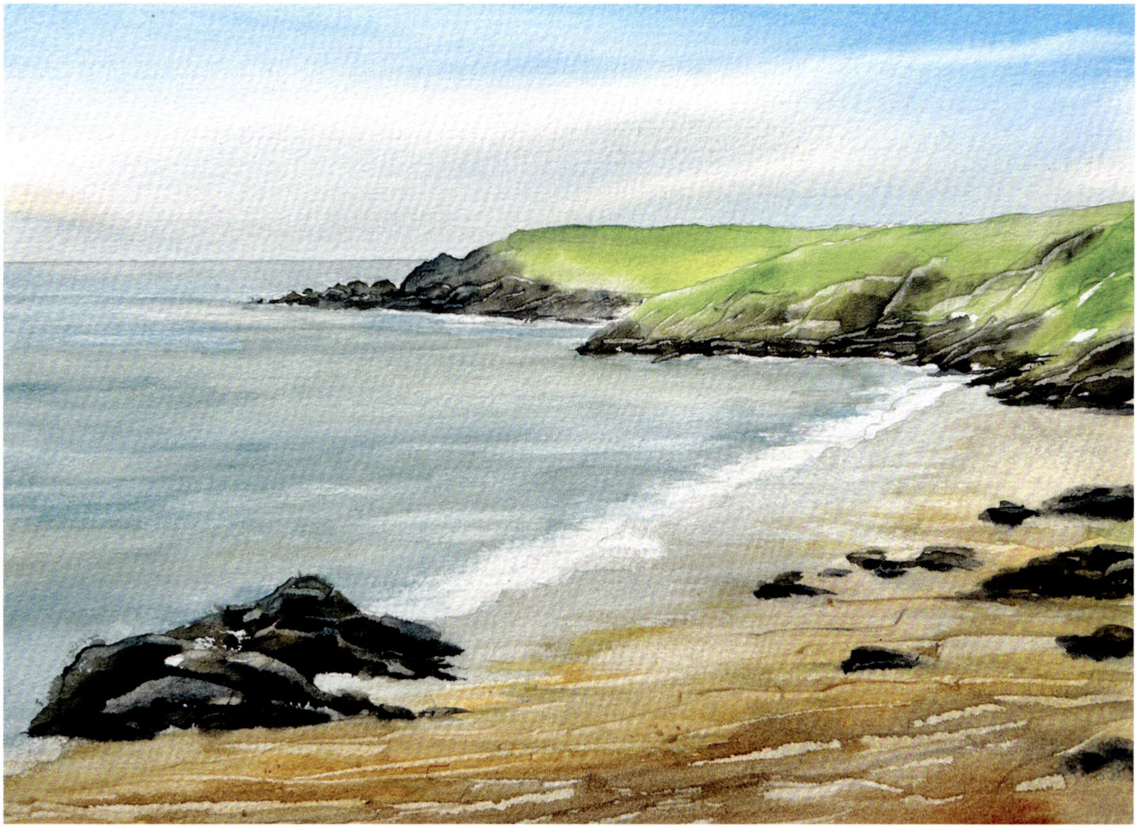

STAGE 4

Mix a very pale glaze of Cerulean Blue, and a mid-value well of Burnt Sienna. Using the size 2 quill brush, paint the water's edge to create a wet sand tideline.

Glaze over the beach with a light-value Burnt Sienna, keeping the value a little darker near the foreground. While it is still damp, use the palette knife to scape in some textural marks and lines. Leave to dry.

Use the size 3 round brush to deepen the shadows at the base of the rocks and headland if needed. Leave to dry.

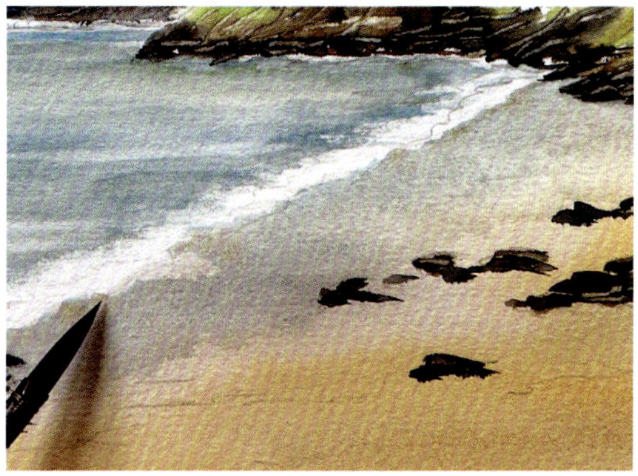

Work the Cerulean Blue glaze up to the unpainted paper to create a subtle contrast between the wet sand and sea foam.

FOCUS ON *Painting Birds*

From the humble gull to the majestic heron, birds are a fantastic way of adding life and movement to a scene. Whether they are up close or far away, singly or in sweeping flocks, they are a sure-fire way to liven up an otherwise static painting.

Setting the Scene

It is tempting to think that focusing on high-level, detailed drawings is the best route to creating beautiful and recognizable bird forms. However, one of the useful facets of painting coastal scenes is that the setting itself does half the work for us. For example, in a beach scene, we would readily expect to see gulls or other common shore birds; so, a few quick, expressive brush marks are all that's needed to denote the rough shape of a flock of gulls, and the viewer's eye does the rest.

Enjoy Yourself!

Of course, you don't need to be an amateur ornithologist to enjoy including birds in your paintings. However, if you like to paint scenes from your local surroundings, it's worth familiarizing yourself with a few of the more common species that frequent your area. Learning to recognize a certain bird by its gait, flight or plumage will help you to develop a deeper understanding of how to simply and effectively capture its nature in pencil and paint.

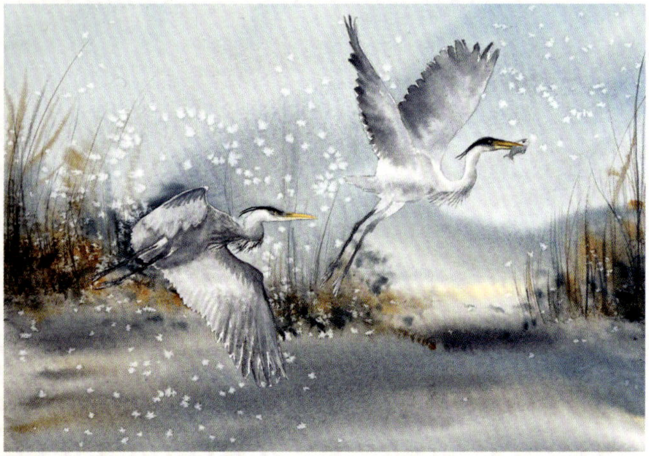

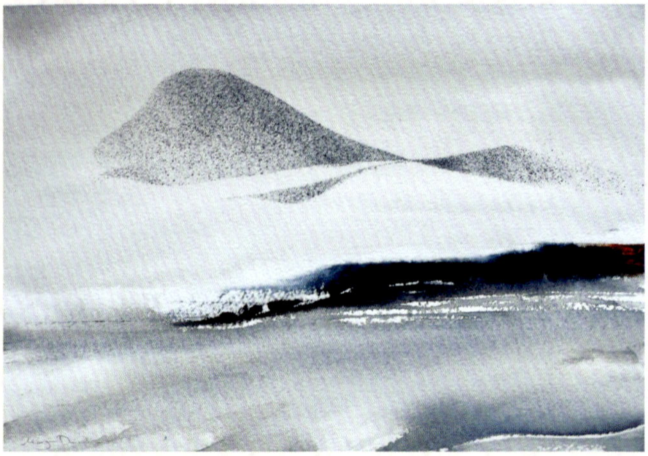

The landscape details are kept deliberately minimal to allow a starling murmuration to take centre stage.

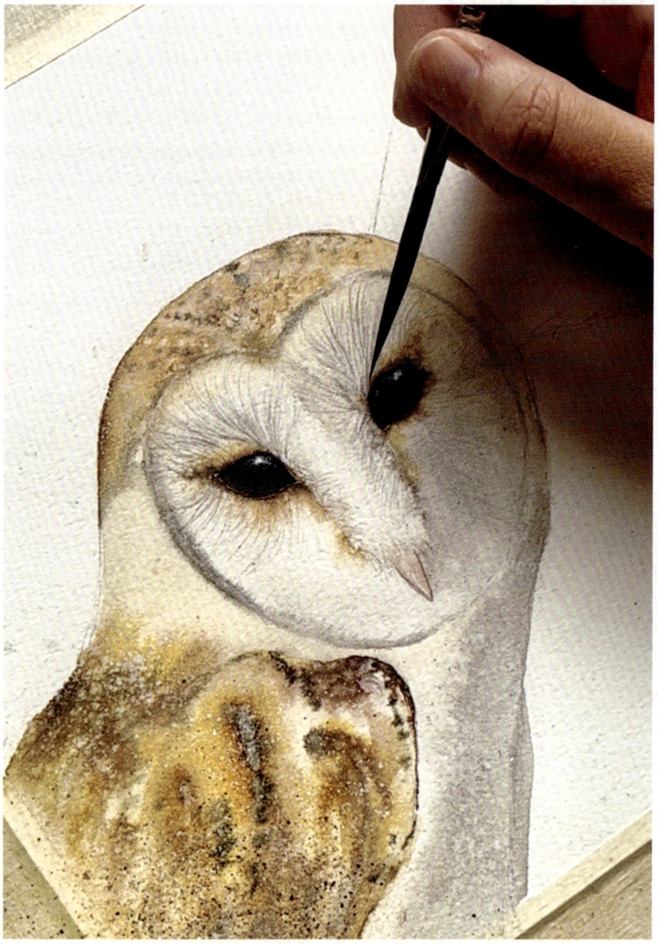

The more you practise painting the things you love, the better you will become – and the more you will enjoy it!

Birds in Focus

The main challenge of adding birds to a landscape setting is deciding on scale. In a painting such as 'The Fisherman' (see pages 74–79), where the bird itself is the focal point, this is obviously irrelevant. However, in a landscape scene that contains features such as boats or cliffs that offer a sense of perspective, it is important to distinguish the scale of the birds you want to paint in comparison to the other features.

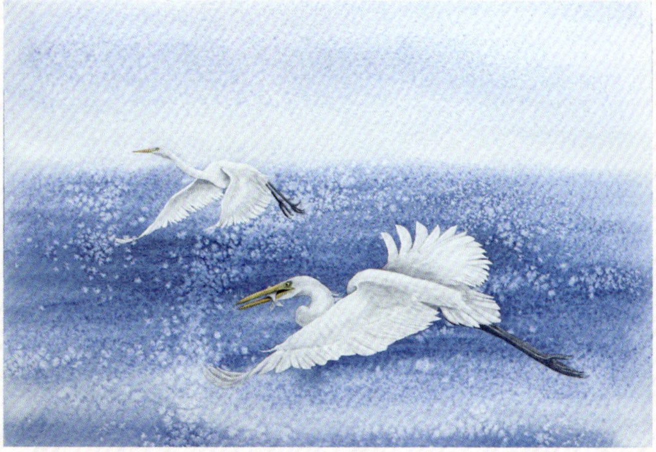

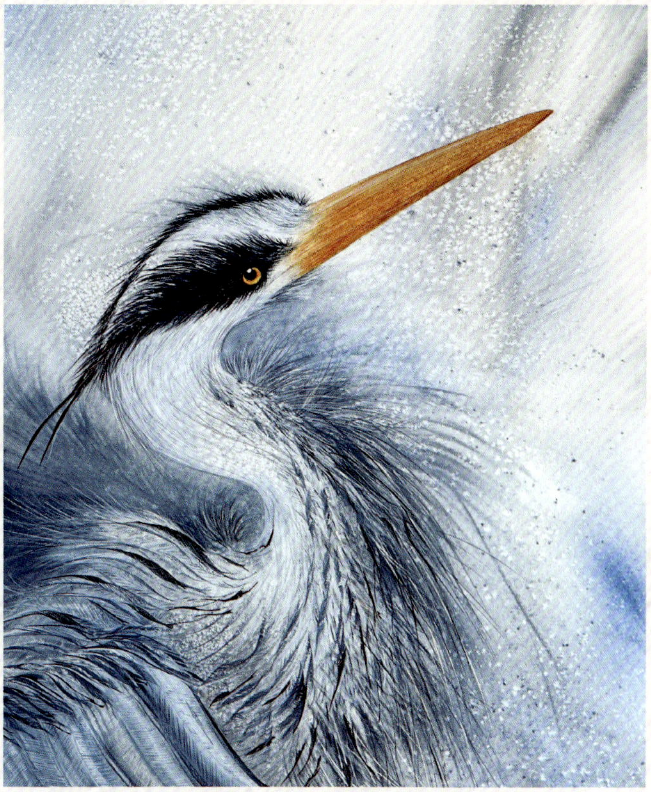

In this painting, the bird is the obvious focus, with the rainy backdrop being a mere suggestion, implied through strong directional brushwork and salt effects.

The temptation is to try to make your bird the focal point by making it large. However, size isn't everything; colour and contrast play key roles in determining where the focal point of your painting lies. For example, a few small white birds painted against the grey of a leaden sky can make a simple yet eye-catching focal point, as a viewer's eye will be naturally drawn to areas of contrasting dark and light. Similarly, in a painting featuring lively colour and light, a simple silhouette can be the most effective way of drawing attention.

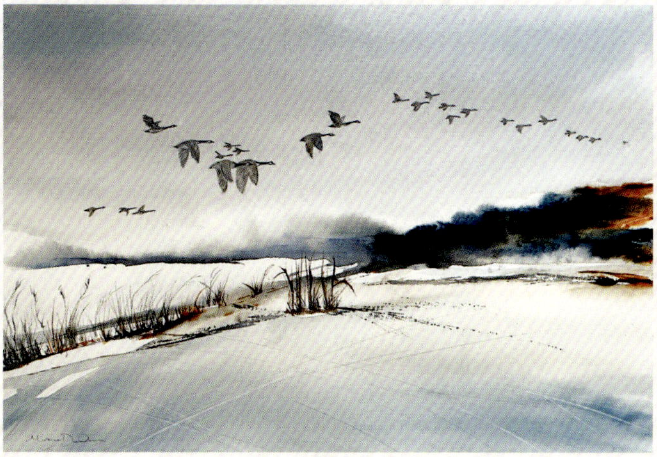

While small, the geese's dark colouring and striking silhouettes make them stand out against the pale sky.

In the UK, what people refer to as 'seagulls' are actually a variety of different birds, including herring gulls, little gulls, black-backed gulls and Mediterranean gulls. These much-maligned creatures are actually intelligent, adaptable, resourceful and beautiful birds.

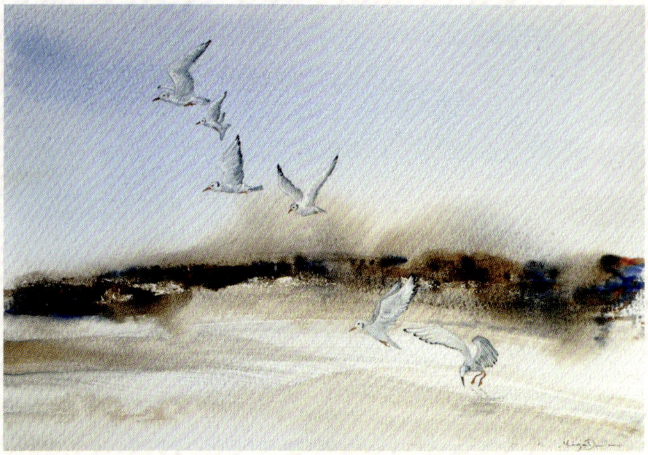

This painting was inspired by my local flocks of black-headed gulls in their winter plumage.

The Fisherman

This project relies on two key elements: one, a soft, impressionistic background of sea and sky, painted in harmonious blues; the second, crisp outlines of this pair of white egrets, which is achieved by using masking fluid.

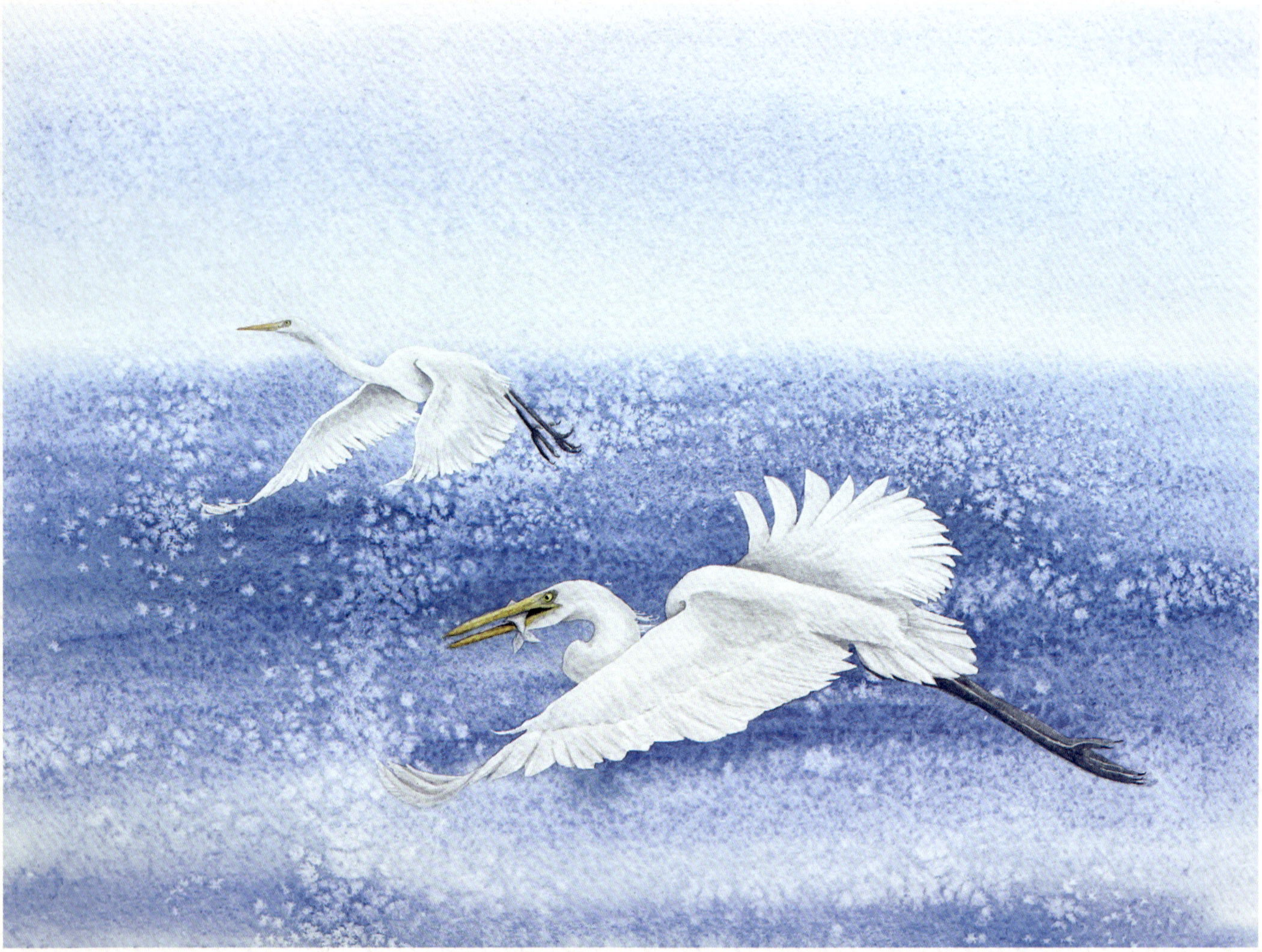

COLOURS NEEDED

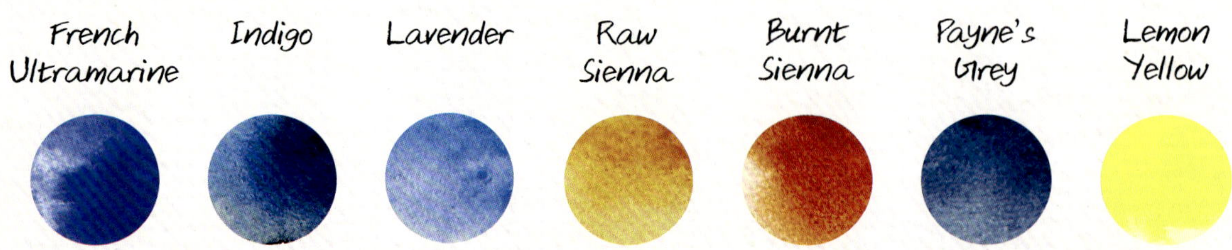

Egrets have long been one of my favourite denizens of the waterways. Whether it be around the cliffs or the edge of the sea, riverbank or estuary, often one of these white-feathered gentlemen can be spotted, strolling unhurriedly along the shingle or winging their way low across the waters. This project is a homage to these beautiful coastal birds. The composition appears simple on the surface, but the key here is the timing of applying the salt (see page 25) in Stage 1.

This project takes advantage of the granulating properties of French Ultramarine, which settles beautifully into the watercolour paper's textured surface and provides a uniquely misty, hazy feel to the sea and sky. This is further enhanced by adding the sprinkle of salt, which adds an extra flurry of texture in the lower two-thirds of the painting, bringing a hint of sea spray and breaking waves beneath the wings of these wonderful birds.

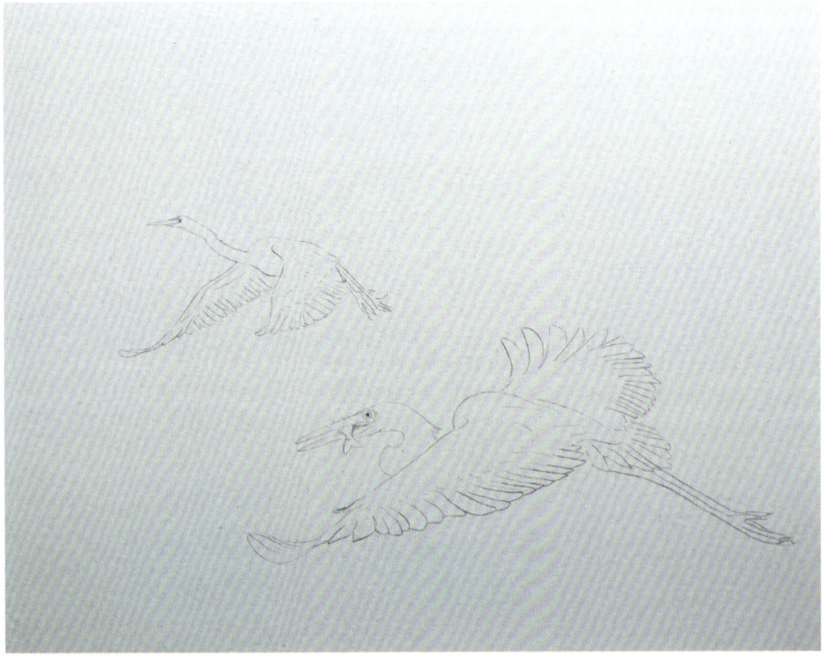

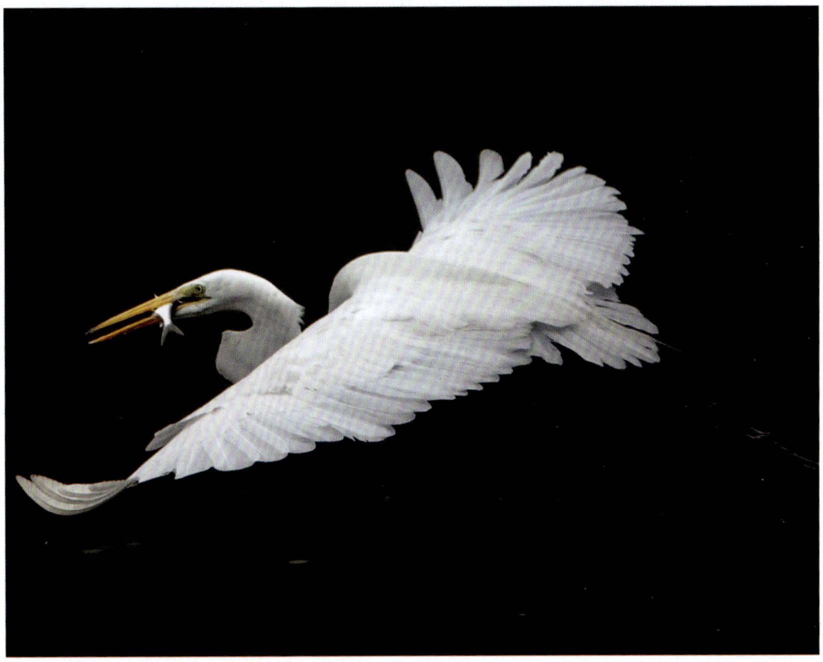

Setting Up

Prepare your paper before you begin by lightly drawing the outline of this pair of egrets using the HB pencil (see page 20). Apply masking fluid to the outlines using an old pointed brush (see page 24). Ensure that the fluid is completely dry before beginning to apply the first wash. Tape your paper to the painting board and lay it flat, ready to begin.

YOU WILL NEED

- *140gsm/300lb hot press watercolour paper*
- *Masking fluid and old pointed brush*
- *Painting board and decorator's masking tape*
- *Sponge or kitchen paper*
- *HB pencil and eraser*
- *Palette with mixing wells*
- *Water spray bottle*
- *Fine table salt*
- *Adhesive eraser*
- *Size 20 mop brush*
- *Size 3 round brush*
- *Size 0 round brush*

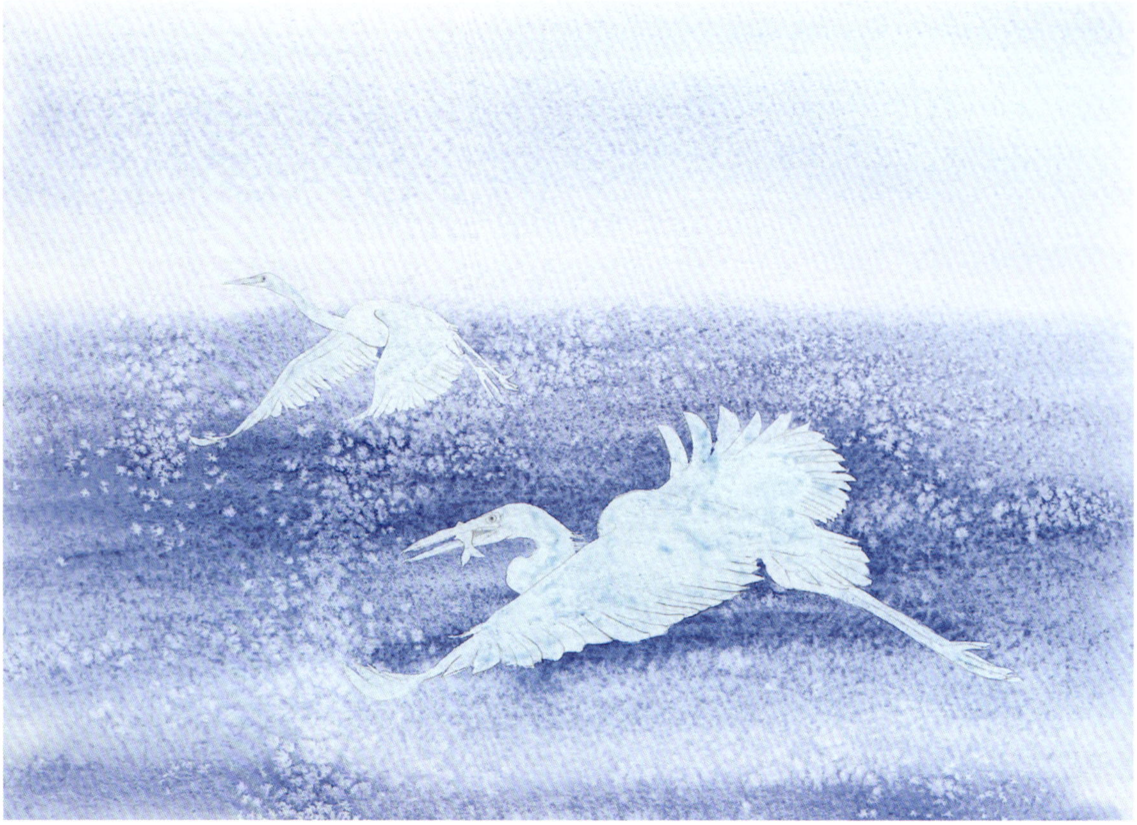

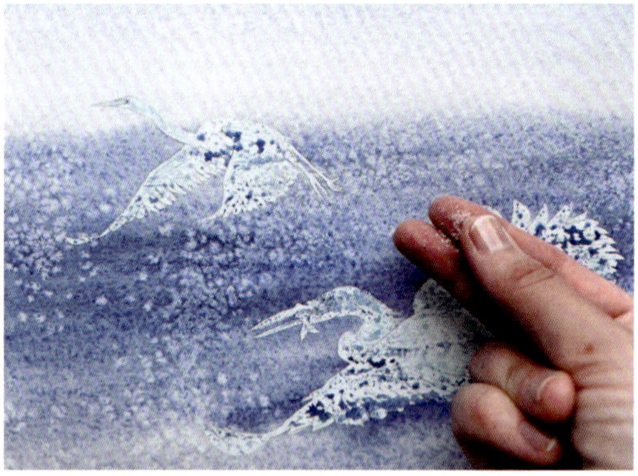

I find the easiest way to apply the salt is to pinch a little between thumb and forefinger from a larger pot, then sprinkle it carefully across the areas of the painting that need it.

STAGE 1

Mix up a large well of dark-value French Ultramarine, and two mid-value wells of Indigo and Lavender. Using the size 20 mop brush, wet the paper all over with clean water and allow to rest for roughly 30 seconds. Take up a good amount of the ultramarine and spread it across the paper in broad horizontal strokes, from edge to edge, across the lower two-thirds of the paper. Sweep a little colour upwards to create the sky, adding more water if necessary, to create a soft, pale sky across the top third of the paper, while still maintaining a deeper colour below.

While the paper is still wet and still using the mop, take up a little of the indigo and lavender, and use the pointed tip of the brush to sweep the colours across the paper to create thinner horizontal bands, creating some variations in tone and hue within the sea. Don't be too worried about flooding the paper with too much paint and water at this stage; this will encourage the ultramarine to granulate.

Once you're happy with the blue tones in the wash, wait until the paper is no longer glossy with water, and apply a sprinkle of salt into the lower third, to create a bloom of pale, freckled marks. Allow to dry fully.

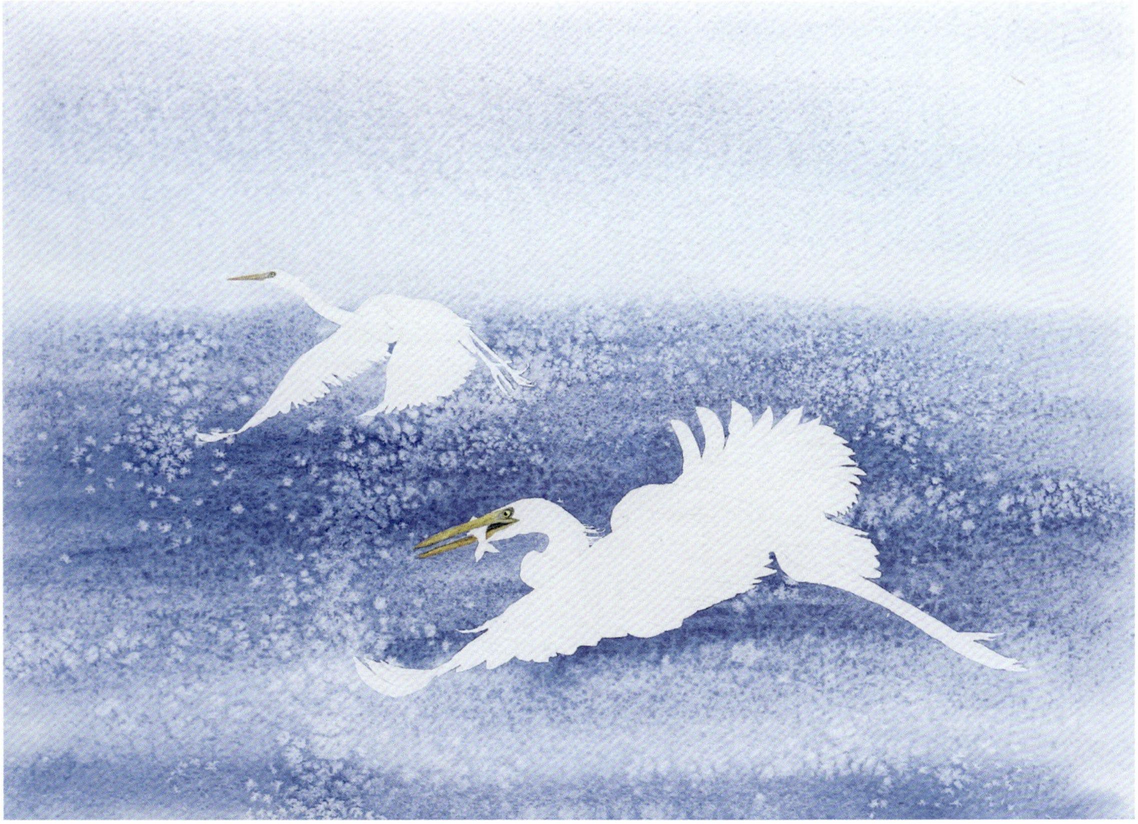

STAGE 2

Once fully dry, wipe down the masking fluid with a sponge or kitchen paper to remove any excess paint sitting on it, before carefully rubbing away the mask from the egrets using an adhesive eraser or your fingertip.

Mix up a little mid-value Raw Sienna, Burnt Sienna and Payne's Grey. Using these three colours and the size 0 round brush, begin adding detail to the bird's face. Start by painting Raw Sienna along the bird's beak, then drop a little Burnt Sienna into the wet paint to add variation and tone. Dilute the colour down as you move up towards the eye, so it becomes less saturated in hue, and dab in a very small amount of Payne's Grey to cool down the yellow-orange tones.

While this dries, use a small amount of Lemon Yellow to paint the eyes of both birds. Use strong Payne's Grey to add the dark pupil, and to shade the area inside the larger bird's beak.

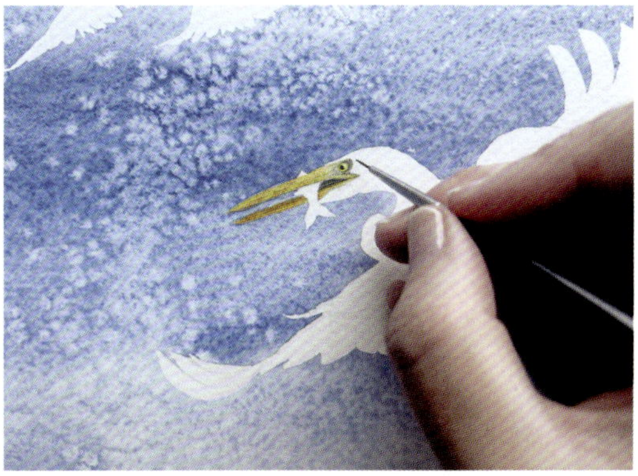

Avoid the temptation to paint the dark pupil directly in the centre of the eye. Instead, paint the pupil a little forward, directing the viewer to look in the same direction as the bird.

Tip

After removing the mask, check the pencil lines you made previously. Sometimes they can be lifted away with the mask, so you may need to re-draw some of them.

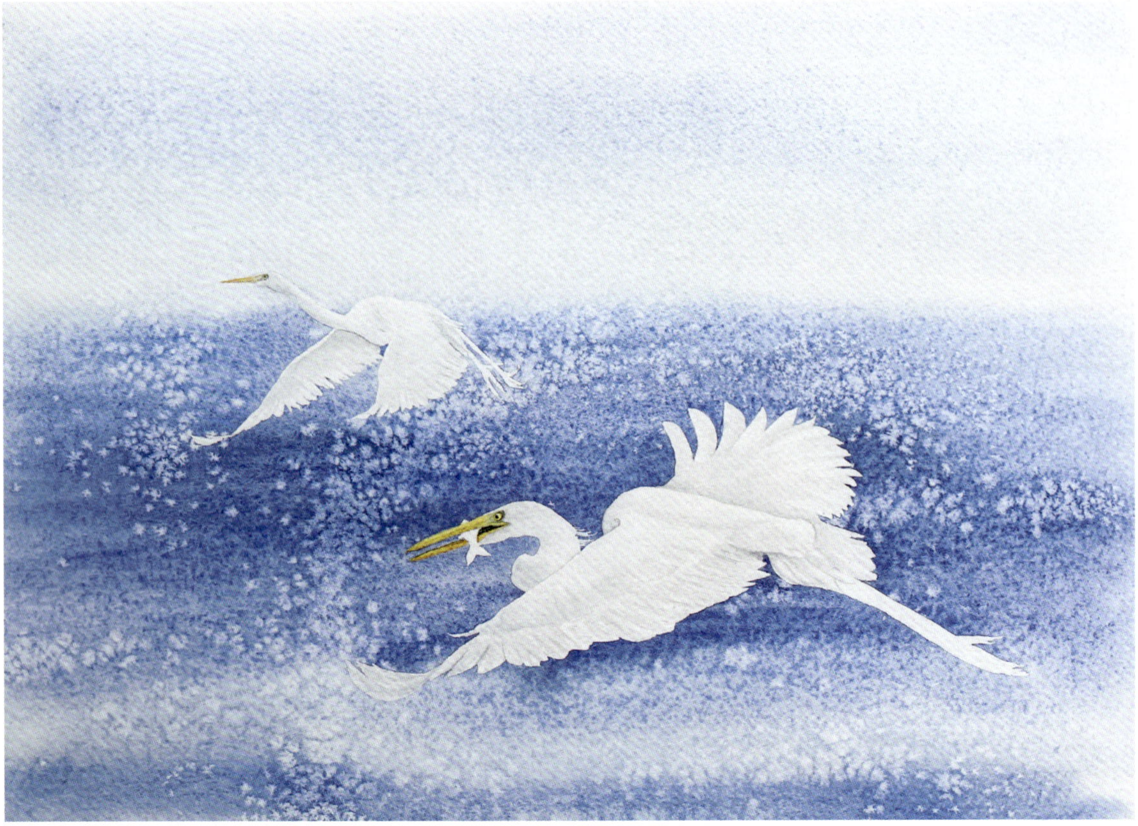

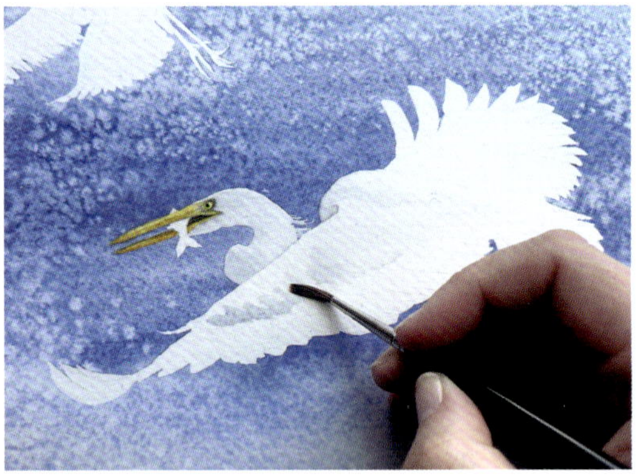

Pay close attention to the directions of your brush marks. Follow the pattern of the bird's feathers as you lay down your shading, particularly in areas across the wing, where the egret's feathers are large and noticeable.

STAGE 3

Mix up a large well of very watery, light-value Payne's Grey, and tint it with a very small amount of French Ultramarine. This colour is for both egrets – their wings, feathers and body – so make sure you have enough.

Essentially, this stage involves painting around the palest areas of bright white on the bird, adding shadows to define shape and form, and using them to emphasize the shape and curve in areas such as the bird's neck and back. Use the size 3 round brush for this, and begin with the larger bird.

Add a little shadow around the egret's face and the bend in the bird's neck. Use clean water to blend and soften any hard lines. Bring the colour down across the bird's back and wings, avoiding any raised areas where the light would naturally catch, such as the wingtips and the highest arch of the bird's body. Continue doing this along to the bird's tail.

Repeat for the smaller bird. Leave to dry completely.

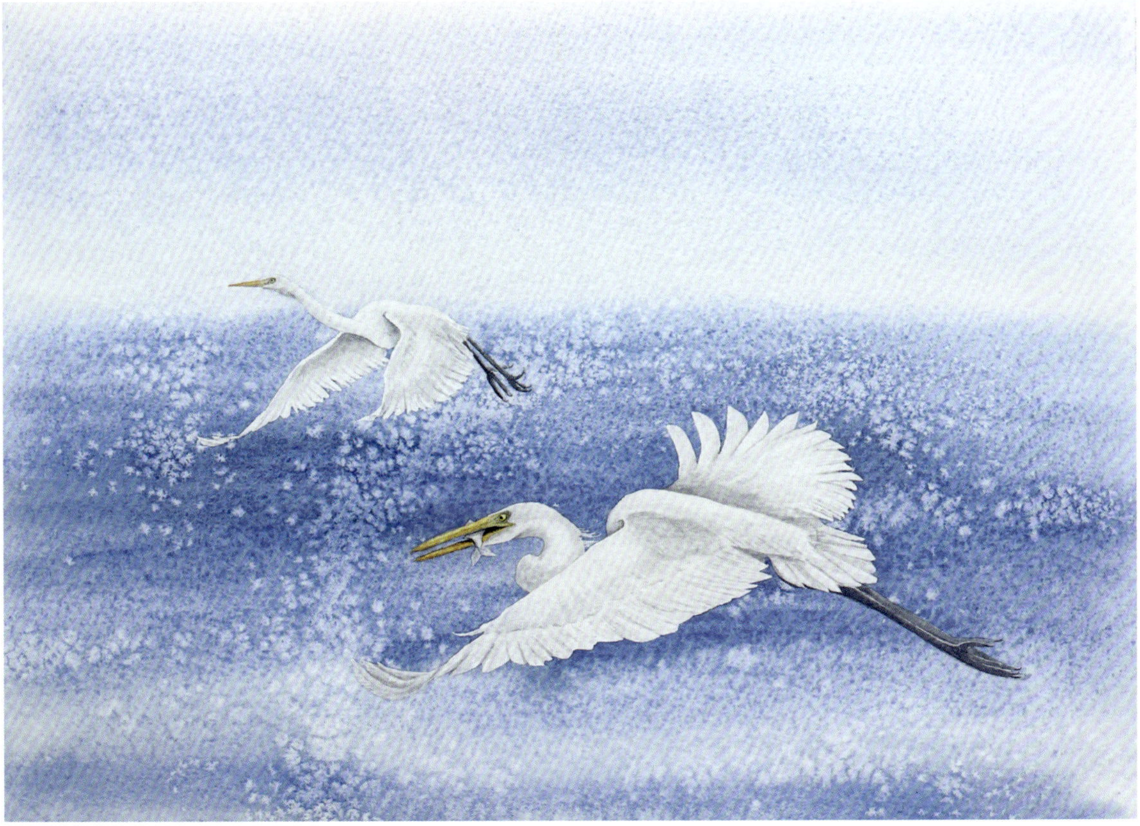

STAGE 4

Use the size 0 round to add colour and detail to the fish in the larger bird's mouth, using a mixture of Payne's Grey and French Ultramarine. Mix up a well of mid-value Payne's Grey and use this to add colour to the bird's trailing legs and feet, using the size 3 round brush to fill them in and the size 0 round brush to add detail and get into any smaller fiddly areas.

Finally, use the size 3 round brush and some more light-value Payne's Grey to go over the areas on the egret's body where the shadows need deepening, such as the crook of the bird's wing and the curve underneath the long neck, to add fullness and definition.

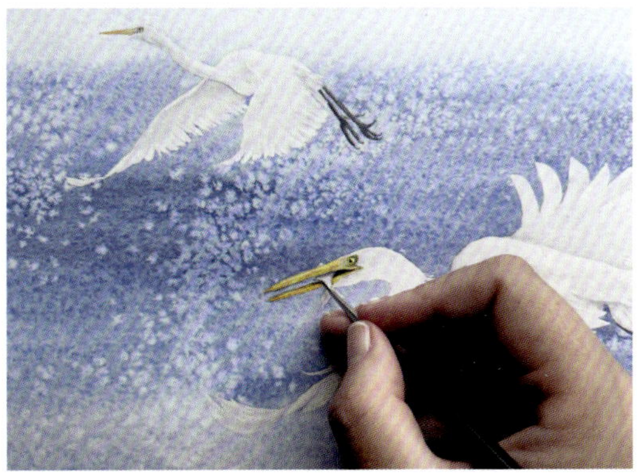

Leave a little glint of white paper on the belly of the fish, to give the impression of the light catching on silver scales.

Tip

A good way to add these final shadows to the egrets is to use multiple layers of light-value paint. Allow each layer to dry in between applications. This will help you build colour gradually, and avoids the risk of these areas becoming too dark.

Sea Fret

There is something magical about the beach when the mist silently rolls in from the sea, muffling the sounds of waves and gulls, obscuring the horizon, and painting everything in softest shades of blue, grey and brown.

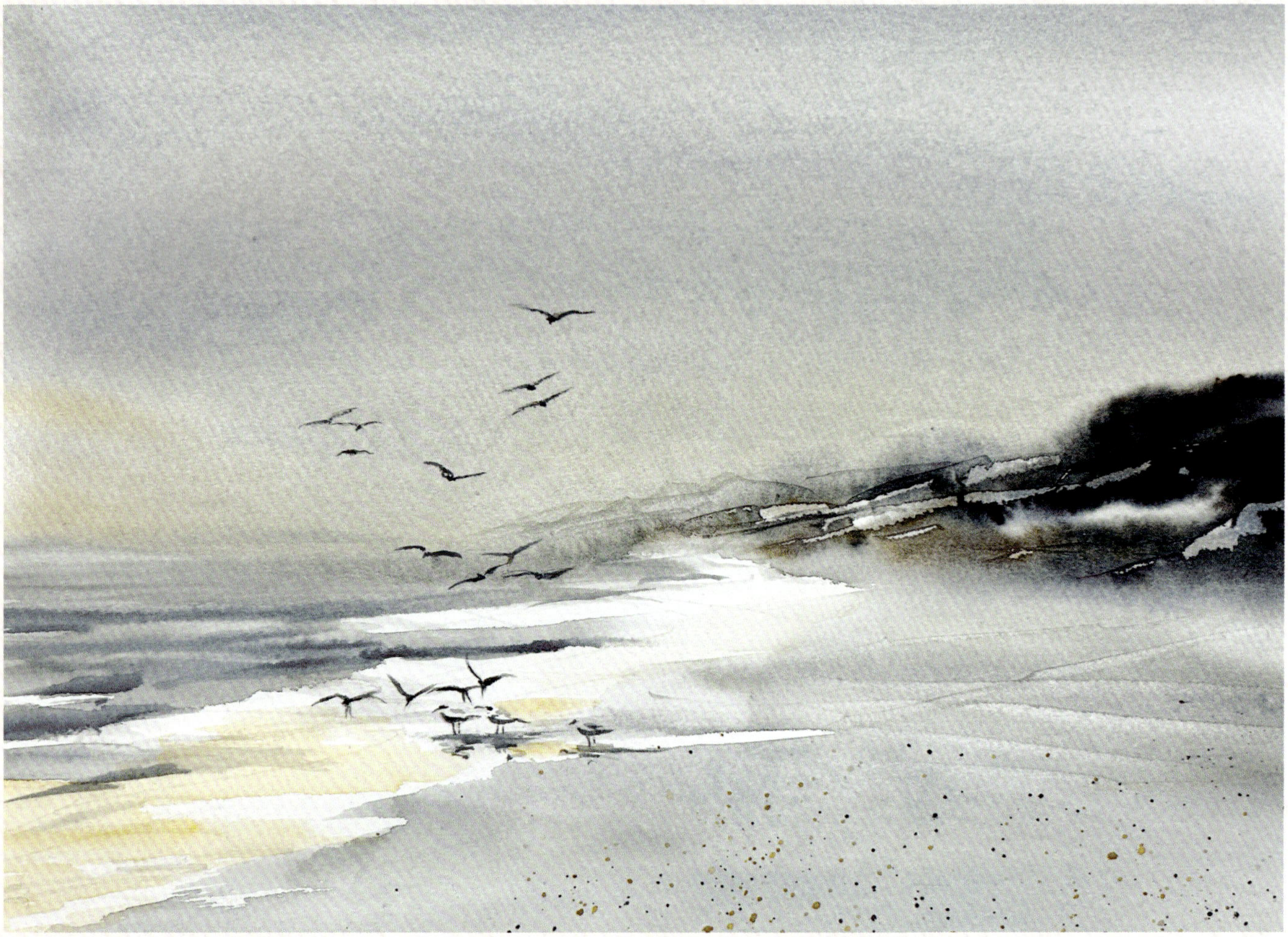

COLOURS NEEDED

Indigo | Payne's Grey | Sepia | Raw Sienna | White Gouache

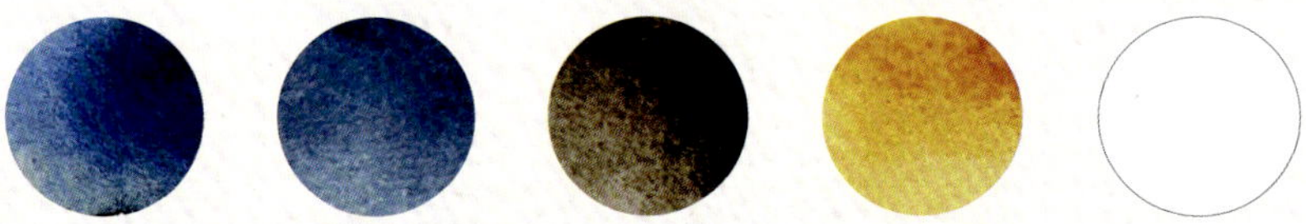

In this project, the first three stages are painted *alla prima*, or in one session, without waiting for things to dry between stages (see page 22). It is important to mix all the colours you need before starting to paint. The wet-in-wet technique (see page 22) will create softly diffused washes and smooth passages of paint that will give a misty and atmospheric impression to the scene. Adding the loose flock of gulls using the wet-on-dry technique (see page 23) and the template (below right) brings this simple but atmospheric painting together beautifully.

Setting Up

Begin by sketching the simple outline lightly onto hot press watercolour paper using the HB pencil (see page 20). The sketch of the shoreline, though very simple, will help you to preserve the small areas of white paper more easily, as you paint the first three stages *alla prima*. Tape your paper to the painting board and lay it flat, ready to begin.

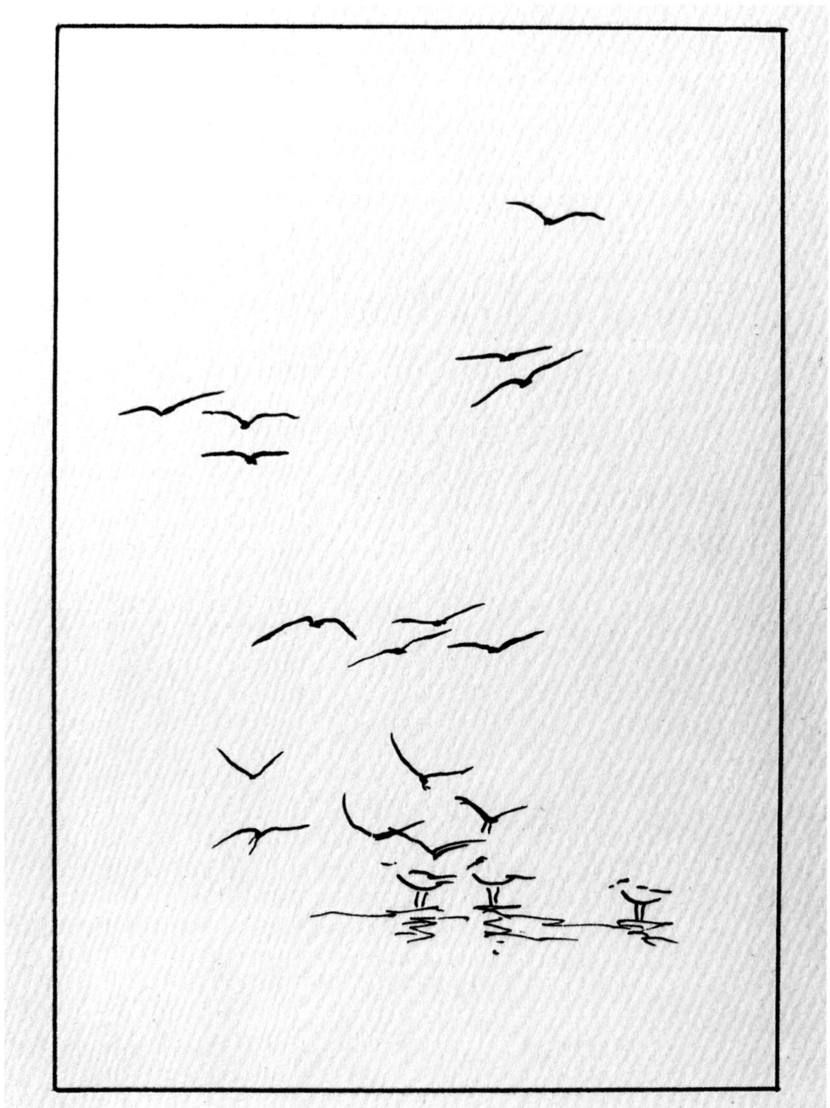

YOU WILL NEED

- *140lb (300gsm) hot press watercolour paper*
- *HB pencil and eraser*
- *Painting board and decorator's masking tape*
- *Kitchen paper*
- *Palette with mixing wells*
- *Palette knife*
- *Tracing paper and 2B pencil*
- *1½in (38mm) mottler brush*
- *Size 2 quill brush*
- *Size 3 round brush*
- *¾in (20mm) flat brush*
- *Size 2 fan brush*
- *Size 0 round brush*

Work around the dry paper at the shoreline with the tips of the brush to preserve the crisp edges of unpainted paper.

STAGE 1

Mix five wells of paint in preparation for Stages 1–3: a large well of light-value grey made from Indigo, Payne's Grey and Sepia; three wells of creamy dark-value paint in Payne's Grey, Indigo and Sepia, and a small well of light-value Raw Sienna.

Wet the paper evenly all over with clean water using the mottler brush, leaving some dry paper streaks at the shoreline on the left, where the pencil marks indicate this. Leave to soak for roughly 10 seconds.

Paint a variegated wash (see page 22) across almost the whole page using the grey mix, starting at the top, adding some of the light value raw sienna into the wash above the horizon, then continuing with the grey. Use horizontal sweeps of the brush to keep the wash nice and flat and leave some areas white for the waves at the shoreline.

Tip

Don't worry if the wash looks a little grainy while wet; this happens because the pigment particles are yet to settle, but once dry everything will soften and diffuse, as in the Stage 3 photo.

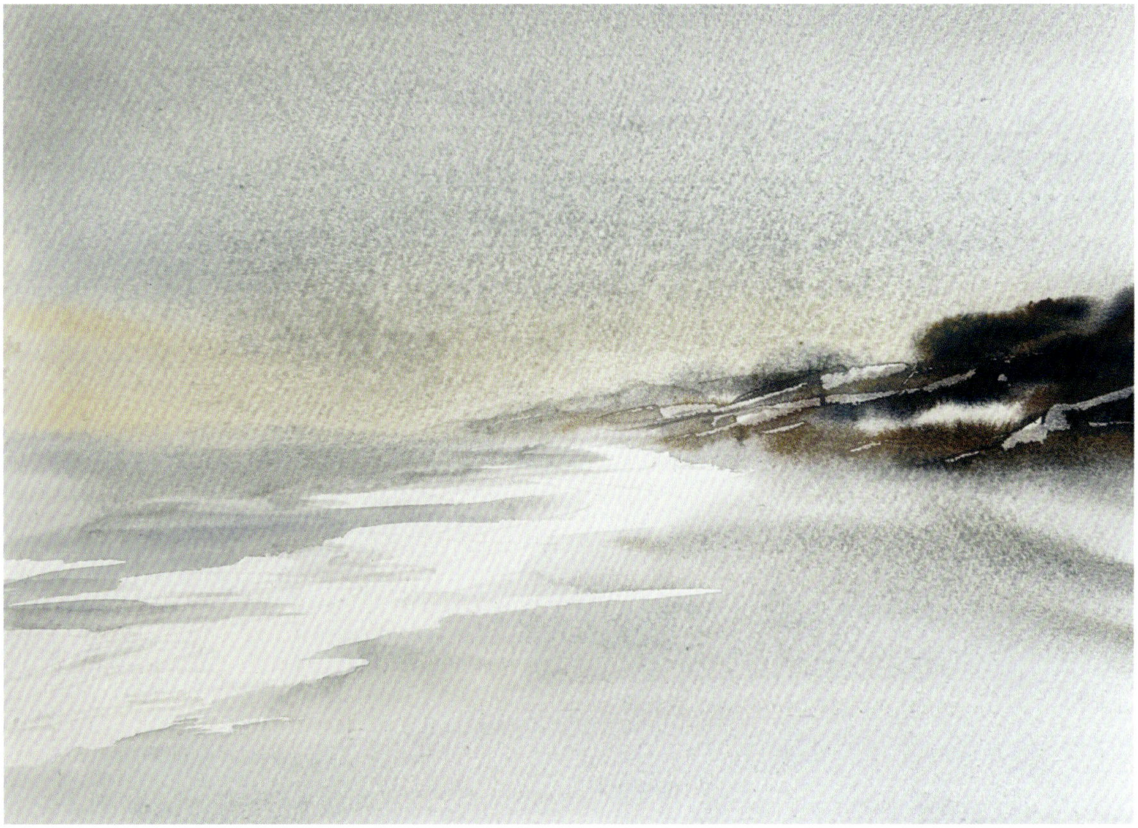

STAGE 2

Without rinsing the brush, dip the tips into all three dark-value colours so they are all on the brush at the same time. Paint the rocky headland with mixed colour brushstrokes (see page 23), turning the brush as little as needed to apply all three colours at the same time, leaving some small gaps so that the lighter wash beneath this rich layer shows through in a few places. Allow the paint to run out and become paler as you reach the middle of the page, which will suggest the effects of mist.

Use the palette knife to scrape through the damp, rich paint to suggest rock strata. Soften the bottom edge with a clean, damp flat brush if needed.

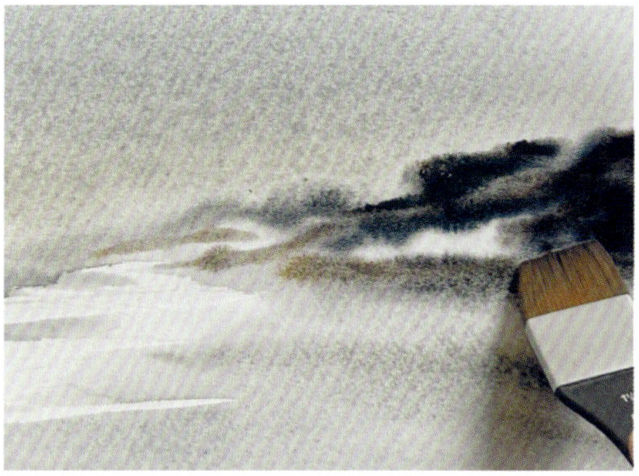

If the right side of the headland looks too pale, dip the brush back into your dark-value colours to deepen it.

Tip

When painting the lighter part of the headland, you can use a small damp brush to soften and lift a little paint if necessary, to create the misty effects.

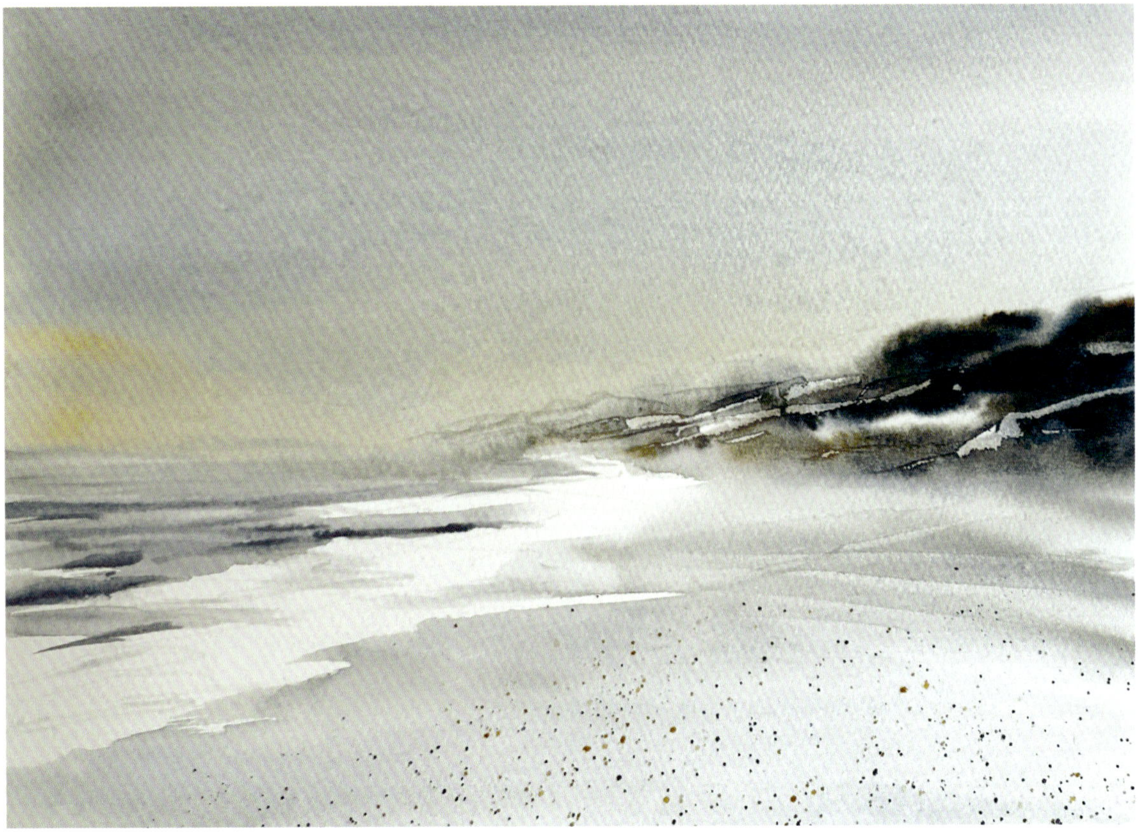

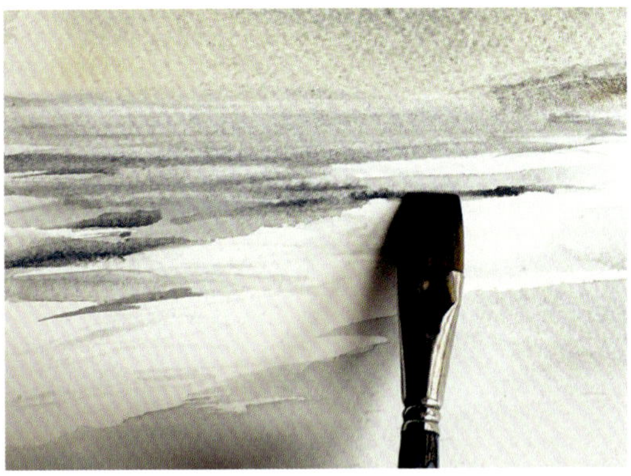

As you darken around the edges of the shoreline, do so carefully to ensure you keep the white highlights unpainted.

STAGE 3

Working quickly while the paper is still damp, rinse the flat brush and wipe it well on kitchen paper to remove all water so it is almost dry. Now use the tip of the brush to lift out a narrow horizon line.

Add some water to the indigo mix to create a mid-value paint, and touch a little of this into the shoreline with the tip of the flat brush, using a side-to-side motion to add a little darker tone to the waves at the shore. Leave the painting to dry completely.

Once dry, add a little water to both the indigo and sepia paint mixes until it is the consistency of ink. Place a sheet of clean paper over the sky and sea to protect them, and use the fan brush to add spatter drops across the foreground for texture.

Tip

Before they dry, you can use kitchen paper to gently dab off any spatter drops that look too large.

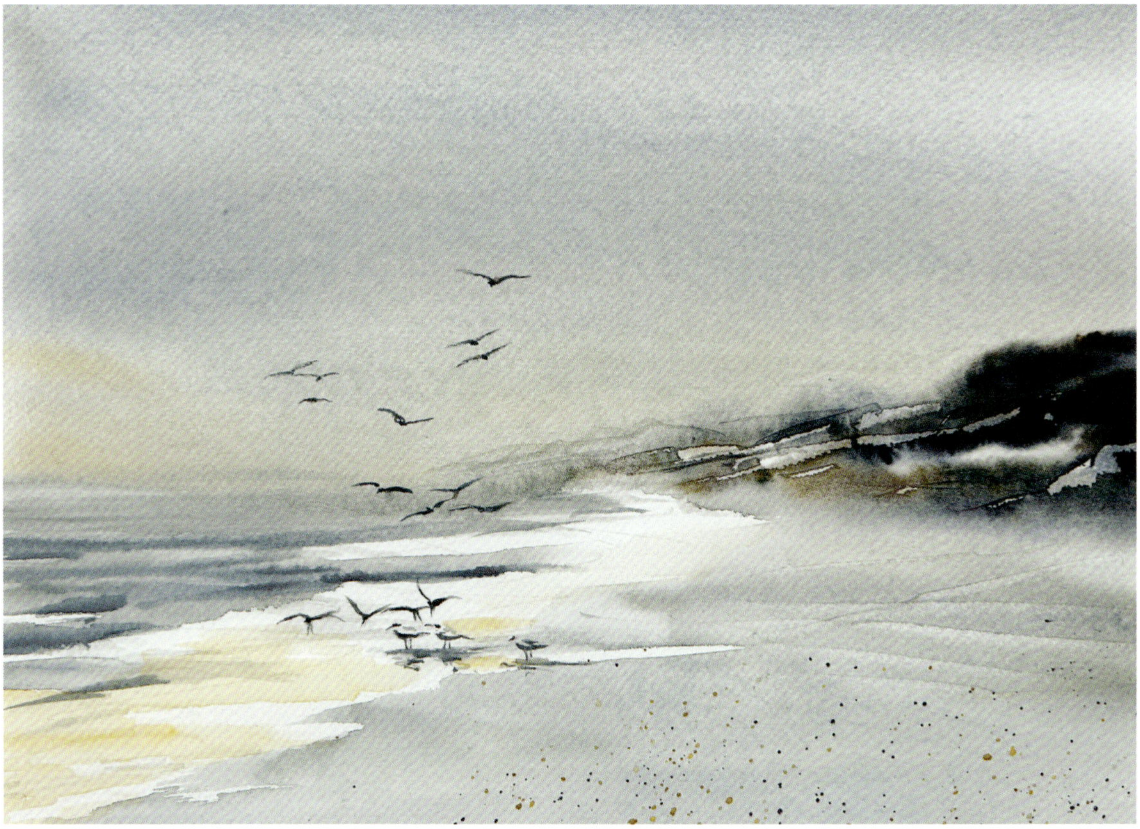

STAGE 4

Copy the template for the flock of gulls on page 81 onto tracing paper, turn the tracing paper over and scribble over it on the back with a 2B pencil to completely cover the traced areas. Turn the tracing paper the right way again, position it on the painting near the shoreline, then carefully draw over the bird shapes to transfer the design lightly onto the painting.

Use the size 0 round brush to paint the birds with Payne's Grey. Leave to dry, then add White Gouache highlights to them.

Once dry, add a few sweeps of light-value Raw Sienna across the wet sand below the birds with the size 2 quill brush. Leave to dry completely.

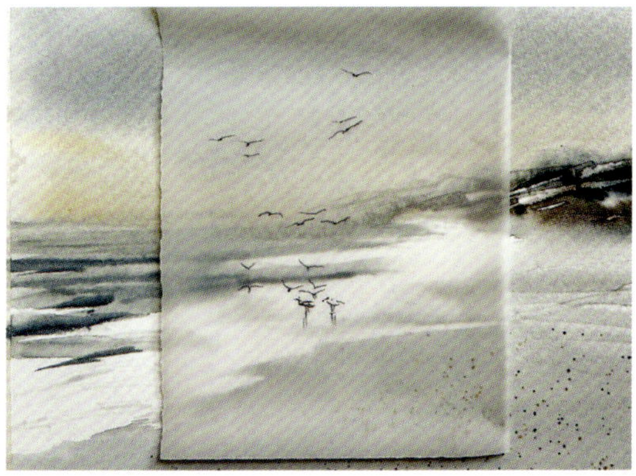

Using transparent overlays of tracing paper like this is a great way to see how something will look before painting it.

Tip

When positioning the gull template, move it around a little until you find the best position for the flock, then transfer the design.

Gulls at Low Tide

In this painting, the sunset colours are muted and soothing, offering a sense of peace, calm and tranquillity. The simple silhouettes of the resting gulls offer a pleasing contrast to the wheeling movement of the distant bird flock in flight.

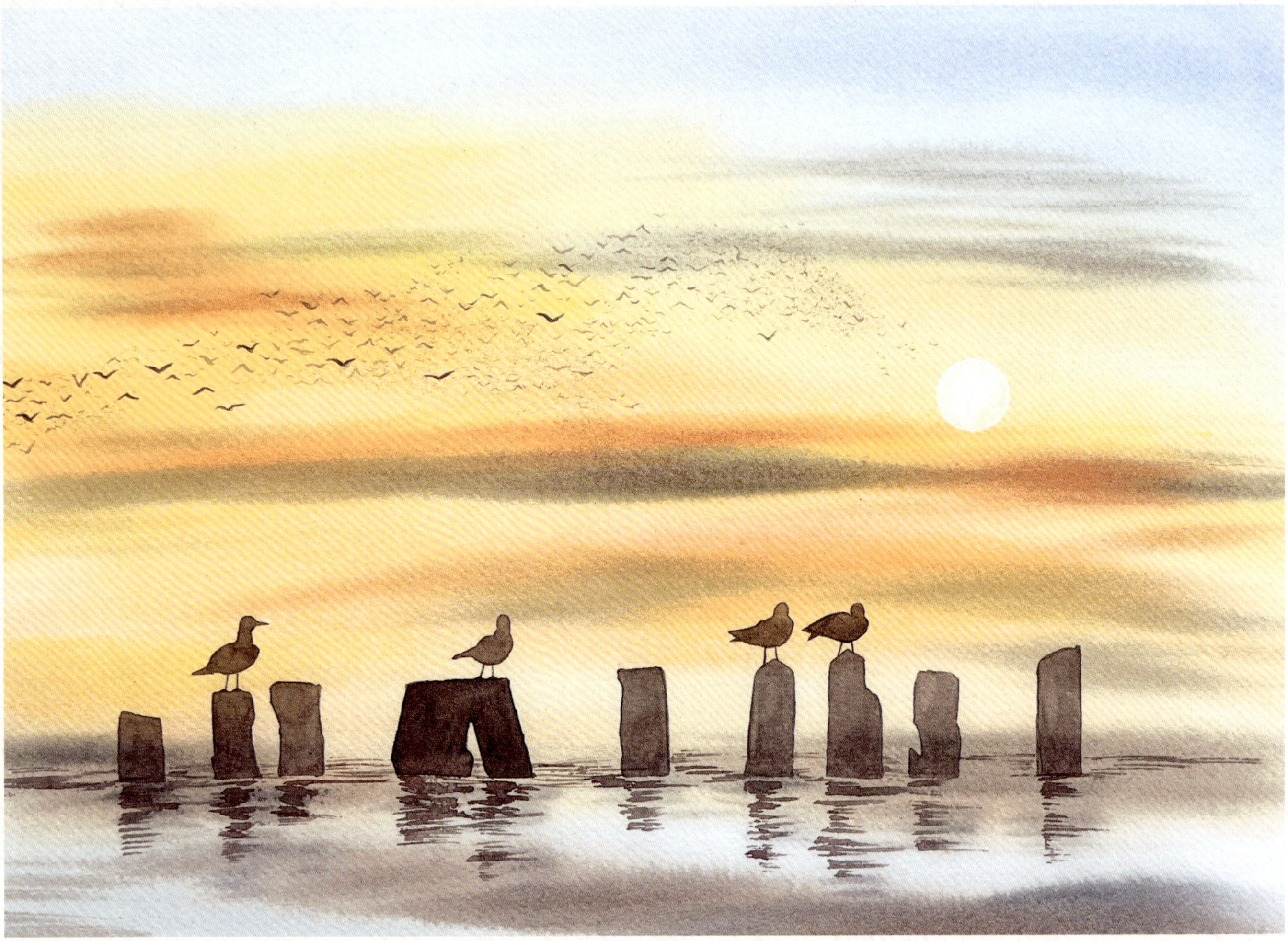

COLOURS NEEDED

Transparent Yellow | Transparent Orange | Lavender | Indigo | Perylene Maroon

Flocks of birds can be tricky beasts to master. This composition calls on aerial perspective (see page 19) to help give a sense of depth and distance within this painting, by using a lighter, paler colour to paint the birds that are further away and therefore smaller.

I based this scene on a beautiful reference photograph, and after deciding to change up the colour palette a bit, I did a preliminary pencil sketch which roughed out the areas of sky I wanted to fill with gulls. Breaking the flocks down into loose oval shapes can help you compose your overall pattern; but while this is a useful way to plan out your painting, do remember that it pays to be flexible when working with watercolour! I ended up changing my original design as I painted, working around the washes of soft sunset colours. Despite this, it was very useful for me to have this sketch as a point of reference when it came to finalizing the overall shape of the bird flock.

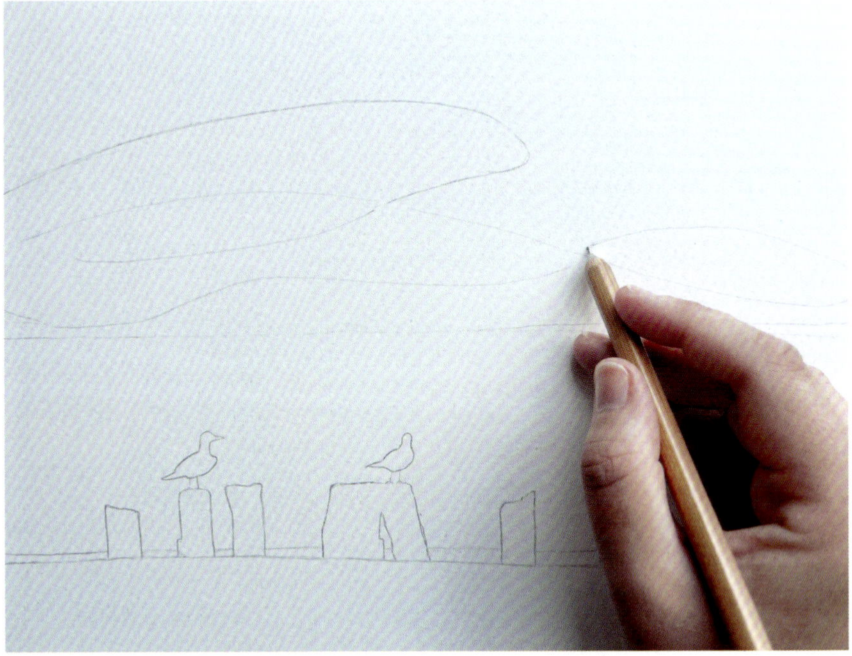

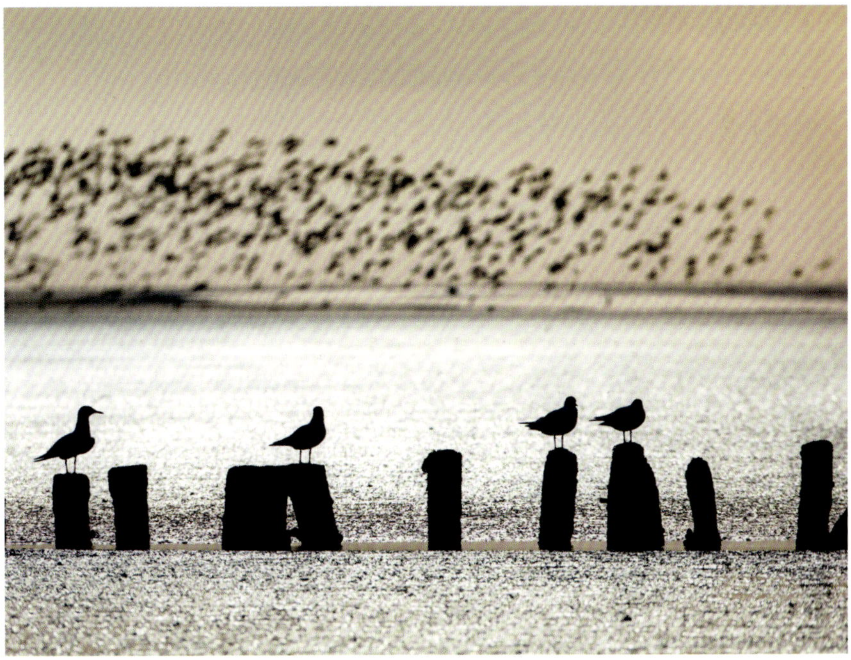

Setting Up

Begin by sketching the outline of the gulls on their posts lightly onto hot press watercolour paper using the HB pencil (see page 20). Tape your paper to the painting board and lay it flat, ready to begin the painting.

YOU WILL NEED

- *140gsm/300lb hot press watercolour paper*
- *Painting board and decorator's masking tape*
- *Sponge or kitchen paper*
- *HB pencil and eraser*
- *Palette with mixing wells*
- *Water spray bottle*
- *Small round coin such as a penny*
- *1½in (38mm) mottler brush*
- *Size 20 mop brush*
- *Size 10 mop brush*
- *Size 3 round brush*
- *Size 0 round brush*
- *Small sword liner brush*

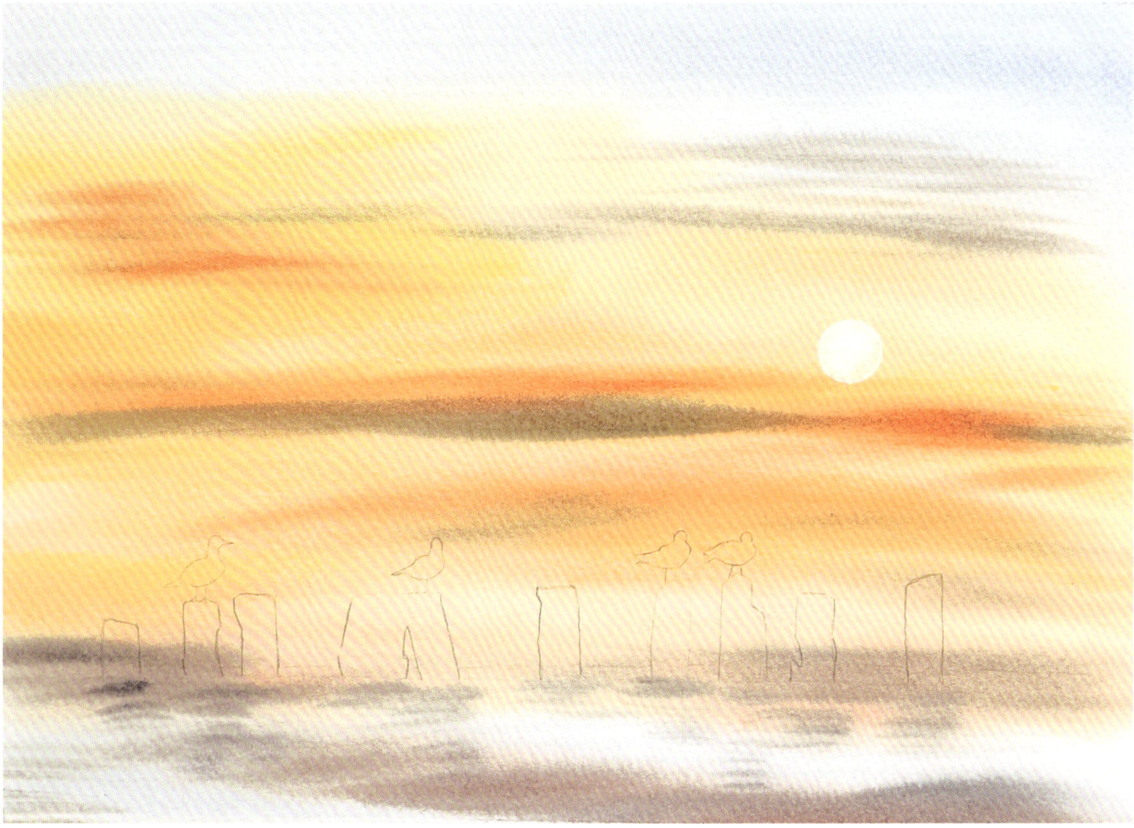

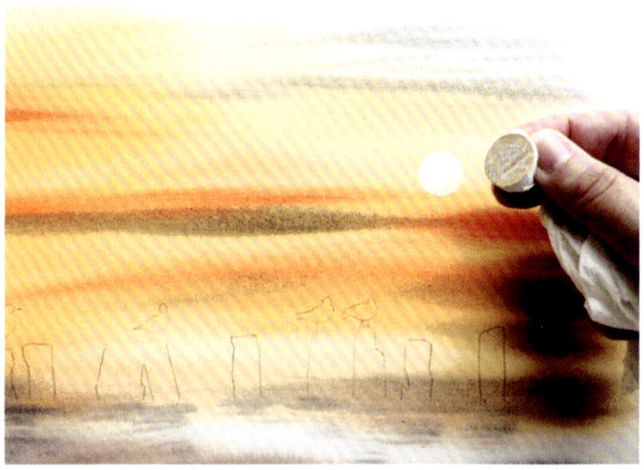

The coin trick works best if your wash is still wet, or at least very damp. If you don't get a clean 'lift' from the coin, you can always use opaque white gouache to brighten your sun once the wash is dry.

STAGE 1

Prepare three mid-value wells of colour: Transparent Yellow, Transparent Orange and Lavender mixed with a touch of Indigo to deepen it. Also prepare a well with mid-value Perylene Maroon. Wet your paper all over using the mottler brush, then use it to apply the lavender mix to the top and bottom areas. Quickly dip the size 20 mop brush into the yellow and begin to fill in the sky using soft horizontal brushstrokes, slowly adding a little orange as you go. While this is still wet, dip it into the maroon and brush this lightly across sections of the sky to deepen the sunset.

In a separate area of your palette, take a little of the lavender/indigo mix and deepen it into a dusky violet hue using the maroon and a touch more indigo. Use this and the smaller size 10 mop to add gentle horizontal shadows across the sky, as well as adding smaller horizontal marks to create some shadowed ripples beneath the pencilled posts.

Finally, use the coin trick (see page 24) to lift a small round sun out of the sky around the upper right third area of paper, then leave to fully dry.

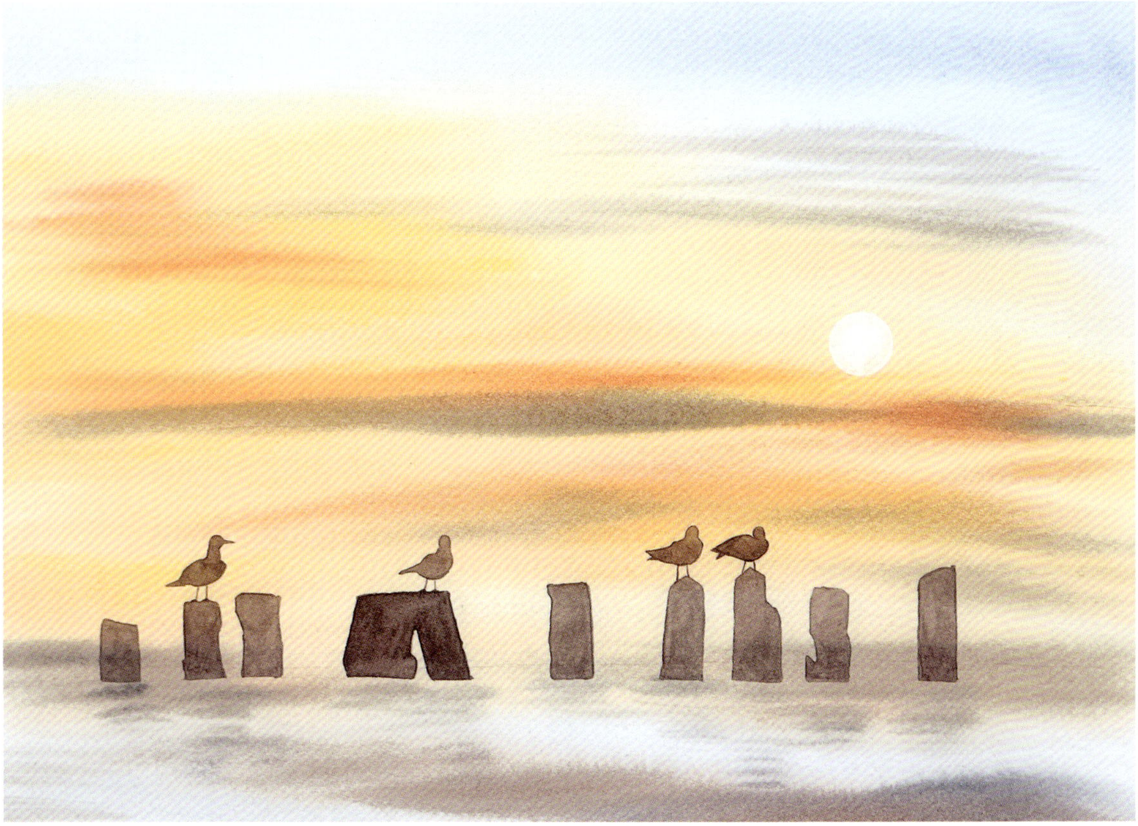

STAGE 2

Mix a light-value shadow colour from Indigo and Perylene Maroon. This should be a purplish-brown hue and not too livid, and the paint needs to be nice and loose in consistency. This is the colour for the rest of the painting, so make sure there is enough!

Using the size 3 round brush, fill in the silhouettes of the posts and gulls, following the pencilled outlines that should still be visible through the wash. Use the size 0 round brush if necessary to tidy up any edges and get into the smaller, more fiddly shapes. Leave to dry.

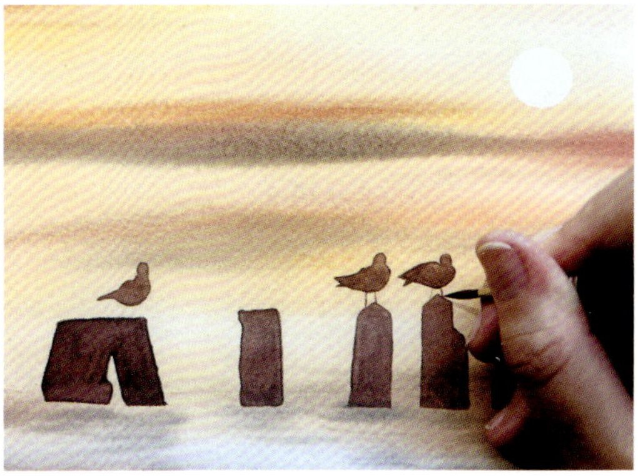

These shapes are all in silhouette, with the sun behind them, so don't worry about details. Concentrate instead on creating crisp, neat outlines and realistic bird shapes.

Tip

Mixing your shadow colour from paints already used in the background wash – in this case from the sunset – is a good way to maintain the colour harmony of a piece.

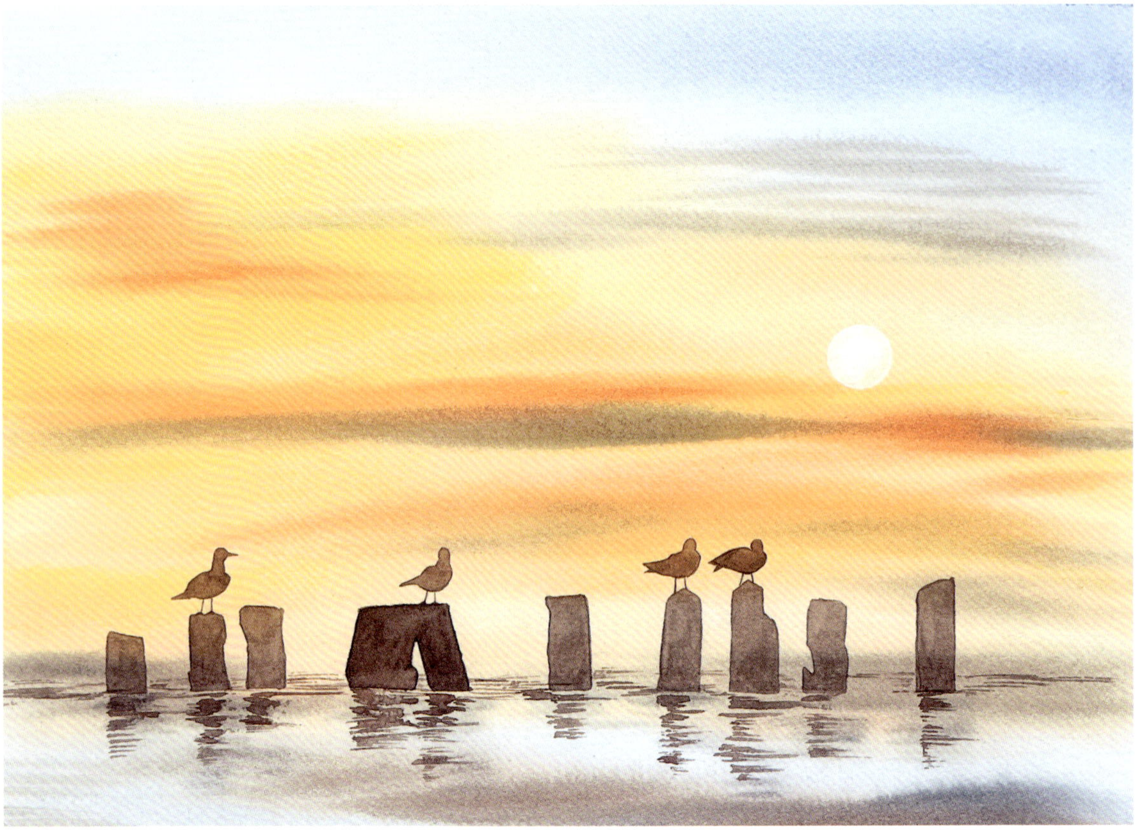

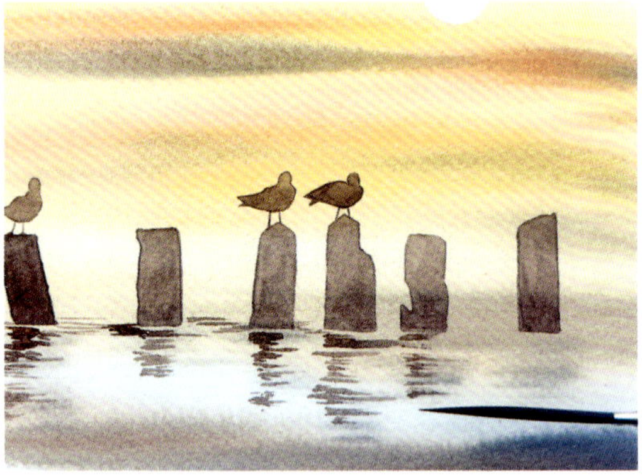

STAGE 3

Take a little of your shadow colour mix, and thin it down a little further using clean water. Use this to add reflections of the gulls on their posts in the lower quarter of the paper, loosely mirroring the shapes you have just painted. Use the size 3 round brush to paint the main areas of colour, and the small sword liner to add a few thinner lines where necessary.

Holding the sword liner brush sideways and lightly tapping the long bristles against the paper is a fun, simple way of achieving loose-looking horizontal marks. Practise on scrap paper before trying this on your painting.

Tip

If the sword liner brush is a bit unwieldy for these thin reflections, try using a regular flat brush instead: hold it upright, so only the crisp edge of the bristles are making marks.

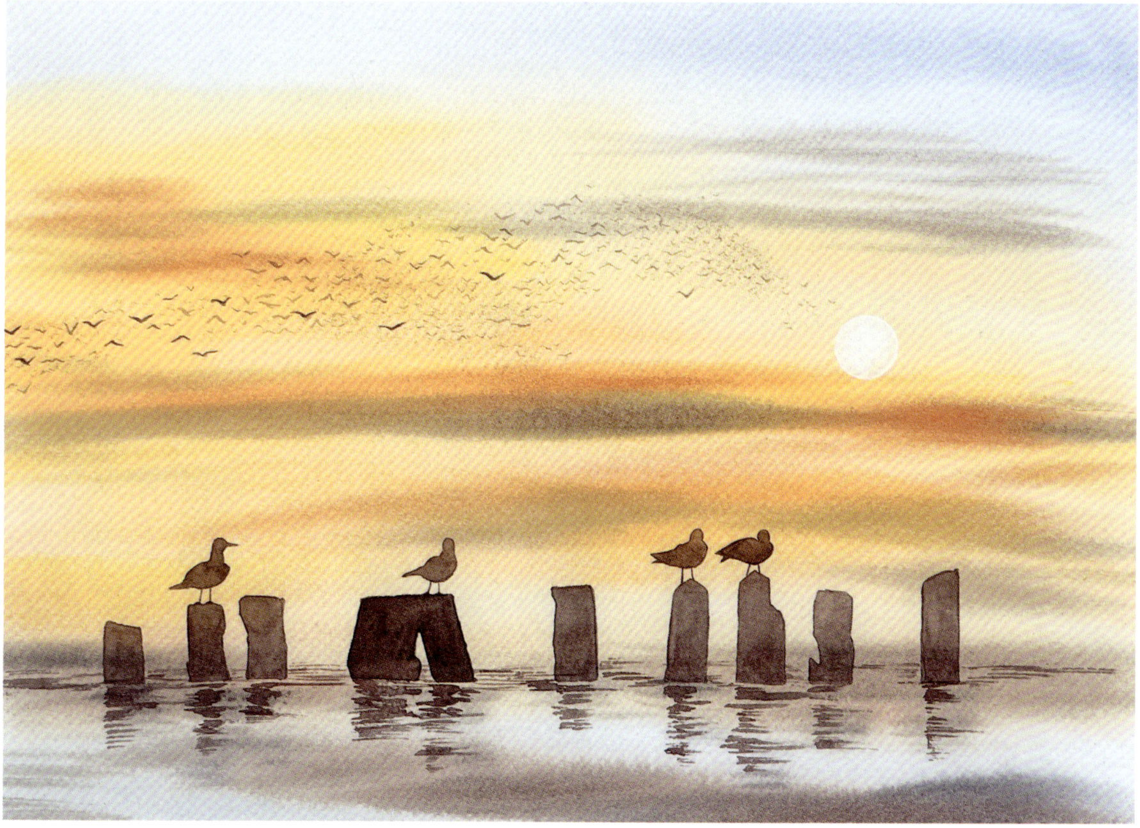

STAGE 4

Paint the flock of distant gulls using the two mixes of dusky violet. Use the darker colour and the pointed tip of the sword liner brush to create the larger birds; by making these a darker value, they appear closer and therefore more distinct.

Once you have added the main 'feature' birds of the flock, fill in the gaps using the paler mix of the same colour and the size 0 round brush. Use a scattering of tiny dots and dashes to denote the very smallest birds that are furthest away in the flock.

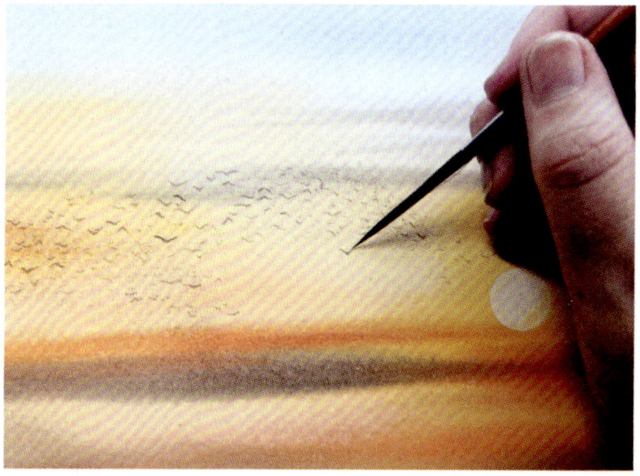

Be sure to vary the shape and wing position of your birds in flight, to help them appear natural and not too regimented.

Tip

You may need to 'guide' your flock of birds around certain features of the preliminary wash (such as very dark clouds), depending on how your Stage 1 turned out. Watercolour has a mind of its own; adaptability is key when things don't quite work out as planned!

Glossary

AERIAL PERSPECTIVE A technique used to add the illusion of depth and distance when drawing and painting landscapes, whereby things look smaller, paler and less distinct as they recede into the background.

ALLA PRIMA An Italian term for a painting approach that involves creating the whole painting in one session without waiting for stages to dry.

ARTISTIC LICENCE Minor changes or deliberate deviations from the standard or real form, made for artistic purposes.

BLEND To merge marks or colours together smoothly.

COLOUR PALETTE A chosen set of colours used to complete a painting.

COLOUR TEMPERATURE The relative warmth or coolness of a colour.

COLOUR WHEEL A circular depiction of primary/secondary colours organized via their relationship with one another.

COMPLEMENTARY COLOURS Pairs of colours that contrast or 'complement' one another; traditionally, the pairing of one primary colour and one secondary colour that is mixed from the other two primaries, e.g. blue and orange.

COMPOSITION The way in which key elements of a painting are arranged so as to be artistically pleasing.

GLAZE A thin, transparent layer of paint brushed over dried paint.

GOUACHE An opaque type of watercolour paint.

HARD EDGES Paint applied so that the edge of the brushstroke remains crisp, usually when painting wet-on-dry.

HIGHLIGHTS The lightest part of the painting, often shown by preserving the white of the paper.

LIFTING OUT A technique in which paint is removed, using a brush or absorbent kitchen paper, to correct mistakes or to lighten certain areas.

LINEAR PERSPECTIVE A method for creating the illusion of depth on a flat surface, whereby all the parallel lines in a painting or drawing converge into a single vanishing point somewhere on the work's horizon line.

LINE WORK The preliminary pencil or ink outlines drawn in preparation for making a painting.

LOOSE PAINTING An expressive style of painting that aims more to capture the 'feel' of the subject, rather than focusing on detail.

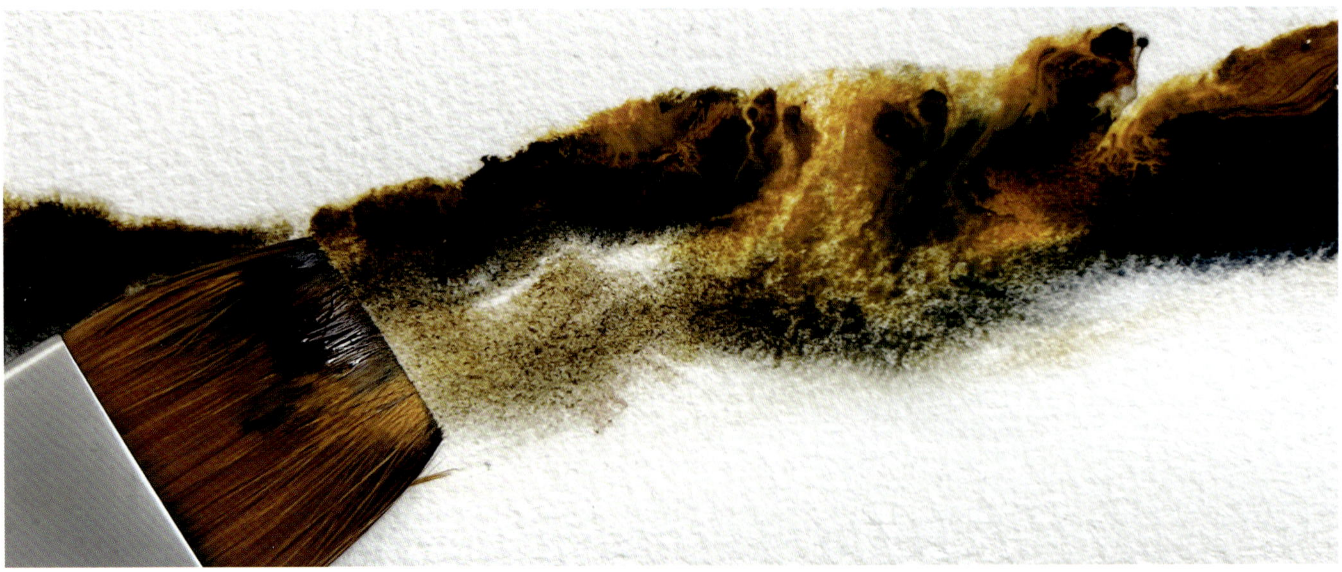

MASKING A technique used to preserve either the original surface of the paper or a layer of paint from subsequent additions of colour.

NEGATIVE PAINTING A method of defining a shape by painting the surrounding space to reveal the shape rather than painting the shape itself.

***PLEIN AIR* PAINTING** A French term for painting (or sketching) outdoors.

PRIMARY COLOURS Colours that cannot be created through mixing other colours: red, yellow and blue.

RULE OF THIRDS A common design guideline to aid a composition by positioning points of interest in the upper or lower thirds of a painting.

SECONDARY COLOURS Colours which can be created by mixing two primary colours, e.g. mixing yellow and blue to create green, red and yellow to make orange, and blue and red to create violet.

SKETCH A rough drawing or painting made to work through preliminary ideas for a painting, used to assist in creating a more polished finished picture.

SOFT EDGES Paint applied so that the edge of the brushstroke softens and sometimes disappears, usually occurring when painting wet-in-wet.

SPATTER A pattern of dots and spots created randomly by tapping a loaded paintbrush over part of the painting.

TEMPLATE A pre-designed pattern used for making copies.

TEXTURE The surface quality of a painting or paper.

THUMBNAIL SKETCHES A series of tiny preliminary sketches used to test out compositional ideas.

TONAL VALUE The lightness or darkness of tones or colours, i.e. how dark or pale a colour is.

VANISHING POINT The point at which converging perspective lines disappear on the horizon.

WASH A thin layer of colour often applied to a larger area than a single brushstroke can cover, e.g. a sky.

WET-IN-WET Painting directly into a wet surface, allowing the paint to soften, blend and diffuse on the paper.

WET-ON-DRY A technique of painting directly onto dry paper without pre-wetting it; or painting onto a wash that has already dried.

Suppliers and Online Communities

UNITED KINGDOM

L. Cornelissen & Son
www.cornelissen.com

Jackson's Art
www.jacksonsart.com

Bromleys Art Supplies
www.artsupplies.co.uk

Cass Art
www.cassart.co.uk

Curtisward Art Supplies
www.curtisward.com

SAA Art
www.saa.co.uk

UNITED STATES

Blick Art Materials
www.dickblick.com

Jerry's Artarama
www.jerrysartarama.com

Cheap Joe's
www.cheapjoes.com

About the Authors

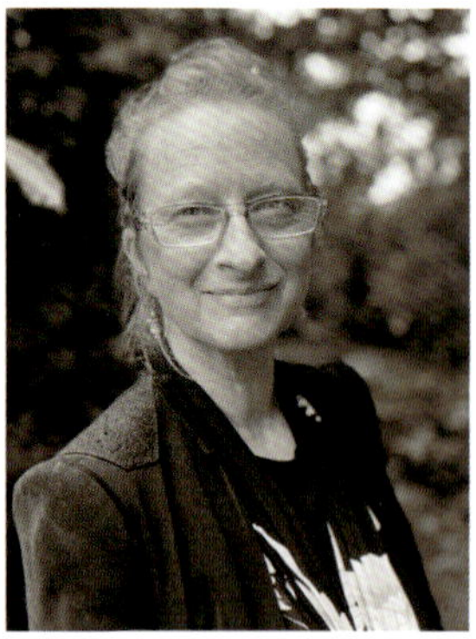

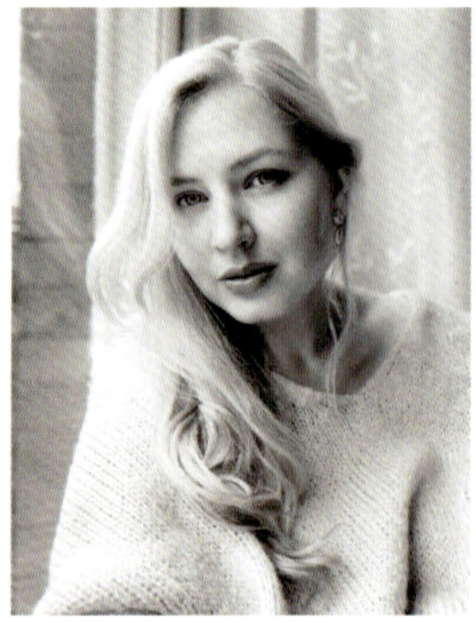

Lois Davidson is an English watercolour artist with over 40 years of experience. Her first book, *Landscapes in Watercolour*, published by GMC Publications Ltd in 2024, is an instructional guide for fledgling painters and a celebration of the natural, rugged beauty of the world around us. She has been painting professionally since 2020, and was shortlisted for the Jackson's Painting Prize in 2021. She offers painting tutorials and watercolour workshops, and runs a popular online art community on Patreon. She sells her paintings across the world and exhibits her work locally and online.

Morgaine Davidson is an avid creative with a passion for art and wildlife. Since graduating from university with a master's degree in English and Creative Writing, she has worked in a variety of different media, experimenting with combining art and the written word. She has penned articles for Jackson's Art Blog, and her fiction has been shortlisted for a number of prizes, including the Mslexia Best Women's Short Fiction 2023. She exhibits her work locally and online, and teaches watercolour painting on Patreon, specializing in capturing the liminal beauty of the natural world.

Together, mother–daughter team Lois and Morgaine run a successful YouTube channel which has over 128,000 subscribers, where they demonstrate traditional and experimental watercolour techniques.

Acknowledgements

Special thanks go to John Horner whose photos and memories of his father Ken Horner inspired the project 'Red Sails,' and our continuing love for traditional Thames sailing barges, and to Mickey Hall whose personal memories inspired the painting of Cambria on page 33. Many thanks to Jonathan Bailey for inviting us to write this book, and to Tom, Ellie and Robin, the wonderful team at GMC Publications Ltd, whose expertise and support have helped turn our vision into a reality. We are also indebted to the many students of watercolour and other fellow artists, who have followed our artistic journeys online and offered endless encouragement.

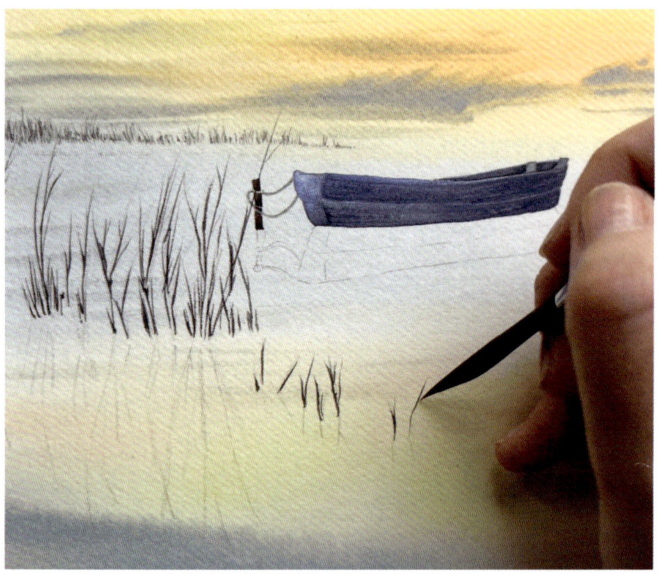

Index

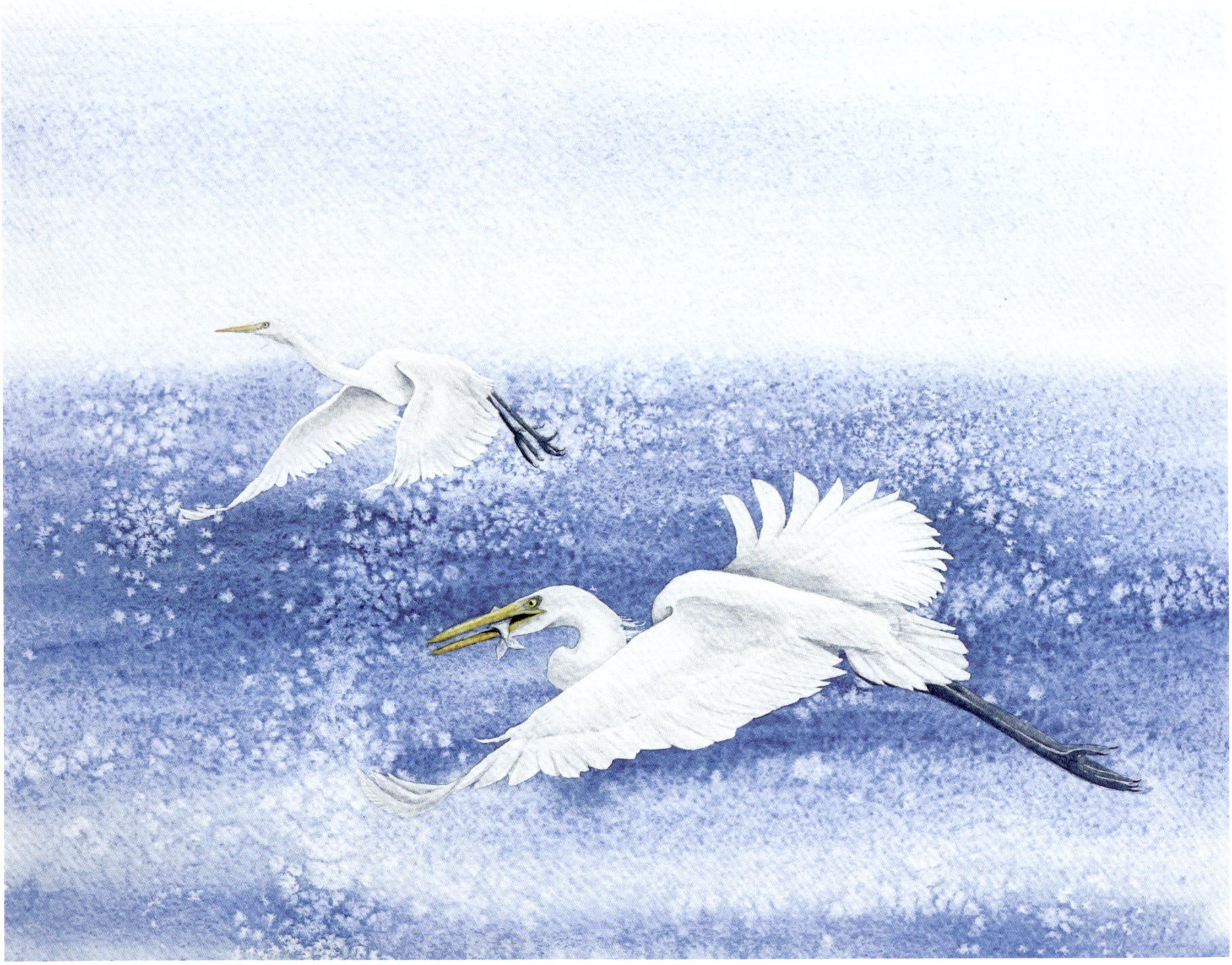

To order a book, contact:

GMC Publications Ltd

Castle Place, 166 High Street, Lewes, East Sussex, BN7 1XU

United Kingdom

Tel: +44 (0)1273 488005

www.gmcbooks.com